In the 1780s and 1790s theatre critics described the stage as a state in political tumult, while politicians invoked theatre as a model for politics both good and bad. In this study, Betsy Bolton examines the ways Romantic women performers and playwrights used theatrical conventions to intervene in politics. Reading the public performances of Emma Hamilton and Mary Robinson through the conventions of dramatic romance, Bolton suggests that the romance of national identity developed by writers such as Southey and Wordsworth took shape in complex opposition to these unruly women. Setting the conventions of farce against those of sentiment, playwrights such as Hannah Cowley and Elizabeth Inchbald questioned imperial relations while criticizing contemporary gender relations. This well-illustrated study draws on canonical poetry and personal memoirs, popular drama and parliamentary debates, political caricatures and theatrical reviews to extend current understandings of Romantic theatre, the public sphere, and Romantic gender relations.

BETSY BOLTON is Associate Professor of English at Swarthmore College. Her articles have appeared in *Studies in Romanticism*, *The Eighteenth Century: Theory and Interpretation*, *English Literary History*, and *Studies in Short Fiction*.

CAMBRIDGE STUDIES IN ROMANTICISM

General editors
Professor Marilyn Butler   Professor James Chandler
University of Oxford   *University of Chicago*

Editorial board
John Barrell, *University of York*
Paul Hamilton, *University of London*
Mary Jacobus, *Cornell University*
Kenneth Johnston, *Indiana University*
Alan Liu, *University of California, Santa Barbara*
Jerome McGann, *University of Virginia*
David Simpson, *University of California, Davis*

This series aims to foster the best new work in one of the most challenging fields within English literary studies. From the early 1780s to the early 1830s a formidable array of talented men and women took to literary composition, not just in poetry, which some of them famously transformed, but in many modes of writing. The expansion of publishing created new opportunities for writers, and the political stakes of what they wrote were raised again by what Wordsworth called those "great national events" that were "almost daily taking place": the French Revolution, the Napoleonic and American wars, urbanization, industrialization, religious revival, an expanded empire abroad, and the reform movement at home. This was an enormous ambition, even when it pretended otherwise. The relations between science, philosophy, religion, and literature were reworked in texts such as *Frankenstein* and *Biographia Literaria*; gender relations in *A Vindication of the Rights of Woman* and *Don Juan*; journalism by Cobbett and Hazlitt; poetic form, content and style by the Lake School and the Cockney School. Outside Shakespeare studies, probably no body of writing has produced such a wealth of response or done so much to shape the responses of modern criticism. This indeed is the period that saw the emergence of those notions of "literature" and of literary history, especially national literary history, on which modern scholarship in English has been founded.

The categories produced by Romanticism have also been challenged by recent historicist arguments. The task of the series is to engage both with a challenging corpus of Romantic writings and with the changing field of criticism they have helped to shape. As with other literary series published by Cambridge, this one will represent the work of both younger and more established scholars, on either side of the Atlantic and elsewhere.

For a complete list of titles published see end of book

CAMBRIDGE STUDIES IN ROMANTICISM 46

WOMEN, NATIONALISM, AND THE ROMANTIC STAGE

WOMEN, NATIONALISM, AND THE ROMANTIC STAGE

Theatre and Politics in Britain, 1780–1800

BETSY BOLTON

CAMBRIDGE
UNIVERSITY PRESS

PUBLISHED BY THE PRESS SYNDICATE OF THE UNIVERSITY OF CAMBRIDGE
The Pitt Building, Trumpington Street, Cambridge, United Kingdom

CAMBRIDGE UNIVERSITY PRESS
The Edinburgh Building, Cambridge CB2 2RU, UK
40 West 20th Street, New York, NY 10011-4211, USA
10 Stamford Road, Oakleigh, VIC 3166, Australia
Ruiz de Alarcón 13, 28014 Madrid, Spain
Dock House, The Waterfront, Cape Town 8001, South Africa

http://www.cambridge.org

First published 2001

Printed in the United Kingdom at the University Press, Cambridge

Typeface Monotype Baskerville 11/12½   *System* QuarkXPress™   [SE]

A catalogue record for this book is available from the British Library

ISBN 0 521 77116 1 hardback

For Nancy Calhoun,
Kristin Bolton
and
Zoe Clare Peyton Jones

three generations of women
who in very different ways
accompanied me
through the writing of this book.

Contents

Illustrations

Acknowledgments

This book has benefited from a wide range of institutional and individual support. In 1995 and 1996, a George Becker fellowship from Swarthmore College helped fund research for this and other projects. Swarthmore colleagues, students, and visitors have also helped shape this project in innumerable ways. Back in 1992, Allen Kuharski in Theater was one of the first people I knew to propose Romantic theatre as a subject worthy of study, while the English department as a whole encouraged me to pursue connections between Romantic men and women writers along with a cultural studies approach to the period. In 1994, Sue-Ellen Case heightened my interest in the politics of theatre and performance and Susan Foster first got me interested in "That Hamilton Woman." Students in an experimental class on "Romanticism and Performance of Gender" made exhilarating connections – and urged me emphatically to restrict the scope of the project. Bruce Grant steered me toward most discussions of nationalism included in these pages. English department colleagues in various reading groups struggled through early chapter drafts: Abbe Blum's incisive questions, Leslie Delauter's undaunted pursuit of issues I wished to abandon, Nora Johnson's exploration of authorship in Renaissance theatre, Carolyn Lesjak's knack for reframing an argument, Ken Saragosa's very different interest in nationalism, Patty White's graceful approach to structure – all helped develop this project far beyond my original conception of it. Nat Anderson provided much-needed moral support; Craig Williamson helped me see an alarming lack of clarity in the penultimate draft. In addition to reading individual chapters several times over, Nora Johnson read through the entire manuscript and offered useful advice and much-needed encouragement while mercilessly attacking excess verbiage.

Participation in the National Endowment for the Humanities' 1995 summer seminar on "Feminism and Enlightenment," directed by Mary Jacobus, provided an intellectual community in which this kind of work held meaning and excitement. In particular, Catherine Burrough's work on Joanna Baillie and Anna Lott's passion for Elizabeth Inchbald fueled my own study of women in Romantic theatre. Mary Jacobus and Catherine Burroughs read an early draft of the chapter on Mary Robinson, and their suggestions helped refine both the argument and the writing. Catherine Burroughs and Anna Lott also read an early draft of the Inchbald chapter and Katherine Kittredge was a generous audience for early work on Emma Hamilton. I have continued to draw support from this community of scholars through long months of further research and revision.

A William Keck fellowship at the Huntington Library in December of 1995 gave me access to the Larpent collection of unpublished plays, which in turn provided material for the prologue, the epilogue, the introduction to farce, and the Cowley chapter. It also vastly expanded my knowledge of eighteenth-century caricatures, and helped me track down some of the verbal satires on Mary Robinson discussed in the fourth chapter of this book. Anyone working with eighteenth-century caricatures owes an enormous debt of gratitude to the work of Dorothy George and her treasure trove of a catalogue. I am also deeply grateful for the generous help of librarians at Swarthmore College, Cornell University, Yale University, the Huntington Library, and the British Library, as well as the staff of the Prints and Drawings Room of the British Museum. The Swarthmore librarians in particular supported my predatory habits with patience and good humor.

Family members have also provided crucial support in the writing of this book, support ranging from typing through construction work to childcare. When I ran into serious trouble with carpal tunnel syndrome, my mother accompanied me to the British Museum's Newspaper Library to help me track and type relevant theatre reviews. My sister Kristin helped reformat various chapters, in addition to painting and sanding a room so I could work in this building site I call home. As I struggled to restart the project, Dot held the baby for long hours so I could think; my father provided print-outs of various drafts, and an analytical ear. Above all, J. read early drafts, listened to endless mutterings about theatre and politics, nagged me to write, accompanied me and the baby to the Prints and Drawings Room of the British Museum, and then held the baby for a few crucial weeks as I revised. In the end, he reformatted the entire book. Thanks also to Valerie Elliston who compiled the index. I am grateful for permission to reprint sections of three articles here. Parts of "Mimicry, Politics and Playwrighting" and "The Farce of Subjection: Elizabeth Inchbald" appeared in *The Eighteenth Century: Theory and Interpretation* under the title "Farce, Romance, Empire: Elizabeth Inchbald and Colonial Discourse" (39.1 [Spring 1998], pp. 3–24). Some paragraphs and ideas in "(Dis)embodied Romance: 'Perdita' Robinson and William Wordsworth" are reprinted from an earlier reading of these two poets: "Romancing the Stone: 'Perdita' Robinson in Wordsworth's London," *English Literary History* 64 (1997), pp. 727–59. Likewise, some paragraphs and ideas within "Patriotic Romance: Emma Hamilton and Horatio Nelson" are to appear in "Sensibility and Speculation: Emma Hamilton" in Katherine Kittredge, ed., *Lewd and Notorious: Female Transgression in the Eighteenth Century,* under contract with University of Michigan Press.

Prologue: the female dramatist and the man of the people

In 1782, George Colman the younger, having written a long poem entitled *The Man of the People*, produced as his maiden effort for the stage a "musical farce" entitled *The Female Dramatist*. The title character, Mrs. Melpomene Metaphor, seems to enact the confusions sketched by Richard Brinsley Sheridan's epilogue to Hannah More's *Fatal Falsehood*:

> A Scene she now projects, and now a Dish,
> Here's Act the First – and here – remove with Fish.
> Now while this Eye in a fine phrenzy rolls,
> That, soberly casts up a Bill for Coals;
> Black Pins and Daggers in one leaf she sticks,
> And Tears and Thread, and Bowls and Thimbles mix.[1]

Confusing a first course and a first act, this combination of housework and playwrighting leaves both realms in disarray. Like Sheridan's epilogue, Colman's play treats the figure of the female dramatist with marked condescension. A young male protagonist promises to bring Mrs. Metaphor to her senses:

Leave the rest to me then – her Conversion is compleat, if I have any skill in Magic – You shall see me transform her into a downright housewife – and by a Single Stroke of my Art, turn her Pen into a Needle, and her Tragedies into Thread papers.(34)[2]

It is tempting to read *The Female Dramatist* as poorly disguised wish fulfilment: Colman, just beginning to write for the stage, may well have been daunted by reigning female dramatists such as Hannah More and Hannah Cowley. London audiences, however, did not share the wish that female dramatists return to their housekeeping: the play was acted only once, on a benefit night. Colman himself remarked that "this Farce was noticed in a very conspicuous manner, – for it was uncommonly hiss'd, in the course of its performance."[3] Arrived at an age of greater

I

maturity, Colman transferred his hostility from the figure of the female dramatist to the farce itself:

> On perusing the manuscript after a long lapse of time, I threw the "Female Dramatist" into the flames, as a fit companion for the "Man of the People"; – and, if this Consumed Couple had belong'd to any Author but myself, he would not, perhaps, have had the folly, or candour, (or whatever else it may [be] call'd), to rake up their ashes. (*Random Records*, 1.112–13)

Perusing Colman's memoirs after a still longer lapse of time, we might pause to ask, what made the Female Dramatist a fit companion for the Man of the People – and what justified burning them both in effigy?

The "Man of the People" immortalized in Colman's youthful verse was the flamboyant politician Charles Fox, famous for his appeal to popular sentiment and his shifting political alliances. Coincidentally, perhaps, in 1782 Fox's name had been publicly linked with that of the former actress and future female dramatist Mary Robinson – though her farce, *Nobody*, produced in 1794, fared little better than Colman's first effort. In 1782, however, Robinson was best known as "Perdita," the abandoned mistress of the Prince of Wales. Her brief affair with Fox seems to have caught the public imagination: contemporary caricatures continued to link this woman of the theatre with the "Man of the People" long after their actual liaison was over. In some prints, Robinson appears as a woman of the people, making possible an unsavory connection between demagoguery and prostitution (the figure of the public woman). In other prints, Robinson is linked both with the prince and with Fox, visually and sexually recording the political alliance between the two men. More generally, however, I think the coupling of Fox and Robinson can be seen as acknowledging the common importance of theatricality – performance, costume, staging – in the apparently disparate practices of politics, theatre, and femininity. Part of what made the "Female Dramatist" of the late eighteenth century a fit companion for the "Man of the People" is the fact that both were politicians: more specifically, both sought to influence public opinion while remaining professionally dependent on public favor. Indeed, as I shall argue in this book, connections between the female dramatist and the demagogue politician were encouraged by the ubiquitous late eighteenth-century analogy between theatre and politics, and by a changing understanding of the "public" addressed by national theatre and national politics alike.

Colman destroyed his own youthful efforts in verse and drama; over the past two centuries, the cultural associations linking his "Consumed

Couple" have also been destroyed, or at least lost to memory and historical record. Thus in sifting through the ashes of Colman's youthful literary pyre, this book also participates in a larger process of historical recovery, the first step of which has been to reconstruct women's participation in late eighteenth-century theatre. Jacqueline Pearson's *The Prostituted Muse* (1988) surveys the literary production and reception of women dramatists over the course of the long eighteenth century. Sandra Richards's *The Rise of the English Actress* (1993) traces the increasing influence and respectability of actresses within English society. Julie Carlson's *In the Theatre of Romanticism* (1994) notes some of the critical connections linking Romantic theatre and politics; in the process, she emphasizes both the influence of Sarah Siddons and the general "surveillance of public women" in the writings of Romantic poets and critics. Ellen Donkin's *Getting into the Act* (1995) underscores the obstacles facing women playwrights within a male-dominated, tightly structured theatre system. Catherine Burroughs's *Closet Stages* (1997) helps expand the boundaries of what we understand as theatre to include closet drama and private theatricals: two arenas in which women had greater influence and control. Judith Pascoe's *Romantic Theatricality* (1997) examines the broader theatricality of romantic culture, exploring the element of staging involved in such disparate events and practices as the 1794 treason trials, the reception of Siddons's star persona, the production of poetry columns in newspapers, and the development of Wordsworth's later public persona.

Much of this recovery work has quite rightly emphasized the constraints under which women struggled to act in the world of late eighteenth-century theatre. Yet one of the most striking features of the London stage in the 1780s and 1790s remains the increased prominence of women playwrights and the continued influence of actresses. Against Donkin's carefully detailed and highly persuasive account of the gender bias against which women dramatists struggled in the latter half of the eighteenth century, we might set the increase in women dramatists over those years. Against Carlson's account of the surveillance of public beauties, we might set Richards's description of actresses' social influence. Striving for the kind of balance available only after extensive historical recovery has already taken place, this book focuses both on the fact of women's theatrical prominence and the possible sources of their unlikely influence. It thus differs from the works mentioned above, first in exploring the opportunities available to women through theatre, and second, in viewing women's theatrical engagement as an explicitly political act.

Discussions of the "bourgeois public sphere" first described by Jürgen Habermas seemed to divide that realm of "rational-critical debate" into the male public domain of coffeehouses, newspapers, and parliamentary debate, and the feminized, private, mixed-class world of the bourgeois novel.[4] Yet theatre, ignored by historians and critics alike as a degraded form, offered an intermediate public sphere, producing political fictions and commentary in a mixed-gender, mixed-class setting. And in this theatrical public sphere women were far more active participants than critics or historians have yet acknowledged. The conservative poet and pamphleteer Hannah More first broke into literary circles with her outrageously popular tragedy *Percy* (1777). Hannah Cowley was first and foremost a dramatist, and only secondarily a Della Cruscan poet. Mary Robinson's literary career as poet, novelist, and dramatist relied heavily on her notoriety as the celebrity actress and public woman "Perdita." The less scandalous Elizabeth Inchbald was also an actress before she turned her hand to drama and fiction. Joanna Baillie was heralded as the "Shakespeare" of the age. Even women less emphatically connected with the stage had ties to it: as Margaret Doody has shown, Frances Burney repeatedly wrote for the stage as well as for a reading public; poet and novelist Charlotte Smith authored one mixed comedy, *What Is She?* (1799), which enjoyed moderate success; Anna Seward carefully divided her verse novel, *Louisa* (1784), into descriptive and dramatic epistles. Even Mary Wollstonecraft wrote a comedy, which William Godwin burned at her death.

Participating in the world of the London stages, these women also engaged the political issues of their times, discussing English imperialism, women's rights, the French revolution, and so forth. Yet such political engagement challenges the accepted wisdom of "separate spheres." If domestic interiors constituted women's proper sphere of influence, why were so many women connected with the very public – and inherently political – world of the London stage? Newspaper critics and politicians commented explicitly on the theatricality of politics during the 1780s and 1790s, and when women writers wanted to mount a political critique, theatricality was a tool which came readily to hand – as Mary Wollstonecraft's famous attack on Edmund Burke demonstrates. But other women writers used theatre and politics more subtly. Parliamentary debates and political show trials invoked conventions of (and direct comparisons with) theatrical performances, while claiming more serious effects; conversely, Hannah Cowley's *A Day in Turkey; or the Russian Slaves* (1791) *dis*claimed political relevance, while mimicking political positions elaborated within those contemporary parliamentary debates.

Women on the Romantic stage also chose to step on to the stage of the nation; this book charts some of their performances and the effects they created. "Staging the Nation," the first part of the book, works to explore the interrelations among genre, gender and nation in the Romantic period. Firstly it traces the ubiquitous Romantic analogy between theatre and nation; secondly it suggests that the ambivalence of this analogy was controlled partly by polarizing spectacle and sentiment; thirdly it examines the ways public women marked the contested border between theatre and politics; and fourthly it considers the forms of farce and romance as cultural containers for larger anxieties about the role of women within the nation.

The second part of the book, "Romancing the State," examines the life performances of public women like Emma Hamilton and Mary (Perdita) Robinson along with the political effects of those performances; it traces the extent to which these celebrity performances were structured according to the conflicting scripts of late eighteenth-century romance. Late eighteenth-century theatrical reception increased the emotional, sexual, and political frisson associated with public performers by blurring the boundaries between stage and life. Thus in reconstructing the performances of public men and public women, I consider how those performances appear, refracted, in letters and memoirs as well as in contemporary caricatures and reviews.

The third part of the book, "Mixed Drama, Imperial Farce," attends to the topical political issues addressed by women's mixed dramas. While romance mingled myth and history, the fabulous and the real, the world of theatre and that of real life, mixed drama disrupted the boundaries between sentiment and farce, tears and laughter, moral earnestness and amoral cynicism. And while romance seemed to focus on the composition of the heroic nation, mixed drama explored the comedy of international relations. Working to recenter the period in its imperial and colonial contexts, the chapters in this part of the book expand our current understanding of Romantic orientalism by exploring the most relevant drama of Hannah Cowley and Elizabeth Inchbald.[5] Arguing that mixed drama allowed women a voice in contemporary political debates as long as they disavowed political intentions, I read Cowley's *A Day in Turkey* (1791) against contemporary parliamentary debates about Britain's role in the conflict between Turkey and Russia. In three of Elizabeth Inchbald's most popular plays, I examine the way a simple inversion of political expectations develops into a more complicated internalization of duplicity as a basis for domestic relations and international affairs alike.

Throughout the book's more general exploration of genre and national agency, I try to stay focused on the materiality and specificity of each woman's theatrical career. The end result, linking cultural studies with detailed readings of texts, suggests new ways of thinking about politics and agency as it revises critical perspectives on literary and dramatic form.

PART I

Staging the nation

CHAPTER ONE

The politics of Romantic theatre

Nation is to modern society as genre is to literature: a messy yet indispensable category of analysis, a gesture toward relationships only loosely defined or definable. If genre can be defined as a set of conventions which allow individual *texts* to "signal their membership in a class," nation might likewise be described as a set of conventions which allow individual *people* to signal their membership within a particular political, social category.[1] Ernest Gellner's working definition of nation, for instance, highlights both the conventionality of a "shared culture" and the importance of signaling and recognizing membership in a given category:

1. Two men are of the same nation if and only if they share the same culture, where culture in turn means a system of ideas and signs and associations and ways of behaving and communicating.
2. . . . A mere category of persons . . . becomes a nation if and when the members of the category firmly recognize certain mutual rights and duties to each other in virtue of their shared membership of it. It is their recognition of each other as fellows of this kind which turns them into a nation.[2]

The political power of such recognition is exceeded only by its formalism, and thus its apparent superficiality.

Indeed, analysts of nations and of genres seem similarly bemused by the arbitrariness, the emptiness of the conventions with which they have to work.[3] Critics like Eve Sedgwick have puzzled over the fact "that a form with the historical stature of the Gothic novel should be so adequately reducible to a formula."[4] Benedict Anderson, for his part, drew attention to the "'political' power of nationalisms vs. their philosophical poverty and even incoherence," noting that "[t]his 'emptiness' easily gives rise . . . to a certain condescension" (*Imagined Communities*, 5). Anderson himself makes the emptiness of nationalism a central part of his argument, pointing to the empty Tomb of the Unknown Soldier as an apt monument to modern national identity, and emphasizing "empty,

9

homogeneous time" as the temporality of modern nationhood. And if bare conventionality is often used to explain the historical adaptability of a genre such as gothic or romance, such an explanation might also apply to nationalism's social and political adaptability. While noting nationalism's unwavering advocacy of respectability, for instance, George Mosse also suggests that "[i]n its long career, [nationalism] attempted to co-opt most of the important movements of the age, to absorb all that men thought meaningful and dear even while holding fast to certain unchanging myths and symbols" (*Nationalism and Sexuality*, 9). Nationalism's capacity for absorption here registers a certain lack of "independent" meaning. At the same time, Mosse's account of nationalism's development emphasizes the somewhat uncanny agency of this imagined entity – its *attempt* to coopt other movements – a feature of nationalism to which we shall return.

The analogy between nation and genre highlights the puzzling appeal of their conventions. What makes the formula of romance repeatedly attractive to its readers? What makes the political formula of fascism persuasive instead of boringly predictable? Differing in content and consequence, these two questions are nonetheless oddly similar in kind. Playing one against the other may teach us something new about each – or remind us of similarities we have forgotten.

This book explores the late eighteenth-century tendency to view the English state as a stage: a place of genre-governed performance both enclosing and addressing a vast, somewhat stylized national audience. Within this spectacular nationalism, I argue, gender functioned as a diacritical mark distinguishing, from the perspective of different writers, good theatre and good models of national politics from bad.[5] The first part of this general introduction examines late eighteenth-century analogies between nation and stage, emphasizing the multifaceted struggle for relative power among audience members, actors, dramatists, and managers of the London theatres. The second section suggests that the ambivalence of the theatrical analogy worked itself out, in critical and political terms, by polarizing sentiment and spectacle. The third section sketches some of the ways public women served to articulate the border between theatre and national politics and thus came to intensify the ambivalence of the theatrical analogy. The final part of the chapter argues that while the theatrical modes of romance and farce were invoked to encapsulate political fears of female power, both forms provided women with new access to political influence and dispute. This introduction ends with a preview of the romance and farce sections which follow, linking (1) the limited agency of actresses with the form of stage romance, and (2) the woman dramatist's critical mimicry of social structures with the form of the mixed drama, or what we might call the sentimental farce.

THE THEATRICAL ANALOGY

Late eighteenth-century discussions of theatre and politics tend to dwell on the theatre's ability to shape a mass of spectators into an audience and, by extension, its power to shape that audience into a nation. In emphasizing the links between politics and the stage, social critics in the 1780s and 1790s drew on a long-established association between theatre audiences and the body politic – an association dating back at least to the "Glorious Revolution." The restoration of the monarchy had, after all, brought with it the restoration of the English stage; the Glorious Revolution, with its newly minted Bill of Rights, gave focus to the analogy between spectator and citizen.[6] One theatrical commentator, writing in 1770, made the analogy between theatrical spectator and the subject of a limited monarchy explicit: "As I address this letter to you in the spirit of the public, I expect to be attended to; for though an histrionic monarchy, you hold your empire on their opinion."[7] Theatre offered a model for a political state in which a socially mixed public held power – if only through the force of its opinions.

By the latter part of the century, however, the great compromise represented by the Glorious Revolution was coming under increased pressure and scrutiny. The Wilkite agitation of the 1760s, an increasing insistence on universal male suffrage, the upheavals associated with the French revolution – all of these threatened to disrupt the treasured stability of the British state. Yet in the turbulent close of the century, theatre critics, politicians, and social commentators continued to refer to the London theatres as a model for national unity. In the revolutionary year of 1789, for instance, the essayist of *The Bystander* claimed that "being the fountain of public taste, it is of national importance that it [the drama] should be kept pure and uncorrupted."[8] In 1793, theatre critic William Woodfall likewise asserted his "thorough conviction that a well-regulated stage was the best possible succedaneum to the laws of a free country."[9] Regulating theatre and preventing its corruption appeared an important part of efforts to stave off or counteract the tyranny of France's revolutionary terror.

Why did theatre – or at least the theatrical analogy – seem so politically charged in this time of perceived crisis? The answer may lie in the

uses to which the analogy could be put. The playhouse as a microcosm
of the state could be used to present an idealized view of English people
coming together as a nation; it could also be used to correct or critique
the performance of politicians, theatre managers, and audience
members. Within the repeated analogy between theatre and nation, elements of spectacle or stock theatricality were used to literalize and thus
discuss the uses and abuses of power in theatre and government alike.
Spectacle made power visible, suddenly open to both criticism and
praise.[10]

These uses of the theatrical analogy differed from earlier accounts of
social theatre or the *theatrum mundi*. Jean-Christophe Agnew has argued,
for instance, that in Elizabethan and Jacobean times, the "theatrical perspective" engaged the radical social uncertainties of market relations; in
this context, the stage analogy encapsulated the "diminishing transparency of social exchange," even as it intensified "the simultaneous
anxiety and exhilaration that this cultural crisis had inspired."[11] By contrast, during the course of the eighteenth century, Agnew suggests that
the "deconstructive dimension of the theatrical perspective was
restrained and recast in a more manageable form" (*Worlds Apart*, 161). In
these more complacent times, theatrical conventions were invoked to
record rather than interrogate "the radical disjuncture between 'gesture'
and 'influence,' between public and private that characterized British life
during the eighteenth century and that, at the same time, explained its
remarkable stability" (160). In his reading of eighteenth-century theatricality, Agnew also argues that the vitality and interpretive force of the
theatrical analogy moved away from drama and toward fiction and philosophy. Yet, as the next few pages should show, the close of the century
witnessed the resurrection of a specifically theatrical analogy: one
focused on the links between theatre and politics rather than those existing between the stage and the market.

This latter-day version of the theatrical analogy emphasized not the
performance on stage, but rather the social and political relations emble-
matized by the larger world of the theatre. Writers invoking the theatrical analogy no longer seemed anxious about the nature of the self or of
social exchange: indeed, they seemed to take for granted the likelihood
that canny entrepreneurs would exploit the audience of stage and nation
alike. Still, anxieties remained. Looking back to the Glorious Revolution,
English theatre offered a model of political stability; looking across the
channel to France, however, theatre seemed inextricable from revolution. Romantic discussions of theatrical relations oscillated between

these two extremes, as commentators and politicians alike attempted to come to grips with new theatrical and political realities.

Romantic invocations of the theatrical analogy presented themselves as descriptively factual, based on contemporary theatre experience as well as on national history, yet they offered a highly mediated view both of spectacle and of power. Accounts of theatre audiences found in dramatic prologues and epilogues must be read within their theatrical contexts: a teasing, flirtatious, sometimes combative situation. A witty prologue could earn a play a favorable hearing; a skillfully written and delivered epilogue could save even an unpopular play from being "damned." Prologues and epilogues wooed their Romantic audiences by relying on ephemeral performance elements: in particular, the mimicry of other actors and celebrities and references to topical events. Portraits of theatre audiences presented in this kind of performative context remain historically contingent: they survive as written relics of what was largely an oral and communal tradition within the theatre. Yet by the end of the century, remarkably similar portraits of English audiences were presented far more seriously by social and political commentators.

Comparisons between the nation and the theatre often emphasized the similar composition of the two forms: players on the London stage shared with political figures of the day the challenge of pleasing (or, at times, appeasing) a large, socially heterogeneous audience. In the 1780s and 1790s, for instance, the various incarnations of the Drury Lane and Covent Garden theatres held between 2,300 and 3,600 spectators – and their potentially massive audiences also included a notable cross section of the population.[12] Yet in stressing the links between political and dramatic audiences, prologues, epilogues, and commentators often replaced contemporary reality with stylized portraits of audience members. In particular, contemporary observers seem to have misrepresented late eighteenth-century audiences in two ways: first by reiterating older views of class distribution throughout the playhouse audience; and second by emphasizing the unruliness of working-class spectators, identified with the "gods" of the upper gallery.

Both prologues and commentators, for instance, frequently stressed the class divisions suggested by the seating areas of box, pit, and gallery. Throughout the Romantic period, Covent Garden and Drury Lane remained the two theatres licensed by royal patent for the performance of spoken drama: they retained, in other words, a monopoly over "legitimate" theatre. In both these theatres, the price of seats varied by location, ranging from the boxes (4 shillings) through the pit (2s 6d) and the first gallery (1s 6d) to the second ("shilling") gallery. The social divisions potentially created by price differences were quickly reified by theatrical prologues, epilogues, and commentaries. In 1755, for instance, Theophilus Cibber compared theatre spectators, "Noble, Gentle or Simple, who fill the Boxes, Pitt and Galleries" with the "K—g, L—rds and COMMONS" composing "that great Body the Nation."[13] Throughout the eighteenth century, such comparisons constituted a critical commonplace, one which emphasized the social divisions reflected and reinforced by the price of theatre seating. Yet that critical commonplace seems only loosely connected to the historical reality of late eighteenth- and early nineteenth-century theatre audiences. The arrest reports of the O.P. Riots in 1809, for instance, suggest a far greater mingling of social classes throughout the playhouse: Marc Baer's analysis of the reports shows apprentices "evenly distributed throughout the theatre" while disorderly clerks and tradesmen were apprehended in the pit (64%) and the boxes (32%).[14] While the riots themselves may well have altered "typical" seating patterns, such reports do suggest that price barriers were far from absolute. Seating patterns did not create exclusive social enclaves.

The second most common misrepresentation of Romantic audiences emphasized the unruliness of working-class spectators in the upper galleries. The London theatres were sometimes seen by contemporaries as subject to the tyranny of the mob: both actors and audience appeared to bow to the whims of the working classes, supposedly positioned in the upper gallery, and familiarly known as "the gods" of the theatre.[15] Foreign or colonial visitors were most apt to call attention to the unruliness of the upper galleries, and of the audience more generally. In 1775 Thomas Campbell, an Irishman visiting London, remarked of a theatrical uproar that "the millionth part of the submissions made by these poor players would have appeased an Irish audience – yea if they [had] murdered their fathers."[16] The German traveler Gebhard Friedrich August Wendeborn likewise noted in 1791 that the "English show their vaunted freedom nowhere more than in the theatres. [. . . There the] aristocrats and commoners are gathered, and the latter are bent on showing that they consider themselves quite as good as the former. The upper gallery controls the whole house, even the actors being compelled to obey orders."[17] Prologues and epilogues supported these claims at least in part by repeatedly bowing to the wishes, if not the judgment, of the upper gallery; actors and dramatists endlessly invoked the favor of those Garrick first nicknamed England's "stout hearts of oak."

Why this gap between conventional, stylized accounts of theatre audiences and the more fluid reality? Several possibilities suggest themselves. Portraying the audience according to fixed notions of class and character may have provided a reassuring sense of stability during a time of great social change and increasing mobility. More specifically, by distinguishing quite rigidly among different sections of the audience, prologues, epilogues, and commentaries allowed for a subsequent synthesis of those audience members into a unified whole. The epilogue to Garrick's "dramatic satire" *Lethe* (1740), for instance, caricatured each section of the audience: the upper gallery with its working-class spectators ("They grin so, one can't distinguish faces!"); the more aristocratic boxes (full of narcissistic beaux and footmen holding places for their masters); and the variety of characters present in the pit. "Here's choice enough: the merchant, soldier, cit, / The surly critic, and the thread-bare wit." The female speaker of the epilogue, looking for a lover, settles on both the soldier and the merchant, confident that the audience as a whole will confirm her choice since it echoes the nation's professional and imperial self-definition: "No doubt you'll all approve my patriotic passion; / My heart is fixed for trade and navigation." The epilogue emphasized the social variety of the audience as a means of validating the nation's unified approval of maritime trade.

While theatrical stereotypes of box, pit, and galleries as distinct social entities were often invoked as a prelude to a projected audience or national consensus, emphasis on the galleries' disproportionate power over the rest of the playhouse stressed both the fabled freedom of the English and the potential dangers of that freedom. The success of politicians' appeals to the people – those of Pitt the elder in the 1750s, John Wilkes in the 1760s, and Charles Fox in the 1780s and 1790s – raised concerns about the power available through (if not exactly to) the masses. Indeed, Fox's appearance in numerous caricatures of the nineties as demagogue politician, a protean "man of the people," suggests how close to the surface such concerns remained. At the same time, Dror Wahrman has shown that in the debates of the 1790s, the political divisions between radical and conservative were mapped on to the social divisions of rich and poor: "[i]n between, the scene was set for the identity of political moderates to be projected onto a social middle, a 'middle class.'"[18] As class (upper, lower, middle) became a marker for political positions, so political anxieties could be projected onto the imagined social structure of the playhouse.

The theatrical analogy compressed into one image national fears and national fantasies: in particular, the fantasy of different classes uniting freely into one nation, and the fear that antagonism between upper and lower classes, or the unruliness of the working classes, might pull the nation apart. The conflation of fear and fantasy meant that the image of political theatre remained highly ambivalent throughout the Romantic period. Both radical and conservative writers invoked the image of the British people coming together as a nation through theatre – even as critical commentaries frequently presented the London play-houses as a place where the nation might come apart rather than come together. Accounts of the theatre as a moral school competed with an emphasis on theatrical deception. Finally, as we shall see in the next section, "bad" theatre, under the title of farce or spectacle, became a label used by both radical and conservative politicians to lambaste their opponents' approach to government.

Commentators' insistence on the healthy diversity of British theatre audiences could be used to support political stances ranging from the radical to the conservative. Mary Wollstonecraft, for instance, in her *Historical and Moral View of the French Revolution* (1794), emphasized the het-erogeneity of English tastes in contrast to French uniformity:

At our theatres, the boxes, pit, and galleries, relish different scenes; and some are condescendingly born[e] by the more polished part of the audience, to allow the rest to have their portion of amusement. In France, on the contrary, a highly wrought sentiment of morality, probably rather romantic than sublime, produces a burst of applause, when one heart seems to agitate every hand.[19]

While Wollstonecraft generally defended the French revolution, she saw such theatrical uniformity as the besetting sin of the French; in her view, England benefited from its spectatorial negotiations and compromises, avoiding thereby the French evils of an absolutism both moral and political.

Somewhat surprisingly, the radical Wollstonecraft and the Tory peer Sir Walter Scott both agreed on the ultimate unity created by the British theatre experience – while both Scott and the radical playwright Thomas Holcroft insisted on the power of drama to "humanize the heart" and civilize the manners of its audience. For Sir Walter Scott, writing in the 1820s,

A full audience attending a first-rate piece may be compared to a national con-vention, to which every order of the community, from the peers to the porters, send their representatives . . . The good-natured gaiety with which the higher

orders see the fashionable follies which they practise treated with light satire for
the amusement of the middling and poorer classes, has no little effect in checking the rancorous feelings of envy which superior birth, wealth and station are
apt enough to engender . . . In short, the drama is in ours, and in most civilized
countries, an engine possessing the most powerful effect on the manners of
society (ellipses: Baer).[20]

Scott's national convention offers a more formal version of Wollstonecraft's
"condescension" and varied relish – by 1820, the shadow of France's revolutionary National Assembly would have fallen only lightly over Scott's
related imagery. Thomas Holcroft, writing as an anonymous theatrical
reviewer in 1783, six years before the French revolution, was far more
extreme in his political analogies:

The Theatre is as well worthy the contemplation of the Philosopher and the
Legislator, as the Man of Taste. We are persuaded it contributes, in its present
state, to humanize the heart, and correct the manners . . . If it is not uniform in
the tendency of its effects, it is because Legislators have never yet been
sufficiently convinced of the power of the Drama, to incorporate it with the
constitution, and make it a legal and necessary establishment; or rather,
perhaps, because some men were fearful, lest while they were erecting the
temple of morality, they should erase the tottering structure of superstition, in
the preservation of which themselves, their children, or their dependents were
materially interested.[21]

While both writers emphasize the social benefits of theatre, over the
course of forty years, Holcroft's rather somber "power of the Drama"
gives way to Scott's "good natured gaiety." So too Holcroft's "material
interests" become in Scott's rhetoric the ostensibly natural attributes of
"superior birth, wealth and station." Strikingly, the same concept
appears to serve opposing ends: Holcroft links the civilizing force of the
drama to a leveling of social classes, while Scott equates theatrical civil-
ity with an acceptance of class difference and of social privilege. The
complacence of Scott's later perspective highlights what was passion-
ately contested during the decades of the eighties and nineties.

Indeed, during that earlier period, the London theatres were often
seen as places where the nation threatened to come apart rather than
come together. Some commentators, for instance, presented tensions
between audiences and theatre managers in terms of a standing conflict
between rulers and ruled. In 1786 one critic promised to force the
theatre's "lordly despots" to a state of "repentance and humiliation for
the enormities of their management, to disrobe them of their habitual
insolence, strengthen their treasury, regulate their manners, abolish their

insolence, purify their minds by the force of irresistible and honest
admonition, and make them finally tremble at the bar of public
justice."[22] The hyperbole of this passage echoes Edmund Burke's rhetorical excesses as he sought in 1785 to impeach Warren Hastings for
abusing his power as Governor of India: Hastings was eventually forced
to kneel, ritually, at the bar of public justice in Westminster Hall in 1788.

Theatrical managers tended to invoke the same political imagery to
protest audience rebellions. Sheridan, a well-known liberal and bad
businessman, seems to have remained largely unaffected by the threat of
violence breaking out within the theatre. But the other most influential
managers of the period – George Colman the younger and John Philip
Kemble – were highly conservative in their politics, especially in their
relationship to theatre audiences. In his *Random Records*, Colman argued
that

> The Dramatick, like the Political Stage, – if it may be compared with that much
> more important scene of action, – may be pester'd and gall'd with incendiaries
> and malignants; – with Radicals who should be uprooted, and Reformers who
> should reform themselves.
> A theatrical Audience being a multitude, it is to be recollected that a small
> part of a multitude can foment "tumult and disorder"; – and in all multitudes
> there are many to be found who are illiberal, capricious, and ill judging, enough,
> to be frequently clamorous about many matters which are not "radically
> wrong" . . . Is it to be conceived that such a heterogeneous body, invested with
> such powers of being turbulent, will not often be so, without just cause?[23]

The manager ruling the theatre is not to blame here: his subjects unjustly
and illogically dispute his control. The "multitude" of theatre politics
seemed impossible to measure, impossible to control: the sheer heterogeneity of its body offered a sufficient explanation for its power of being
turbulent.

Politicians as well as theatrical managers invoked the theatrical
analogy both as an ideal and as a means of critique. Edmund Burke, for
instance, invoked the theatrical analogy at moments of political crisis,
first as a means of schooling his fellow politicians in proper conduct,
then as a means of educating "the people" or public opinion. In 1783,
for instance, urging reform of England's East Indian empire, Burke
claimed that the fate of the reform bill "will turn out a matter of great
disgrace or great glory to the whole British nation. We are on a conspicuous stage, and the world marks our demeanour."[24] Burke's metaphor
used public opinion to manipulate parliamentary performance, inviting
members of parliament to see themselves as actors under the scrutiny of

a demanding audience. At the same time, the image suggested that these political actors could lead "the whole British nation" to the glory of principled moral action. Seven years later, in his *Reflections on the Revolution in France*, Burke slanted the analogy in the opposite direction, presenting theatre as a "school for morality," in which the form of tragedy taught audiences to accept the trappings of monarchy as essential garments constituting "the wardrobe of a moral imagination."[25] Burke's argument in *Reflections* suggests some of the ambivalence associated with the analogy between nation and stage: the claim to public attention unevenly balanced by the threat of empty theatricality. In an age of spectacular theatre and politics, a well-stocked wardrobe might well outweigh less flashy appeals to a "moral imagination."

This ambivalence meant that the theatrical analogy could also be used to criticize politicians, both as actors on the stage of the nation and as managers of the national drama. Richard Brinsley Sheridan, combining the roles of politician, playwright, and theatrical manager of Drury Lane theatre, made an especially tempting target for critique, as his parliamentary performances were occasionally reworked into plays commenting on contemporary politics. Asked for his opinion of Sheridan's *Pizarro* (1799), for instance, prime minister William Pitt the younger is said to have responded: "If you mean what Sheridan has written, there is nothing new in it, for I heard it all long ago at Hastings's trial."[26] Sheridan's speeches at the Hastings impeachment worked to link colonial corruption to monarchical power while claiming for the opposition party the high moral ground of family values and economic disinterest. *Pizarro*, Sheridan's translation of Kotzebue's *Rollas Tod*, attacked Spanish colonialism in Peru along similar lines. But in translating politics (the Hastings impeachment) into theatre (the sentimental, popular, and profitable *Pizarro*), Sheridan could be seen as exploiting the public in much the same way the conquistadors had exploited America, or Hastings had exploited India. James Gillray's caricature "Pizarro" conflated the playwright with the villain of the piece, emphasizing Sheridan's financial gains from his political drama (plate 1). Imagining the nation as a theatre thus could be used to draw attention to the unscrupulous use entrepreneurs might make of both forms.

Overall, the conflicted analogy between theatre and state deployed in the 1780s and 1790s captured both a fantasy of the British coming together as a nation, schooled by their drama, and the fear that the nation was coming apart, that the drama of national identity was nothing but a spectacular fraud, a deception. More specific than earlier

Plate 1 James Gillray, "Pizarro contemplating over the product of his new Peruvian Mine." June 4, 1799.

versions of the "theatrical perspective" described by Agnew, this emphasis on political theatricality could be used to criticize particular models
of government or, indeed, particular politicians; it also provided a critical topos, a commentator's commonplace within which anxieties could
be aired: especially anxieties about republicanism, class antagonism,
and more generalized social unrest. Oscillating between a model of
national concord and one of class disruption, between praise for theatre
as a school for morality and scorn of its spectacular deceptions, the
theatrical analogy encapsulated the ambivalent appeal of early Romantic
nationalism.

SPECTACULAR SENTIMENTS

Critics and politicians sporadically attempted to resolve the ambivalence
of the theatrical analogy by distinguishing the evils of spectacular
theatre from the sentimental virtues of heartfelt, moral political action.
In practice, however, both theatre and politics appealed to the public
through a combination of sentiment and spectacle. Praise for the
instructive morality of sentimental drama or politics, like the corre-
sponding denunciations of theatrical and political spectacle, must therefore be taken with a large pinch of salt. In fact, Romantic nationalism
relied on spectacle both in appealing to the public's patriotic sentiments
and in projecting a sentimental code of honor: benevolent mastery of
domestic and international affairs.

In discussions of politics and theatre, however, the polarity between
sentiment and spectacle prevailed. Politicians used the contrast between
theatre as an education and theatre as a fraud to promote their own
visions of political order while condemning those of their opponents.
Edmund Burke, for instance, complained that the French revolution
(and its English supporters) relied too heavily on spectacle:

Plots, massacres, assassinations seem to some people a trivial price for obtain-
ing a revolution. Cheap, bloodless reformation, a guiltless liberty appear flat
and vapid to their taste. There must be a great change of scene; there must be
a magnificent stage effect; there must be a grand spectacle to rouse the imagination grown torpid with the lazy enjoyment of sixty years' security and the still
unanimating repose of public prosperity. (*Writings and Speeches*, 156)

Here, spectacle and stage effect compensate for the mental and aesthetic
inadequacies of Burke's opponents: only torpidity and laziness, he
implies, could find public prosperity a flat, vapid, unanimating spectacle. For Burke, the French National Assembly – produced by revolution,

spectacular in its openness to women and the working classes – could be compared only to the lowest forms of English theatre: French politicians act "the farce of deliberation with as little decency as liberty. They act like the comedians of a fair before a riotous audience" (*Reflections*, 161). As Romantic audiences and theatre managers were repeatedly criticized for preferring spectacle and pantomime to the tragedies of Shakespeare, so Burke condemned the French people and revolutionary government for a failure of dramatic taste and decorum.

Yet Thomas Paine, in criticizing the monarchical governments that Burke wished to defend, associated monarchy rather than representative governments with spectacle and farce: he compared monarchical privi- lege and power with

something kept behind a curtain, about which there is a great deal of bustle and fuss, and a wonderful air of seeming solemnity; but when, by any accident, the curtain happens to open, and the company see what it is, they burst into laugh- ter. In the representative system of government nothing of this can happen. Like the nation itself, it possesses a perpetual stamina, as well of body as of mind, and presents itself on the open theatre of the world in a fair and manly manner. Whatever are its excellencies or defects, they are visible to all. It exists not by fraud or mystery; it deals not in cant and sophistry; but inspires a lan- guage that, passing from heart to heart, is felt and understood.[27]

Paine and Burke desired very different forms of government – but each writer envisioned his political ideal in terms of a manly, open, heartfelt theatre, defined against the farcical spectacle he used to describe the opposing system of government. Spectacle and farce were both asso- ciated with negative models of political theatre: models which saw the people cheated by their leaders *and* models which imagined the multi- tude revolting against just leadership. Sentiment, meanwhile, manifest in terms such as "manly" or "open" and phrases such as "passing from heart to heart," remained a catch-all form for a complicated blend of political stances. As Claudia Johnson puts it, "what and how one feels is a matter of public consequence, and as such subject to one's own as well as to other people's surveillance. During the 1790s, in short, sentimental- ity is politics made intimate."[28] Theatre both evoked and betrayed the promise of such political intimacy.

Sentimental politics relied on natural feeling and familial relations to provide a model for political action; like the theatrical analogy itself, this model had both radical and conservative political implications. The "natural" feelings of benevolence and pity, for instance, may have seemed egalitarian at heart, yet they required victims for their exercise.

As summarized by Robert Markley, eighteenth-century sentimentality was "at least in part a masculinist complex of strategies designed to relegate women to the status of perpetual victims, biologically constrained by their hypersensitivity and emotionalism to passive suffering and sociopolitical docility."[29] Claudia Johnson likewise emphasized sentiment's dubious chivalric reliance on "the spectacle of immanent and outrageous female suffering" (*Equivocal Beings*, 15). In political contexts, sentiment frequently invoked female suffering as a national call to action. In 1786, for instance, launching impeachment proceedings against Warren Hastings for colonial corruption, Edmund Burke delivered an impassioned speech describing in excruciating (and largely unsubstantiated) detail the rape and torture of women in Rangpur: the torture of Rangpurian men prepared for the rape scene which rhetorically sealed Burke's argument. Four years later, publishing his *Reflections on the Revolution in France*, Burke again used the spectacle of female sexual vulnerability to argue his case: he described Marie Antoinette, first as radiant Dauphiness, then as queen, fleeing her bed to fall, erotically disheveled, before the feet of her similarly threatened king. For Burke, such spectacular appeals to the public sense remained harnessed to his vision of the "moral imagination"; conversely, one might argue, Burke's moral imagination placed a radical reliance on the spectacle of female vulnerability.

Sentiment's attempts to save its victims ranged from the politically progressive to the politically conservative. Attributing "the American revolution against patriarchal authority" partly to the widespread reading of sentimental literature in the colonies, for instance, Jay Fliegelman has argued that "[t]he problems of family government addressed in the fiction and pedagogy of the period – of balancing authority with liberty, of maintaining a social order while encouraging individual growth – were the larger political problems of the age translated into the terms of daily life."[30] More specifically, Fliegelman suggests that the sentimental novel's critique of parental tyranny provided a revisionary model of England as (bad) imperial parent to its colonial offspring. Yet Burke's *Reflections on the Revolution in France* presented the state-as-family in terms that emphasized the analogy's conservative power:

We have an inheritable crown; an inheritable peerage; and an house of commons and a people inheriting privileges, franchises, and liberties, from a long line of ancestors . . . In this choice of inheritance we have given to our frame of polity the image of a relation in blood; binding up the constitution of our country with our dearest domestic ties; adopting our fundamental laws into the bosom of our family affections; keeping inseparable, and cherishing with the warmth of all their combined and mutually reflected charities, our state, our hearths, our sepulchres, and our altars. (119–20)

In Burke's formulation, the inheritance of private property seems to produce both state and family, and to tinge both with the warmth of domestic affections, the maternal image of the familial bosom.

Laying claim to the ideologies of sentiment, political writers like Burke and Paine invoked theatre while damning spectacle – which is to say they invoked an idealized theatre, one which ran counter to contemporary social and political realities. Yet at first glance Romantic theatre fashions seem to recreate, or rather produce, the very opposition between heartfelt theatre and tawdry spectacle invoked by these politicians. Critical pronouncements attacked both sentiment and spectacle, but in antagonistic ways, and spectacle bore the brunt of the critics' wrath.

Dramatists from Garrick on had turned to spectacle as a means of pleasing their audiences, while nonetheless complaining in advertisements, prologues, epilogues, and the drama itself that spectacle degraded the stage. The prologue to Garrick's *Miss in Her Teens* (1747), for instance, begins with the complaint, "Too long has farce, neglecting nature's laws, / Debased the stage and wronged the comic cause."[31] Sentimental dramatists and critics could object to spectacle more consistently. A character in Hugh Kelly's sentimental *School for Wives* (1773), for instance, insisted on the instructive power of comedy: "unless we learn something while we chuckle, the carpenter who nails a pantomime together will be entitled to more applause than the best comic poet in the kingdom."[32] Wordsworth's complaint in his preface to the *Lyrical Ballads* (1802) put in extreme terms a more general concern: he argued that both the literature and the "theatrical exhibitions of the country" had "conformed themselves" to the general public's "craving for extraordinary incident," to a "degrading thirst after outrageous stimulation." If the efficient cause could be attributed to "great national events which are daily taking place," the result was nonetheless a mental "state of almost savage torpor."[33] Overall, dramatists and critics largely agreed that spectacle – a reliance on scenery, costumes, music, lighting, and other stage effects – was designed to appeal, through physical sensation, to the lowest common denominator within the audience: the "children great and small" to whom Colman the younger addressed his dramatic romance, *Blue Beard*.[34]

Against the childishness, crude vulgarity, and blunted sensibilities produced by a spectacularized theatre, critics set the excessive (and untheatrical) refinements of sentiment. A capacious yet peculiar form, sentimental drama has resisted definition for over 200 years. As Colman the elder noted, in the eighteenth century the term was used more as a stock complaint than as a precise description: "the most offensive weapon of Modern Criticism is some *reigning word*, with which every literary Rifleman arms himself, and does dreadful execution . . . I am old enough to remember when the word Low was this Scare-crow . . . At length, however, the word *Low* has been restored to favour, and the term SENTIMENT in its turn has fallen into disgrace."[35] Late eighteenth-century critics attributed to sentimental drama a capacity to educate or elevate its audience in moral terms; at the same time, they complained that sentimental drama was untheatrical or novelistic, that its plotting (or "fable") was weak, relying on artificial quandaries and improbable reforms.[36] Oliver Goldsmith's famous attack on sentimental comedy includes a description which seems fair in outline, though pointed in tenor and detail:

In these plays almost all the characters are good and exceedingly generous; they are lavish enough of their tin money on the stage; and though they want humour, have abundance of sentiment and feeling. If they happen to have faults or foibles, the spectator is taught not only to pardon, but to applaud them, in consideration of the goodness of their hearts; so that folly, instead of being ridiculed, is commended, and the comedy aims at touching our passions, without the power of being truly pathetic.[37]

Both proponents and opponents of sentiment would surely agree that sentimental characters were notable for their goodness, their generosity, and their feelings, and that the drama addressed the emotions or passions of the audience. Even some of Goldsmith's more specific complaints point to recognizable features of the drama: when he complains that sentimental characters "are lavish enough of their tin money on the stage," for example, he points to an element of artificiality often noted by critics and drama historians. Goldsmith went on to assert that "those abilities that can hammer out a novel, are fully sufficient to raise the characters a little" and produce a sentimental drama – and indeed, this was one of the most frequent complaints raised against sentimental comedy. Some ten years earlier, William Whitehead's sentimental comedy *The School for Lovers* (1762) had been described by the *Monthly Review* as "rather a Conversation-piece than a comedy" (158); six years after Goldsmith's essay, *Town and Country* described Elizabeth Griffith's

The Times (1779) as "far too sentimental for the stage," the reviewer going on to state that while the play "would have afforded a good ground-work for a sentimental Novel, it is not calculated for a dramatic representation" (xi, 660). In a period of great ambivalence toward spectacle, however, this critique of unstageability was less damning than might at first appear. Indeed, in presenting monarchical or representative government as a mode of open, heartfelt, manly theatre, Burke and Paine relied on established norms of sentimental drama to invoke a paradoxical ideal of antitheatrical theatre.

The apparent opposition between sentiment and spectacle collapses upon closer inspection, however. For one thing, spectacle was ubiquitous in late eighteenth-century theatre, so that the most sentimental drama imaginable was necessarily received within a spectacular context. An evening at the theatre toward the close of the eighteenth century typically began with music, progressed through a prologue, mainpiece performance, entr'acte entertainment, an epilogue to the mainpiece, and ended with an afterpiece. Many of the more spectacular elements of the evening underlined connections between the theatre and the nation, and thus attempted an appeal to national sentiments *through* spectacle. Popular options for entr'acte entertainment included nationalistic displays such as patriotic songs, or symbolic processions. Afterpieces, too, might be as simple as a "spectacle" of a recent battle or political event; other common afterpiece forms (farce, pantomime, opera, and ballet) frequently referred, in depth or in passing, to recent political events. In 1793, for instance, the year Britain first declared war on France, Covent Garden offered a series of afterpieces addressing military affairs, including *HARTFORD BRIDGE; or the Skirts of the Camp*; *THE RELIEF OF WILLIAMSTADT; or, the Return from Victory*; *THE INVASION; or, all Alarm'd at Brighthelmstone*; *THE SOLDIER'S FESTIVAL; or, The Night before the Battle*, and musical interludes such as *TRUE BLUE* and *TO ARMS, or the British Recruit* ("To conclude with a Representation of the Grand Fleet under Sail"). A handful of Covent Garden titles from 1798, when invasion fears were running high, tell a similar story: *ENGLAND PRESERV'D*; *BRITISH FORTITUDE; or, An Escape from France*; *RETALIATION; or the Citizen a Soldier*; *BRITONS ROUSED! or, Citizen Soldiers*. The playbill for this final performance specified the three scenes of the spectacle to emphasize their topical interest:

Scene I. A View of a Camp. Officers – Incledon, Townsend, Betterton, &c. *Scene II.* The Advance of the Army, Slow Time. They form a half moon, and go through the Manual Exercise [*sic*]. *Scene III.* A Sham Battle. They divide; when the mode of attack and defence in street-firing, so necessary to be practised and known at this critical period, will be exactly represented. To conclude with *God save the King*.

As these examples suggest, theatrical spectacles were often designed to appeal to the emotions of the audience as well as to their senses: in particular, to patriotic feelings of loyalty or pride – or fears for national defense.

If stage spectacle often addressed serious national concerns, "serious" drama was often staged in spectacular forms. Shakespeare was already a national idol, but in practice even his plays had been spectacularized. In the words of Hugh Kelly's prologue to *The Romance of an Hour* (1774), "Shakespeare is great – is exquisite – no doubt – / But then our carpenters must help him out." Or as a character in Colman's *New Brooms* (1776) put it, "Begar, dere was more moneys got by de gran spectacle of de Sha-kes-peare Jubilee, dan by all de *comique* and *tragique* of Sha-kes-peare beside, *ma foi!* – You make-a de danse, and de musique, and de pantomime of your Sha-kes-peare, and den he do ver well."[38] Conversational and domestic, sentimental drama resisted the encroachment of fabulous stage sets, but even sentimental comedies often included songs and sometimes dances. Indeed, by the 1780s and 1790s sentiment was more likely to appear as one element within a particular dramatic piece than as its reigning genius.

More intrinsically, though, sentiment as a mode of thought itself relied on a particular kind of spectacle: a scene of suffering or a familial tableau, to which the spectators, on stage and off, were expected to respond with "luxurious tears" and active or passive "benevolence." Straddling the literary and theatrical public spheres, sentiment incorporated a reliance on spectacle into the forms of the essay and the novel; conversely, it incorporated the act of spectatorship into the world of eighteenth-century theatre. While theatre critics traditionally complain of sentiment's unstageability, literary critics have noted sentiment's insistent theatricality, and its political investments.[39] The rather static theatre of sentiment – this staging of spectatorship – seems in some ways ideally suited to political invocations of the theatrical analogy. Honing the role of onstage spectator, politicians modeled for their public the proper responses to political tragedy and comedy alike.

WOMEN ON THE STAGE OF THE NATION

As it produced conflicted and illusory models of national unity, the theatrical analogy also helped articulate one crucial intersection between women and national politics during the Romantic period. At first glance, women marked out the boundary between the political and the dramatic stages: ostensibly absent from politics, women were highly visible in the spectacular theatre of the period. Yet to contemporaries that boundary must have seemed alarmingly fragile, frighteningly permeable. Women's spectacular presence on the dramatic stage became increasingly difficult to separate from their influence in other realms – especially because women's presence on the Romantic stage signified in a wide variety of ways, ranging from the sentimentally vulnerable to the politically manipulative. Indeed, women's status on the stage of the nation intensified the ambivalence of the theatrical analogy: in a display of vulnerability, women could be used to summon up the chivalric values of the nation; portrayed as politically powerful or manipulative, they embodied the internal corruption and the vulnerability to theatrical deception against which the nation must be guarded.

Romantic discussions of women, theatre, and politics remained focused on the scandal of women's visible participation, emphasizing the role of the actress and occluding that of the female playwright. According to Raymond Williams, the late eighteenth-century "uncertainty in dramatic forms combined with the strong fashionable element in the audience to produce a concentration of interest on actors as such." [40] This concentration of interest both fed and was fed by what Sandra Richards has described as "the rise of the English actress" during the eighteenth century; by the end of the century popular actresses could command not only public attention but also respect. If Sarah Siddons alone could be equated, however vulgarly, with the Archbishop of Canterbury, lesser actresses like Harriet Mellon or Elizabeth Farren might nonetheless marry into the nobility, or simply take a prominent place in society. More generally, the star system of late eighteenth-century drama, mingling newspaper "puffs," portraits, caricatures, and so on, drew attention to actresses and their remarkable social mobility, while actresses' celebrity memoirs helped establish their public through the medium of print as well as that of public performance. [41]

The sharp-tongued Frances Abington may serve to demonstrate some of the social power available to a canny actress; her roles also begin to demarcate the shifting boundary ostensibly separating a woman's power on stage from her power in the nation. Abington's social power was inseparable from her spectacular visual presence on stage. In an age when actors largely provided their own costumes, an actress's elegance in dress style could itself become a marketable commodity. W. D. Archenholtz, a German visitor to London, noted that Abington has invented for herself an occupation quite particular. As she possesses the most exquisite taste, she spends a good part of the day in running about London, to give advice on the dresses and new fashions. She is consulted like a Physician and fee'd in the handsomest manner. There is no marriage celebrated, and no entertainment given, where her assistance in regulating the decorations is not requested. In this way she is said to make annually nearly fifteen hundred pounds a year. It is quite sufficient in London to say "Mrs. Abington has worn this" to stop the mouths of all Fathers and Husbands.[42]

Abington's skillful promotion of spectacle outside the theatre as well as within it suggests how permeable the boundaries of the theatre could be, and how central a role was played by spectacle – costume, decoration, display – in high society's understanding of its own rituals.

Frances Abington's prominence among the fashionable set, combined with her skill in mimicry, made her a valuable epilogue speaker, especially for plays of more style than substance. Let us glance for a moment at John Burgoyne's *Maid of the Oaks* (1774), precisely the kind of theatrical spectacle *against* which theatrical and political commentators defined their national, dramatic ideal. The (sentimental) drama itself was largely the reworking of an aristocratic spectacle. According to Ralph G. Allen, "Burgoyne's play had been created . . . for the express purpose of showing off some spectacular scenic effects – in this case, some topical scenes by De Loutherbourg of Lord Stanley's celebrated fête champêtre, including views of the pavilion designed by the brothers Adam for that most remarkable of social events."[43] The play's reliance on spectacle did not go unnoticed. In November 1776, the *London Magazine* denounced *Maid of the Oaks* along with Garrick's *Christmas Tale* as "two of the vilest compositions, taking them in their different ways, that ever disgraced an English stage," and as "repeated scenes of mummery, nonsense, and absurdity." The prologue and epilogue that Garrick wrote to frame *Maid of the Oaks* attempted to obscure its ephemeral and limited claim to public attention by exaggerating the link between theatre and politics. The prologue, for instance, offers one of the strongest eighteenth-century articulations of the theatrical analogy:

> With more than pow'r of parliament you sit,
> Despotic representatives of wit!
> For in a moment, and without much pother,
> You can dissolve this piece, and call another!
> As 'tis no treason, let us frankly see,
> In what they differ, and in what agree,
> The said supreme assembly of the nation,
> With this our great Dramatic Convocation!

> Business in both oft meets with interruption:
> In both, we trust, no brib'ry or corruption;
> Both proud of freedom, have a turn to riot,
> And the best Speaker cannot keep you quiet.

The epilogue continued the analogy, with the speaker, Mrs. Abington, addressing the theatrical house as if it were the lower house of parliament. Having compared the play with a bill before parliament, she then moved the vote:

> You that would pass this play, say *Aye* and save it;
> You that say *No* would damn it – the *Ayes* have it.

According to one contemporary viewer, Abington "speaks the epilogue in a masterly fashion. In it she compares the boxes with the Upper House, and the pit and gallery with the Lower, gesticulating, murmuring and whispering, so that it was a pure joy to see her."[44] Abington's political mimicry succeeded largely because of its transgression of boundaries, but that transgression helped reinforce the very boundaries it challenged. To see a woman "doing" the political would have exaggerated the gap between women and politics even as it temporarily closed that gap. The unthinkable appeared on stage – but its appearance was merely laughable.

Indeed, laughter and mockery repeatedly marked the boundary between women and politics, as negative responses to women's political actions were expressed through caricatures and songs filled with references to spectacle, theatre, and actresses of dubious moral reputations. Ironically, perhaps, one of the celebrity women most notorious for her political stands was not an actress but an aristocrat – yet her political activities produced strangely theatrical responses. In 1784, Georgiana, Duchess of Devonshire, crossed the boundaries of female propriety by canvassing on behalf of Charles Fox in the hotly contested Westminster election – and making a political spectacle of herself seems to have translated into becoming an actress by association. Caricatures criticizing the Duchess of Devonshire's political activity repeatedly linked her with actresses of dubious morality (or physical charms) and by extension with the burlesque election represented in Samuel Foote's political farce *The Mayor of Garrat* (1763).

Caricatures linked the Duchess of Devonshire with two women known both for their theatrical predilections and (ironically or not) for their political positions: the Hon. Mrs. Hobart, later Lady Buckinghamshire, and Mary Robinson. The connection with Mrs.

Hobart was explicit, and from one perspective unexceptional: caricatured elsewhere for her role in private (aristocratic) theatricals, Mrs.
Hobart canvassed on behalf of Sir Cecil Wray, Fox's opponent in the
1784 election, and thus functioned as a female political foil to the
duchess. Yet while the duchess herself typically appears both beautiful
and refined, Mrs. Hobart represents a far grosser sense of female sexuality. In "Madam Blubber's Last Shift" (British Museum Sat 6561), for
instance, she is shown traveling to the hustings by means of hot air: the
flatulence trapped by her voluminous skirts. In Rowlandson's "The Poll"
(plate 2) that same vulgarity taints Hobart's political opponent: the
duchess forsakes her dignity in riding a political seesaw balanced by this
private and political actress. The politicians they support pull down on
either side of the seesaw, yet the women's own political "weight" threatens to decide the contest. Indeed, as one of the election songs put it,

> Since women of fashion govern the State
> And you Mrs. Hobart, have sure the most weight
> I wonder you've no better candidate
> Than Sir Cecil Wray.[45]

Connections drawn between Georgiana and Perdita were far more
subtle and indirect, but perhaps more damning in the long run. As I have
noted, in the 1780s Mary (Perdita) Robinson was an actress best known
for her affairs first with the Prince of Wales and then with Charles Fox.
Caricatures continued to link Robinson both with the prince and with
Fox long after each affair was over – largely, it seems, to register the prostitution of politics, the dissipation of these two public men. On October
16, 1783, for instance, an anonymous print entitled "Florizel and
Perdita" (plate 3) presented the two erstwhile lovers as two halves of a
single portrait. On the left, the prince wears the ribbon and star of the
Garter; on the right, Robinson's breast juts aggressively and unnaturally
out of her shirt: the "conjunction" of the public man with the public
woman visibly dishonors the former. Perhaps the most interesting part
of this print, however, is the versatility with which the pairing of public
man and public woman could be applied: one of the most effective caricatures criticizing the political activism of the Duchess of Devonshire
simply reapplied the earlier portrait of "Florizel and Perdita" to this
clearly analogous situation. "Cheek by Joul; or the Mask" (plate 4) is
somewhat more decorous than its prototype: as a member of the aristocracy, the duchess takes the prince's place on the left side of the print,
and the commoner Fox takes the place of his lover Perdita. In this print,

Plate 2 Thomas Rowlandson, "The Poll." April 12, 1784.

Plate 3 Anonymous, "Florizel and Perdita." October 16, 1783.

the duchess's breasts are not exposed – but by drawing an analogy
between the noblewoman's somehow illicit connection to Fox and
Robinson's affair with the prince, the caricature reduces all public
women to prostitutes and conduits between political men. The fact that
Georgiana as a major Whig hostess served as "platonic confidante" to
both Fox and the Prince of Wales is here rendered sexually suspect,
aligned with Mary Robinson's rather more carnal knowledge of both
men.

If "Cheek by Joul" relies in part on the scandalous reputation of a
demi-monde actress to pillory a duchess, another pair of caricatures underscores the perceived connection between Mary Robinson and the
Duchess of Devonshire. The British Museum's copy of "The Rivals; or,
the Man and Woman of the People in Conjunction" (plate 5) dates from
June 19, 1788, but Dorothy George suggests this may be a reprint of a
caricature first issued in 1782. At the center of the print, Colonel
Tarleton, another of Robinson's lovers, holds the prince by the hair with

Plate 4 Anonymous, "Cheek by Joul; or the Mask." May 3, 1784.

a sword at his throat, as the prince exclaims, "Stop, Colonel, Charley has decided it." At the left of the print, Fox carries Perdita away on his shoulders. The caricature emphasizes the grotesquery of the mingled figure of public man and public woman "in conjunction." Fox's legs are half as thick again as those of the prince; his upper body, obscured by Perdita's legs, seems greatly foreshortened, his shoulders appearing about where the middle of his rib cage might be expected; on top of a thick neck, he sports the head of a fox, its tongue sticking out. Perdita's legs are rigid, her bustle sticking out stiffly behind as she holds Fox's head under the chin. The two appear almost as a single body, a centaur-like creation – except for the (phallicly positioned) fox's head. The conjunction of public man and public woman produces a creature of dubious gender as well as dubious humanity. Thomas Rowlandson's "Every Man Has His Hobby Horse" (plate 6) replays this conjunction of the man and woman of the people, but with a difference. The public man and public woman remain quite visually distinct in this print, perhaps in order to emphasize not the monstrosity of this pairing but its scandalous sexuality. Both the Hobby Horse of the title, and the fact that Fox is "riding" the duchess, suggest a sexual union between these political allies, although the print itself remains relatively discreet. Granted, Fox's hand strays a bit too near the duchess's breast, and the exposed breast of Mungo's woman, along with her summation of Fox as "a good Man – for the Ladies," keeps sexual exposure in the foreground of the print. The racial mixing of Mungo and his woman likewise underlines the sexual taboos broken by the imagined pairing of patrician duchess and demotic politician.

Indeed, Rowlandson at one point planned to invoke the link between Perdita and Georgiana to debase the duchess still further – linking her not with the prince or Fox but with the republican publican, Sam House. John Brewer has shown how references to the mock elections at Garrat were used in 1784 to attack the Duchess of Devonshire's support of Fox.[46] Linking Sam House, a figure for male plebeian politicians, with the patrician duchess served to emphasize the gap between upper and lower classes as it stressed the differences between public man and private woman. Yet the link between House and the duchess remained for the most part fairly circumspect. Rowlandson's "Lords of the Bedchamber" caricature (BM Sat 6529) suggests that such circumspection was achieved by censorship, if only self-censorship. In Rowlandson's original sketch for the caricature, Sam House says to Fox, "Open House Charly for ever with me. Do bring Madame Perdita toNight We'l be

Plate 5 [?J. Baldrey], "The Rivals; or, the Man and Woman of the People in Conjunction." June 19, 1788; probably reprinted from 1782.

Plate 6 Thomas Rowlandson, "Every Man Has His Hobby Horse." May 1, 1784.

damned jolly over a Pot of – ."[47] House's coupling of Fox and Perdita
suggests a further linking of himself with the duchess: the sexual intimacies evoked by the first pair could be applied to the second. Such a suggestion may well have seemed too extreme upon reflection; the final
caricature omits the comment.

As an aristocrat campaigning for "the Man of the People,"
Georgiana, Duchess of Devonshire, offered one of the most striking
challenges to the exclusion of women from the public realm of politics;
her actions were rebuked in part by caricatures equating her with an
actress of dubious reputation. If the prevalence of the theatrical analogy
meant that actresses' stage presence sometimes carried a political
charge, women engaging in political activities could also be chastised by
allusions to actresses, to theatre, and to spectacles such as the mock elections at Garrat. If women helped to mark the boundary dividing theatre
and politics, under close examination that boundary proved only too
obviously fragile. Rebuking public women for their independence, critics
and caricaturists shored up the distinction by returning to an old, familiar script: the antitheatrical equation of actress and prostitute.

While women visibly on the stage of the nation or the London theatres drew critical and political fire – what Julie Carlson has called "the
surveillance of women on the public stage" – women writers engaged the
theatrical analogy in less visible but no less controversial ways. Mary
Wollstonecraft denounced the theatricality at work in Burke's *Reflections
on the Revolution in France*; Elizabeth Inchbald, Hannah Cowley, and others
wrote plays engaging contemporary political events. For the most part,
female dramatists and women writers invoking theatre were spared the
kinds of public critique and control suffered by actresses: in fact, the
intense public scrutiny of actresses may well have diverted attention away
from female dramatists. Ironically, of course, dramatists were much
better positioned than actresses for social and political critique: female
playwrights could largely control the *mise-en-scène* of their plays, and they
chose the words actresses could only deliver. Yet as Ellen Donkin has
shown, female playwrights had to run the gamut of a masculinist theatre
system before their plays had a hope of production: the censorship implicitly and explicitly exercised in this way may have reduced male fears of
women's political engagement through written drama.

Occasionally, however, critics saw politics at work even in drama presented as apolitical. As we shall see, Hannah Cowley struggled to defend
her mixed drama *A Day in Turkey; or the Russian Slaves* (1791) from complaints that it displayed political sentiments: Cowley felt that this charge

of "politics" had robbed the play of a royal command performance (and by extension, robbed the playwright of increased profits). Two years later *The True Briton* attacked Elizabeth Inchbald's comedy *Everyone Has His Fault* (1793) as subversive, because it seemed to support a woman's right to choose her own marriage partner. Certainly the comedy articulated a general discomfort with women's shifting social and political positions. Within the play, for instance, the patriarch Lord Norland says to his divorced ward: "What are you now? Neither a widow, a maid, nor a wife. If I could fix a term to your present state, I should not be this anxious to place you in another."[48] While the end of the play shows divorced and dissatisfied marriage partners returned to one another, the expression of dissatisfaction itself seemed subversive to *The True Briton*. Under public attack, Inchbald resisted being pigeonholed a subversive writer, retaining for herself a mobility and independence denied her female characters. In a published reply to *The True Briton*, Inchbald insisted that her instincts for professional survival were too strong for her to have produced a subversive play: "had I been so unfortunate in my principles, or blind to my own interest, as to have written anything of the nature of which I am accused, I most certainly should not have presented it for reception to the manager of Covent-Garden theatre."[49] Like Cowley, Inchbald was canny enough to maintain a pose of political innocence; even more than Cowley, however, she articulated the economic interests underlying this particular feminine pose. The careers of female dramatists depended on their political innocence or neutrality – yet their plays might well engage political issues within a pose of female domesticity.

SCRIPTING THE NATION

Key political theorists like Jean-Jacques Rousseau and Edmund Burke may have felt as lost as Lord Norland when it came to "fixing a term" to women's present state, yet they were quick to name the generic shape of women acting out. Indeed, both Burke and Rousseau inveighed against women's political power by associating women with a particular kind of negative theatricality. Rousseau linked women's power with that of the masses by presenting "spectacle" as the means by which public opinion – far more powerful than law as a means of controlling public morality – was formed and altered. In his *Lettre à d'Alembert sur les spectacles*, first translated into English in 1759 and "immediately popular," Rousseau argued that contemporary French theatre presented only "romances"

staged under the name of *drames*: "a natural effect of this sort of play is
to extend the empire of the fair sex, to make women and girls the pre-
ceptors of the public, and to give them the same power over the audience that they have over their lovers."[50] Rousseau suggested that the
gendered inversion of power relations shown through stage romance
could spread outside the theatre, and went so far as to picture candidates
for office having to seek the support of actors in order to succeed: "the
elections will take place in the actresses' dressing rooms, and the leaders
of a free people will be the creatures of a band of histrions. The pen falls
from my hand at the thought" (123). With this image of illicit couplings
behind the stage, sexuality, theatricality, and politics appeared at once
inseparable and monstrously conjoined.

Burke, criticizing the revolution of which Rousseau was the patron
saint, nonetheless agreed with Rousseau's critique of female power. If
Burke condemned the French National Assembly as "comedians at a
fair," his elaboration of their theatricality highlighted the role of women
in the revolution's inversion of power relations:

> they act amidst the tumultuous cries of a mixed mob of ferocious men, and of
> women lost to shame, who, according to their insolent fancies, direct, control,
> applaud, explode them; and sometimes mix and take their seats amongst them;
> domineering over them with a strange mixture of servile petulance and proud
> presumptuous authority. As they have inverted order in all things, the gallery is
> in the place of the house. (*Reflections*, 161)

As the revolutionary audience takes the stage, refusing to remain passive
spectators, women "lost to shame" appear as domineering and presump-
tuous as the ferocious men more predictably associated with revolution.
For Rousseau, theatrical "romances" made women into lawgivers
through their influence over social behavior and public opinion; for
Burke, the farce of revolution could be summed up in the image of
shameless, domineering women directing the National Assembly or
forcing the return of the royal family to Paris.

In what follows I explore the two forms of dramatic romance and farce
as touchstones for the intersection of women, nationalism, and drama
during the Romantic period, highlighting the different shapes taken by the
ambivalent force of the theatrical analogy within these two forms. Male-
authored dramatic romances tackled the problem of women's role in the
nation, while female-authored sentimental farces explored international
relations through the lens of domestic affairs. As Burke's and Rousseau's
writings suggest, both theatrical modes were invoked to encapsulate fears
about women's political power – yet both forms also offered women access

to political affairs. In dramatic romance, actresses gained a temporary prominence and a quasi-political role by virtue of their theatrical roles. Sentimental farce, meanwhile, offered women writers a set of forms and dramatic conventions associated with social and political critique.

The next section of this book focuses on the figure of the actress or public woman and the form of dramatic romance; its introduction attempts to articulate the cultural logic structuring the frivolous, illogical form of romance. Dramatic romance constituted a truly minor offshoot of late eighteenth-century drama – yet in its intense and self-conscious theatricality, it raised questions about national identity, and about the power or agency available to individuals within a nation. Inaugurated by Garrick's *Cymon* (1767) and including such forgettable productions as Burgoyne's *Richard Cœur de Lion* (1786) and Cross's *The Apparition* (1794), the form of dramatic romance relied heavily on staging; it appealed to audience desires for spectacle through exotic or historical sets, through processions and pageantry demonstrating state power, and through heroines at once powerful and dependent – or demonstrably flawed. Indeed, dramatic romances offered women an emblematic role in the nation – the role of a symbol representing national identity – only to suggest that women were inadequate to that role.

Within a handful of plays and a more general set of cultural images and expectations, dramatic romance enacted the ambivalence evoked by spectacular nationalism in sequential terms: first the attractions of the nation were made flesh, embodied by an actress or public woman; then the woman herself was purged from the spectacle of the nation or the nation's power. And as women were excluded from the national spectacle, the dark side of the theatrical analogy – that nationalism was a cheat and a deception, that the nation was coming together only to be controlled by its lowest orders – could also be purged. Within the scapegoating logic of dramatic romance, then, actresses were first privileged, then punished. Yet the main chapters within part two focus on two public women – Emma Hamilton and Mary Robinson – who used their moments of privilege and prominence to alter the shape of national romance before (and sometimes after) the sequential logic of romance demolished their claim to public influence.

Moving from women on stage to women behind the scenes, the final section of the book examines female dramatists' use of farce or mixed drama to comment on national policy and international affairs. Again, the introduction to this section attempts to articulate the logic and Romantic associations of the form: its status as staged caricature, attacking both political and social foibles, as it challenged the force of even its own insights. Relying on inversion, allusion, and exaggeration for its effects, Romantic farce remained a revisionary (or, more harshly, a parasitical) form, best read in relation to the forms it relentlessly debunked. In this book, I am mostly interested in the relationship between farce and sentiment. While sentimental ideology equated the governing of a nation with that of a family in order to stress the emotive force of a just paternalism, farce played off the possibilities for domestic and international misrule suggested by common stereotypes of family discord. Romantic farces also presented national character in terms of crude stereotypes – and often reduced international affairs to the level of those stereotypes. Slavish Frenchmen, passive oriental women, despotic Sultans, the just and feeling Englishman: through these stereotypes, major political events became fodder for comedy. Conversely, the combination of farce and sentiment in Romantic "mixed dramas" tended to raise questions about the justice of various kinds of international action: Britain's colonial projects in India and southeast Asia, for instance; or Britain's divided loyalties in a territorial war between Russia and Turkey. Chapters on Hannah Cowley and Elizabeth Inchbald emphasize the ways these female dramatists mingled social and political critique, the way their plays both highlight and undercut the contemporary overlap of sentimental and imperial ideologies.

Given the wide range of Romantic theatre experimentation, it may seem ludicrous to focus on just two minor, ill-defined, and overlapping forms. Yet I would argue that the very lack of seriousness associated with romance and farce, their minor status, allowed for the presentation of ideas and opinions unthinkable within more canonical or established forms. The similarities as well as the contrasts between romance and farce on the one hand and melodrama on the other may be instructive here. Melodrama, after all, subsumed central elements of both romance and farce: in particular, the emblematic narrative of romance, the exaggerations of farce and some of its humor. Yet melodrama upstaged the kind of self-critique available through humor, or even frivolity, with its serious moral claims. In melodrama, sentimental morality prevailed: as Raymond Williams has pointed out, twentieth-century readers may object to the form of sentimental drama, yet they share most of its fundamental assumptions. In short, we tend to approach the frivolity of farce and romance through the morality of sentiment; the epilogue to this book takes the opposite view, considering the victory of sentiment from the perspective of farce and romance, and recalling the critical perspectives preserved within these frivolous minor forms.

PART II

Romancing the state: public men and public women

CHAPTER TWO

Varieties of romance nationalism

Georgiana, Duchess of Devonshire, pilloried in dozens of caricatures for her support of Charles Fox in the 1784 Westminster elections, seems to have been partly vindicated by Fox's eventual victory. Thomas Rowlandson, one of her most persistent (graphic) critics, marked the victory with an etching entitled "Liberty and Fame introducing Female Patriotism to Britania" (plate 7). As Linda Colley has noted, Liberty and Fame seem to be restraining rather than supporting the duchess – and "patriotism" may well have summoned up radical political associations in 1784.[1] Yet despite its ambivalence, the print remains remarkable for its joint presentation, on a single plane of imaginary existence, of Britannia, embodiment of the nation, and Georgiana, whose body had attracted all too much attention in the preceding election. Ostensibly endorsing the actions of this "female patriot," however, Rowlandson's caricature more effectively removes her from the realm of political action into a restrained world of mythological and symbolic significance.

Fifteen years later, on the twelfth of February 1798, Covent Garden staged as its afterpiece a patriotic pageant, featuring the onstage audience of "Britannia seated in Clouds, attended by Commerce, Plenty and Neptune." Before this rather optimistic vision of the national wellbeing, a series of historically significant scenes were enacted. Roughly a third of those scenes portrayed women's participation in Britain's heroic destiny: "RICHARD CŒUR DE LION imprisoned in Germany, & liberated by the Voluntary Contributions of his fair Countrywomen . . . EDWARD AND ELEANORA – The affectionate Wife sucks from her Husband's arm the Venom of a poisoned Arrow, by which Edward was wounded in Palestine . . . HENRY V – The Triumphs of Agincourt, and his Marriage with Catherine." As Gillian Russell has noted, the pageant "was staged at one of the crisis points in the war between Britain and France: the mutinies at the Nore and Spithead had occurred the previous summer, a French invasion was in the offing, the government was

45

Plate 7 Thomas Rowlandson, "Liberty and Fame introducing Female Patriotism to Britania." May 25, 1784.

facing acute problems in financing the war, and Ireland was in a state of virtual rebellion." Russell also suggests the pageant was "mainly aimed at the female members of the audience."[2] For my part, I am struck by the clarity with which the pageant splits women's nationalism into the separate roles of actor and spectator. Britannia's stillness on stage under-writes her monumental role of symbolizing the nation; active women, ranging from selfless, anonymous volunteers to more heroic queens, are carefully subordinated to the service of their kings.

Like Rowlandson's caricature, this pageant tackled two interwoven questions: (1) how to stage the nation; and (2) how to accommodate women within that spectacular nationalism. Obviously, the answer failed to produce immortal drama – yet this pageant, and the stage romances to which it is loosely related, did work to create one version of female patriotism, one account of the agency available to women within the British nation. The most persuasive account of romance nationalism to date, Marlon Ross's "Romancing the Nation-State," excludes women from the writing of romance nationalism and implicitly aligns them with the passive role of national symbol.[3] Yet Mary Robinson and Emma Hamilton both laid claim to an active – albeit problematic – role in national politics through their larger-than-life performances as heroines of romance. To understand how romance both facilitated and invali-dated their claims to political agency, we need to acknowledge the inter-nal tensions and contradictions of romance nationalism, and its relationship to a wider range of late eighteenth-century romance. Persuasive and coherent as Ross's account of romance nationalism undoubtedly is, it nonetheless equates romance with an "internally har-monized, though varied, whole" (72), thus occluding both the inner ten-sions of the form and its distinctly unharmonious history.

In the next few chapters, I want to present the minor, almost acciden-tal form of dramatic romance as another model of romance national-ism, one which relied on publicity and spectacle, on the transgression of boundaries between the stage and the nation, and on the interweaving of fiction or theatre with real life. Yet to understand the logic of dra-matic romance, we need to approach it within the larger, conflicted context of eighteenth-century romance. In reading the performances of Emma Hamilton and Mary Robinson, I will argue that both women drew on the mingling of fact and fantasy associated with the feminized prose romance; that their male counterparts appealed instead to the romance nationalism suggested by chapbook romances and their male readership; and that Hamilton's and Robinson's rise and fall in public prominence echoed the rhythms established by the theatrical form of dramatic romance. In this chapter, meanwhile, I hope to provide the necessary background for those more specific readings, while suggesting that romance provided a form of nationalism and a kind of public sphere at odds with the generally accepted accounts of each.

ROMANCE, NATIONALISM, AND THE PUBLIC SPHERE

We might begin by acknowledging that grounding English nationalism in romance dramatically affects the trajectory imagined for the nation. If, as Benedict Anderson suggests in *Imagined Communities*, the rise of nationalism is linked not just to the development of "print languages" but to the particular print forms of the realist novel and the newspaper, where does romance fit into this equation? According to Anderson, "we see the 'national imagination' at work in the movement of a solitary hero through a sociological landscape of fixity that fuses the world inside the novel with the world outside" (30). The newspaper, meanwhile, presents participation in the nation as an act of consumption: the daily obsolescence of the newspaper creates an "extraordinary mass ceremony: the almost precisely simultaneous consumption ('imagining') of the newspaper-as-fiction . . . [T]he newspaper reader, observing exact replicas of his own paper being consumed by his subway, barbershop, or residential neighbours, is continually reassured that the imagined world is visibly rooted in everyday life" (35–36). Anderson suggests that the realist novel and newspaper together helped produce "that remarkable confidence of community in anonymity which is the hallmark of modern nations" (36). It seems hardly accidental that the anonymous community produced by print capitalism here appears confidently, visibly masculine.

Like Anderson's vision of early modern nationalism, the bourgeois public sphere described by Jürgen Habermas relies heavily on the print forms of the newspaper and the novel to produce a male community in which social differences were temporarily ignored. In *The Structural Transformation of the Public Sphere* Habermas suggests that the public sphere, a realm of human interaction distinct from state, family, and economic endeavors, came into being over the course of the eighteenth century. In England, a literary public sphere composed of coffeehouses, journals such as the *Spectator*, and bourgeois novels such as Richardson's *Pamela* provided a context for social conversation focused on individual subjectivity and inner freedom. Alongside this literary public sphere, there developed a political public sphere, consisting primarily of parliamentary debates, the political press, and coffeehouse conversations, to discuss and critique political decisions in light of the public good. For Habermas, the public sphere provided an opportunity for rational-critical debate within a space where social inequalities were bracketed; one's personal circumstances were in principal excluded from the conversations conducted in coffeehouse discussions and political journalism. Yet Habermas also grants the limitations of the bourgeois public sphere: its agent or speaker was simply the bourgeois head of household, deriving autonomy and political power from his role within the family, his power over women, children, and servants.[4]

Habermas's bourgeois public sphere of rational-critical debate is obviously quite distinct from Anderson's national community in anonymity, but both theorists envision a political force ("the nation," "public opinion") arising in the eighteenth century out of a newly imagined sense of (male bourgeois) community, experienced through the print forms of journalism and fiction. In eighteenth-century England, however, romance developed a contrapuntal rhythm at odds with this particular history of cultural consumption and rational-critical debate. Against the sociological fixity of the newspaper and domestic novel, one might set the fantastic shape-changing and mythical mobility of romance as presented on stage and in print. Against the coffeehouse culture of rational-critical debate, one might set the "enchanted ground" of romance, experienced in a variety of public spaces ranging from the massive patent theatres to lowly street fairs to the reading "closet." Like the newspaper and the novel, romance offered its readers and spectators a particular mode of community; unlike the public sphere and the imagined nation, however, the community produced by romance was based on shared enjoyment of ostensibly unbridled fantasy. At the same time, the varied forms of publicity offered by print and stage romance emphasized rather than bracketed social differences: "peasants" were thought to read chapbooks and attend street fairs; women and servants were seen as reading prose romances while male scholars read medieval verse romances. Dramatic romances attempted to appeal to these distinct audiences *ensemble*, but only in published debates over the effects of romance did anything like Habermas's rational-critical public sphere begin to take shape. Even there, written responses to romance worked to separate the cultured from the crude, the sophisticated from the naïve, the rational critic from the raving enthusiast. If eighteenth-century romance offered fantasies of heroic power untrammeled by the limits of time and space, critical discussions of romance carefully distinguished the writers, those capable of critical self-determination, from the uncritical audience, those enthralled, almost literally captivated by the deceiving promises of romance.

The next few pages briefly sketch five different kinds of eighteenth-century English romance, marketed to distinct audiences and associated in varied ways with the imagined community of the nation. I start by considering chapbooks and vulgar stage romance respectively as extra-literary and extra-theatrical public spheres. Treated with amused condescension by men of letters, chapbooks and stage romance nonetheless developed a communal fantasy of national identity as embodied but unbound by physical limitations; they also provided an entry into print culture and public performance – two important media for political activism in the Romantic period. I then consider the contested public sphere of literary romance, noting ways the romance revival worked to counter the popularity of feminized, Frenchified prose romance with a nationalistic social history of medieval verse romance. Finally, I suggest that the minor theatrical form of dramatic romance provided something like a palimpsest of these other forms. Like chapbooks and the popular stage, dramatic romance emphasized exotic scenery and transformation scenes over literary value. Like its prose counterparts, dramatic romance presented women as protagonists or in roles of political power – but like the romance revival, dramatic romance replaced scenes of female dominance with those of state pageantry. The last third of this chapter offers a close reading of two popular dramatic romances: Garrick's *Cymon* (1767) and Colman's *Blue Beard* (1798). I argue that these plays staged the seductive attractions of the nation through the figure of the public woman, then abjected the negative theatricality of spectacular nationalism by disciplining that willful female figure. In subsequent chapters, I suggest that the logic of dramatic romance influenced the reception of public women acting on a national as well as a theatrical stage. Women's political prominence seemed inseparable from their sexual exposure, and such exposure always entailed a radical loss of respect. Yet because the romance of the nation repeatedly took shape through – and in opposition to – the figure of the public woman, the performances of public women could nonetheless alter the shape of romance and the imagined community of the nation.

CHAPBOOKS AND STAGE ROMANCE

Over the course of the eighteenth century, "the masses" were thought to enjoy romance in the written form of chapbooks: booklets of twenty-four pages, roughly printed and accompanied with crude woodcut illustrations – not unlike the modern comic book. On the popular stage, the same material appeared as farce, pantomime, and vulgar spectacle. Both forms – chapbook and stage romance – popularized the older traditions of medieval verse romance. Chapbook tales, for instance, were produced through a series of adaptations and compressions. At the end of the sixteenth century, "hack" writers such as Richard Johnson and Samuel Rowland had produced "modernized" and abridged versions of various medieval romances. In the early years of the Restoration, such romance adaptations were further abridged and rewritten, gradually taking shape as chapbooks. Over the course of the eighteenth century, these chapbooks proliferated until they came to be the most accessible form of print culture, seen as literature for children and the working classes alike.[5]

Theatrical romance, meanwhile, moved from the conventions of prose romance to a more vulgar staging of chapbook tales. The early Restoration stage had featured first the intrigues of "Spanish romance" and then the noble tragedy of Dryden's heroic drama, adapted in part from the French heroic romances of Madeleine de Scudéry. Dryden's defense of stage romance emphasized the imaginative power of the form, but even in his time, romance improbability was more commonly associated with farce than with heroism: over the course of the long eighteenth century romance drew ever closer to farce.[6] Henry Fielding's prologue to the farce *Tom Thumb* (1730) pointed to the blending of romance and folk culture produced by early eighteenth-century chapbooks as it mockingly proposed the heroes of these unsophisticated tales as the proper heroes for English tragedy:

> *Britons*, awake! – Let *Greece* and *Rome* no more
> Their Heroes send to our Heroick Shore.
> Let home-bred Subjects grace the modern Muse,
> And *Grub-Street* from her Self, her Heroes chuse:
> Her *Story-Books* Immortalize in Fame,
> *Hickathrift*, *Jack the Giant-Killer*, and *Tom Tram*.

Fielding's call to fellow Britons highlights the nationalism of romance: favorite chapbook heroes included St. George of England, Bevis of Southampton, and Guy of Warwick. The ever-popular *Seven Champions of Christendom* developed an international pantheon of heroes who periodically united to make war on Arab nations and to save Europe from pagan invasions – but even within this pantheon, St. George was clearly first among champions. Still, transformed into heroes of chapbook romance, Bevis, Guy, and St. George did actually rub shoulders with Jack the Giant-Killer and Tom Hickathrift – a situation with comic potential Fielding was quick to grasp.

Fielding's *Tom Thumb* recorded an important turning point in the history of stage romance, even as it helped create that turning: by the middle of the eighteenth century, critical disapproval had largely driven heroic romance off the legitimate stages. Less dignified venues remained, however. Henry Carey and John Frederick Lampe's *Dragon of Wantley* (1737) mocked the use of romance in contemporary opera with astounding success – a success which paradoxically seems to have encouraged the production of romance spectaculars on the operatic stage. Less dignified still lay the fair at Smithfield: in *The Theatre of Compliments* (1688), Bartholomew Fair is described as containing "valiant St. George and the Dragon, a farce." And in the *Dunciad* (1728), Alexander Pope mocked Elkanah Settle with his performance at the Fair: "Reduced at last to hiss in [his] own dragon."[7] In ballad form, romance material was sung on city streets, maintaining a link between romance and performance.[8] More generally, in street fairs and on small, popular stages, romance appeared inseparable from farce, as St. George the Dragon-Slayer and Jack the Giant-Killer relied on audience participation to compensate for theatrical shortcomings.

Chapbooks and stage romance offered their audiences participation in a communal fantasy: one based on shifting and exotic locales, transformation scenes, heroic powers, and chivalric stances. National heroes like St. George, Bevis of Southampton, or Guy of Warwick slew dragons, fought Moors, rescued (and married) fair damsels, undertook quests involving years of chastity (which nonetheless passed in seconds of real time), occasionally aided the poor and downtrodden and more consistently gained riches and rewards as they traveled the world. The imagined national community produced by chapbook and stage romance was one embodied by a hero, but unbound by normal physical limitations. With the turn of a page, the drop of a painted backcloth, or an announced change of scene, our hero might fly from Egypt to England; with equal ease, he might take on an animal guise or disappear from sight altogether. Whatever challenges he faced or humiliations he suffered, however, the hero could be counted on to triumph in the end. Embodying the fantasies and aspirations of the nation, the romance hero was necessarily unbeatable.

Popular engagement in chapbook and stage romance is almost impossible to reconstruct: those who wrote of these forms had a vested interest in downplaying their appeal and influence. Writerly responses to chapbooks presented them as a pre- or sub-literary mode of publicity; cultured responses to stage romance likewise distinguished the form from theatre proper. I want to suggest, however, that these forms may have operated as extra-literary or extra-theatrical public spheres, providing not a model of rational-critical debate, but a realm of shared fantasy. In *Public Sphere and Experience*, Negt and Kluge sketch the political potential of such fantasy. Arguing that "by virtue of its mode of production, fantasy represents an unconscious practical criticism of alienation," they stress fantasy's connection to real, lived experience in terms that emphasize its fragmentation, transposition, and mobility – all dominant features of romance.[9] They go on to argue that "all escapist forms of fantasy production tend, once they have reached a certain distance from reality, to turn around and face up to real situations. They establish themselves at a level definitively separated from the production process *only if* they are deliberately organized and confined there by a valorization interest" (36). Of course, popular forms of eighteenth-century romance remain in historical record largely because of literate attempts to organize and confine them. We know almost nothing of how popular audiences responded to stage romance, what one woman said to her neighbor in the pause between scenes, or how transformation scenes, like pantomimes, might have addressed topical issues. As a matter of historical record, chapbook and stage romance appear escapist, apolitical. In the writings of cultured men, chapbook and crude stage romances amuse children of all classes, but limit the lower classes by appealing to their crude beliefs and blinding them to political realities. Men of letters described a differentiated reception of romance, as if they themselves could see through the illusions of romance, but working-class readers and spectators could only accept romance at face value.

Even within this kind of written record, however, the accessibility of chapbooks (and the presentation of chapbook material on popular stages) established romance nationalism as a common aesthetic for a wide range of the population. Many working-class readers might have joined the poet John Clare in asserting that chapbooks "were the whole world of literature to me and I knew no other."[10] Yet literary lions such as Samuel Johnson, Edmund Burke, William Godwin, and Robert Southey also learned to read from the chapbook version of *The Seven Champions* and other abridged romances. Wordsworth and Coleridge even insisted that children be raised on romance rather than more rational forms of instruction. Coleridge, for instance, wrote to Thomas Poole on October 16, 1797: "Should children be permitted to read Romances, & Relations of Giants & Magicians, & Genii? . . . – I know no other way of giving the mind a love of 'the Great' and 'the Whole.'"

Yet since taste was seen as a natural marker of class, eighteenth-century men of letters needed to distinguish their cultured appreciation for chapbook romance from the uncultured liking of the masses. George Crabbe, for instance, emphasized the importance of romance in his own childhood even as he imagined the effects of romance in humbler settings: he described chapbooks as "Romances in sheets" their "coats in tatters"; these were "the Peasant's joys, when, placed at ease, / Half his delighted offspring mount his knees."[11] The difference between the poet Crabbe and the peasant's family lay in the fact that Crabbe's own history included a stage of growing beyond romance, a time when "Enchantment bowed to Wisdom's serious plan." Wordsworth in book five of the *Prelude* similarly sketched a stage of "the Poet's" life in which love of the marvelous gave way to a love of words and language. The peasant was distinguished from the scholar, the poet, and the gentleman by his inability to move beyond the enchantments of romance. Men of letters presented themselves as having outgrown their credulity, but they retained the magic of romance by nostalgically idealizing childhood simplicity, a simplicity also associated with impoverished peasants.

The same kind of double standard applied to the reception of stage romance. Henry Fielding's prologue to *The Author's Farce* (1730), for instance, implied that stage romance abolished its audience's freedom of response. Fielding's verse presented romance not as imaginative participation in the nation's destiny, but rather as the extortion of public support in the name of patriotism:

> Or when, in armour of Corinthian brass,
> Heroic actor stares you in the face,
> And cries aloud with emphasis that fit, on
> Liberty, freedom, liberty and Briton!
> While frowning, gaping for applause he stands,
> What generous Briton can refuse his hands?
> Like the tame animals designed for show,
> You have your cues to clap, as they to bow.[12]

Literally enthralled by the staging of romance nationalism, the general public supposedly loses its ability to respond critically – an ability which Fielding himself clearly retained. In the 1805 *Prelude*, Wordsworth casts a similarly critical eye over the larger theatrical context of stage romance. He describes a visit to "Half-rural Sadler's Wells" where romance takes its place among "singers, rope-dancers, giants and dwarfs, / Clowns, conjurors, posture-masters, harlequins" (*Prelude* 7.288–94). The romance on stage features "The champion, Jack the giant-killer – lo!" and the poet emphasizes the crudity of its illusions:

> He dons his coat of darkness, on the stage
> Walks, and achieves his wonders . . .
> . . .
> His garb is black, the word
> "Invisible" flames forth upon his chest!   (*Prelude* 7.302–9)

Invisibility becomes hypervisible, drawing attention simultaneously to the impossibilities of romance and the inadequate theatrical resources of Sadler's Wells. Yet the poet entertains himself with greater sophistication in watching the audience's suspension of disbelief:

> Nor was it mean delight
> To watch crude nature work in untaught minds,
> To note the laws and progress of belief.   (*Prelude* 7.296–98)

Crude theatricality becomes crude nature to these "untaught" spectators: their beliefs, mediated by the poet's condescension here, seem equally crude and undiscriminating.

The model of a socially differentiated reception of romance had clear political implications. When Edmund Burke, for instance, proclaimed in his *Reflections on the Revolution in France* (1790) that the age of chivalry is dead, he harked back to the values of romance from a perspective which explicitly took into account modern economic analysis, the antithesis of romance. He presented the French revolutionaries, by contrast, as unable to think beyond the illusions of romance:

Rousseau . . . had perceived that to strike and interest the public the marvellous must be produced; that the marvelous of the heathen mythology had long since lost its effect; that giants, magicians, fairies, and heroes of romance which succeeded had exhausted the portion of credulity which belonged to their age; that now nothing was left to the writer but that species of the marvelous which might still be produced, and with as great an effect as ever, though in another way; that is, the marvelous in life, in manners, in characters, and in extraordinary situations, giving rise to new and unlooked-for strokes in politics and morals. I believe that were Rousseau alive and in one of his lucid intervals, he would be shocked at the practical frenzy of his scholars, who in their paradoxes are servile imitators, and even in their incredulity discover an implicit faith. (283–84)

Burke paints the revolutionaries as credulous even in their incredulity: they may undo the church, but they accept the marvels of romance uncritically. The pamphlets developed in the wake of Burke's *Reflections* operated according to a similar logic: each writer attempted to show his opponent seduced by the illusions of romance, while emphasizing his own broader views. Only "the (uneducated) people" and the politically blind were seen as vulnerable to the follies of romance.[13]

CONTESTED HISTORY: PROSE ROMANCE

For the most part, men of letters responded to chapbooks and stage romance with affectionate condescension, but the world of literary romance generated a full-blown critical debate, opposing English rationality to French delusions while nonetheless retaining the nationalistic appeal of romance heroism. Throughout the eighteenth century critics worried about the French influence of prose romance, especially upon a readership largely composed (as it was thought) of women and servants. From the 1760s onwards, a small group of scholars known retrospectively as the romance revivalists, urged a return to a purer, more English form of romance: the verse romances of the Middle Ages, as yet untranslated and therefore inaccessible to all but a handful of antiquarian scholars. Prose romances mingled history and fantasy, interspersing historical events and fictional episodes; revivalists read medieval romances through the lens of recent history. International in focus and setting, prose romances gave women a certain social dominance; filled with tales of foundlings and heroes in disguise, they suggested fantasies of social mobility, or freedom from the constraints of social status. Romance revivalists by contrast read into verse romance a social history of English and foreign cultures, in which women remained in need of protection, and the working orders vanished from sight. Overall, the revivalists proposed a vision of the nation not unlike the hero of a chapbook romance – mobile, subject to startling transformations, at once embodied and unbound – but this vision developed against the international exoticism, illogic, and social mobility which prose romances were thought to disseminate among an audience of women and servants.

Indeed, if the eighteenth-century community of romance readers (like that of newspaper readers) might be said to form, "in their secular, particular, visible invisibility, the embryo of the nationally imagined community" (Anderson, *Imagined Communities*, 44), this could only be a matter of urgent concern for eighteenth-century men of letters. Women, children, and servants were considered the primary readers of prose romance, and (gentlemen) critics believed them incapable of distinguishing fiction from reality. In generic terms, the shifting and delusory landscapes of prose romance disallowed the "sociological fixity" that would come to be associated with the realist novel: heroic romances notoriously mingled fact and fantasy. Lord Chesterfield, for instance, complained that in *Grand Cyrus*, *Clelia*, and *Cleopatra*, three celebrated Romances, there is some true history; but so blended with falsities, and silly love-adventures, that they confuse and corrupt the mind, instead of forming and instructing it. The greatest Heroes of antiquity are there represented in woods and forests, whining insipid love-tales to their inhuman Fair-one, who answers them in the same style . . . I would just as soon believe, that the great Brutus, who expelled the Tarquins from Rome, was shut up by some magician in an enchanted castle, as imagine that he was making silly verses for the beautiful Clelia, as he is represented in the Romance of that name.[14]

Such a disruption of history and gender norms, such a trivialization of heroism, could only be French in nature – and one central strand of English nationalism took shape in opposition to such foreign forms. William Owen was not the only critic to insist of prose romance that "*France* first gave Birth to this strange Monster, and *England* was proud to import it among the rest of her Neighbour's Follies. A Deluge of Impossibility overflow'd the Press."[15] In an apparently irresistible gesture, the literary form of romance was repeatedly conflated with the monstrous or illusory figures which swelled its pages. A reviewer of *Peregrine Pickle* in the *Monthly Review* complained of "that flood of novels, tales, romances, and other monsters of the imagination, which have been either wretchedly translated, or even more unhappily imitated, from the *French*, whose literary levity we have not been ashamed to adopt, and to encourage the propagation of so depraved a taste." Yet if such monstrous figures seemed to threaten England's national character, the reviewer consoled himself and his audience with the idea that "this forced and unnatural transplantation could not long thrive in a country, of which the faculty of thinking, and thinking deeply, was once, and it is to be hoped, has not yet entirely ceased to be, the national characteristic."[16] British reason would eventually overcome French romance.

In the meantime, women and servants were seen as particularly vulnerable to the French perversion of reason. In 1751 William Owen suggested that Fielding's fiction had finally "persuaded the Ladies to leave this Extravagance to their *Abigails* with their cast Cloaths. Amongst which Order of People, it has ever since been observ'd to be peculiarly predominant."[17] In 1754, however, Richard Berenger was still worried by women's adherence to the conventions of romance:

I know several unmarried ladies, who in all probability had been long ago good wives and good mothers, if their imaginations had not been early perverted with the chimerical ideas of romantic love, and themselves cheated out of the charities (as Milton calls them), and all the real blessings of those relations, by the hopes of that ideal happiness, which is no where to be found but in romances.[18]

Romance distracted women from their duties, diverted them from their proper social roles – and threatened to corrupt servants in similar ways. As late as 1787, Thomas Munro would assert that sentimental Abigails, heroic footmen, and rhetorically adept shoemakers were "the characters which do a material injury to that part of the nation, who, when they have shut up shop, wet their thumbs and spell through a novel. A love-sick chambermaid is enough to ruin half the sisterhood; an intriguing apprentice is the torment of master tradesmen; and the high-flown notions of honour, which are inculcated by 'Johnny with his shoulder-knot' will set a couple of tailors a duelling."[19] Prose romances, encouraging waste and insubordination among subordinate classes, might well lead those less well off to question "the real blessings" of established social relations, or to claim the privileges of the upper classes, even the dubious privilege of duelling. Indeed, Munro went on to point the moral at established social privilege: "Should delicacy of thinking become too common, we may drive the lawyers from their quibbles, and how then are we to get those little odd jobs done for ourselves and our estates, so convenient for our families, and so beneficial to our landed interests?" The issue might be addressed lightly, but it was seen as serious. Hugh Blair's 1762 lecture "On Fictitious History" insisted that "any kind of writing, how trifling soever in appearance, that obtains a general currency, and especially that early pre-occupies the imagination of the youth of both sexes, must demand particular attention. Its influence is likely to be considerable, both on the morals and taste of a nation."[20] Prose romance, however trifling, had become in some sense the imaginative coin of the realm. To claim the nation, men of letters had to find ways of reclaiming romance.

The romance revival, driven by the work of Richard Hurd, Thomas Percy, and Thomas Warton, helped reestablish an elite sense of the national community by harnessing romance to England's epic destiny, to a particular version of history which remained inaccessible to the masses. The scholars of the romance revival purged romance of its French and feminizing influences by becoming interpreters – and polishers – of inaccessible texts, addressing their work to other men of letters. After reading Richard Hurd's *Letters on Chivalry and Romance* (1762), for instance, Thomas Percy wrote to Richard Farmer that he was "glad to find a taste for the Old Romances . . . not among the common

Readers, where it would do hurt" but "amongst our Critics and Poets. Mr. Hurd's Letters place them in a very respectable light."[21] Percy and Warton, followed by Joseph Ritson, George Ellis, and Sir Walter Scott, all emphasized the antiquity of the medieval verse romances, and their legitimacy as a national cultural heritage, in implicit opposition to the French perversions of the heroic prose romances. Women's role in romance was also carefully contextualized and reconsidered: the prominence and power accorded women in even the medieval verse romances were registered by revival scholars as a more general legacy of chivalric society, linked to women's vulnerability in times of war, and usually contrasted with the poor treatment women received in Roman days, or in "Mahometan countries." Yet while the romance scholars touted the virtues of the medieval verse romances – texts that in their "authentic" forms became available to a reading public only in the early years of the nineteenth century – their readings of those verse romances were heavily influenced by earlier critical debates over the Frenchified, feminized heroic prose romance.

Richard Hurd's *Letters on Chivalry and Romance* (1762), for instance, mounted a defense of Spenser's *Faerie Queene* (1590, 1596) against the detractions of French neoclassical criticism. As his title suggests, Hurd read the poem as a mixture of political history (chivalry) and literary form (romance). Presenting a political history of romance, Hurd's *Letters* sketched the interplay between politics and imagination both in the creation of romance and in the history of its reception. Hurd's famous conclusion pitted imagination and allegory against more pedestrian politics and reason:

Under this [allegorical] form the tales of faery kept their ground, and even made their fortune at court . . . But reason, in the end, (assisted however by party, and religious prejudices) drove them off the scene, and would endure these *lying wonders*, neither in their own proper shape, nor as masked in figures.

Henceforth, the taste of wit and poetry took a new turn: And *fancy*, that had wantoned it so long in the world of fiction, was now constrained, against her will, to ally herself with strict truth, if she would gain admittance into reasonable company.

What we have gotten by this revolution, you will say, is a great deal of good sense. What we have lost, is a world of fine fabling.[22]

Fancy – the unacceptable fancy of romance – is here feminized, and Hurd oscillates between championing this wanton damsel in distress, and joining with other (men) of reasonable company to "constrain" her.

In general, the revival scholars constrained the feminine fancy of romance by emphasizing history over imagination, representing contemporary events and recent history through the lens of England's epic past. Even the ungainly form of romance, with its anachronistic mingling of gothic and crusading elements, could be used to establish for England (and its constitutional structure) a principle of historical adaptation, accretion, and inclusiveness. Thomas Percy, for instance, emphasized the nationalistic appeal of his collection of popular ballads in these terms: "the English reader . . . will here find a faithful picture of his Saxon Ancestors, as they existed before they left their German forests: Here he will see the seeds of our excellent gothic constitution and will perceive the original of many of the customs which prevail among us at this day."[23] This emphasis on *German* heritage was hardly incidental: as Hurd deprecated not only French neoclassical values but also the Frenchified court of the Restoration, so Percy emphasized the Saxon rather than the Norman or Celtic ancestry of the English. It may be worth noting that George III, crowned in 1760, became the first Hanoverian king raised in England: synthesizing a German and an English cultural heritage, he presided over a heterogeneous kingdom of English, Welsh, Scots, Irish, and North American subjects. Similarly mingling past and present, Thomas Warton's account of the social conditions informing romance could well have been applied to – or adapted from – the British conquest of India: "In the early ages of Europe, before many regular governments took place, revolutions, emigrations, and invasions were frequent and almost universal. Nations were alternately destroyed or formed; and the want of political security exposed the inhabitants of every country to a state of eternal fluctuation" (*History*, xxvi–xxvii). Published in 1774, Warton's *History* followed close on the heels of the Regulating Act of 1773, designed to limit the East India Company's tendency to produce political fluctuations and irregular governments.

While the romance revivalists read romance through the lens of recent history, however, they also insisted that the imaginative freedom associated with romance be maintained and nourished in men of letters: imaginative expanse formed part of England's epic and imperial destiny. Addison's influential *Spectator* papers on the Imagination were an important authority here, especially no. 419 (July 1, 1712), which described "the Fairie way of writing" and a delight in "Witchcraft, Prodigies, Charms and Enchantments" as a characteristic trait of the English:

Among all the Poets of this Kind our *English* are much the best, by what I have yet seen, whether it be that we abound with more Stories of this Nature, or that the Genius of our Country is fitter for this sort of Poetry. For the *English* are naturally Fanciful, and very often disposed by that Gloominess and Melancholly of Temper, which is so frequent in our Nation, to many wild Notions and Visions, to which others are not so liable.[24]

If Addison began the trend of associating romance and enchantment with the "genius" of England, he was also responsible, in a slightly different context, for a phrase that became a standard topos of romance. In no. 417, Addison had compared the diverse effects of Homer, Virgil, and Ovid upon the imagination of the reader: he claimed that "when we are in the *Metamorphosis*, we are walking on enchanted Ground, and see nothing but scenes of Magick lying round us" (III.564). Richard Hurd, invoking Addison's authority for his own national reading of romance, quoted directly from no. 419, but in breaking off the quotation, he brought the fanciful nature of romance more allusively into play: "We are upon enchanted ground, my friend; and you are to think yourself well used that I detain you no longer in this fearful circle" (*Letters*, 54). Conflating the "enchanted ground" Addison had found in the *Metamorphosis* with English fancy, Hurd made the phrase into a touchstone for English romance. "Enchanted ground" as the topos of romance encompassed both the force of native superstition and the sense of England as a nation blessed with special imaginative powers – powers which recognized no national boundaries other than their own.

Yet if the romance revival harnessed the vital excess of the form to England's epic destiny, it also presented epic as dependent on romance and its imaginative power. So too the potential power of nationalism depended on its ability to appropriate popular forms, popular loyalties, popular beliefs. As Richard Hurd put it, "[w]ithout admiration (which cannot be effected but by the marvellous of celestial intervention . . . or by the illusion of the fancy taken to be so) no epic poem can be long-lived" (*Letters*, 102–3). If eighteenth-century scholars were ultimately concerned with the nationalist claims of epic (and the epic claims of nationalism), romance seemed to infuse such nationalism with interest and admiration as it harnessed the powers of fancy and superstition to more civilized and civilizing ends.

DRAMATIC ROMANCE

Commercial rather than political in design, dramatic romances worked to exploit a wide range of contemporary interests in romance. It must be said, however, that dramatic romance remains an eminently minor theatrical form, inaugurated by a single writer with a single play. In 1767

David Garrick, acquainted with some of the romance scholars through Johnson's literary club, turned the scholarly revival of romance into more commercial channels with *Cymon; a Dramatic Romance*. Drawing on the conventions of prose romance, *Cymon* mingled characters from drastically different walks of literary life: Merlin and the knights of chivalry rubbed shoulders with pastoral shepherds and shepherdesses, as well as characters such as Urganda and Fatima, whose names recalled the exotic romances of the *Arabian Nights*. Like chapbooks and the romance revival, however, *Cymon; a Dramatic Romance* worked to discipline and restrain women's volubility and power. Above all, Garrick's dramatic romance emphasized stage spectacle, presenting among other wonders, an enchanted palace and a tower that went up in flames before sinking to the stage floor. His prologue explicitly subordinated drama to theatrical spectacle –

> As for the plot, wit, humor, language – I
> Beg you such trifles kindly to pass by;
> The most essential part, which something means,
> As dresses, dances, sinkings, flyings, scenes –
> They'll make you stare.

Over the next few decades a handful of plays followed *Cymon*'s lead, presenting exotic stage spectacles – "which something mean" – cobbled together with a little rough, impromptu plotting. Romance – associated with exotic and historical settings, heroic action, inconsistent and discontinuous plots, and sudden transformations – offered a description rather than a justification of such theatrical froth. Indeed, Hugh Kelly's prologue to *The Romance of an Hour* (1774) echoed the earlier insouciance of Garrick's prologue to *Cymon*:

> Let critics proudly form dramatick laws,
> Give me, say I, what's sure to meet applause;
> Let them of time, and place, and action boast,
> I'm for a devil, a dungeon, or a ghost.[25]

Some plays, like Garrick's *Cymon* and George Colman's *Blue Beard* (1798) explicitly presented themselves as dramatic romances; Burgoyne's *Richard Cœur de Lion* (1786) appeared as an "historical romance"; Cross's *The Apparition* (1794) as a "musical dramatic romance." Other plays, like Garrick's *A Christmas Tale* (1773) or George Collier's *Selima and Azor* (1776), simply exploited contemporary demands for exotic stage spectacle. Prologues to still other plays invoked Romance in their presentation of the scenes to come. Boaden's prologue to *Fountainville Forest* (1794), adapted from Radcliffe's *The Romance of the Forest*, presented his plot as "Caught from the Gothic treasures of Romance," while Matthew Lewis described the "fair enchantress . . . Romance" as the presiding spirit of *The Castle Spectre* (1798).

Of course, almost all of these plays can be accommodated within other theatrical categories. *The Castle Spectre* and *Fountainville Forest* have both been described as "gothic drama," while *A Christmas Tale* and *Blue Beard* were both written to address, somewhat tangentially, audience demands for a Christmas pantomime. For his part, Allardyce Nicoll included all of these plays from the 1780s and 1790s under the general category of melodrama, stressing "the spectacular nature of the setting, the love of gloom and mystery, the excess of artificial sentimentalism, the hopelessly unnatural poetic justice and the general air of pathetic morality," along with the characters of villain, distressed heroine, hero, and comic sidekick. For Nicoll, these categorical decisions were based not on titles, but on "the general tone and atmosphere of each play."[26]

In describing these plays as dramatic romances rather than melodramas, I am privileging their self-declared frivolity over the more earnest claims and gloomy atmospheres of established melodrama. I also hope to register some of the similarities linking stage romance to chapbook, the feminized prose romance and the romance revival. Like chapbooks and more vulgarly available versions of stage romance, dramatic romance appealed to its audience through exotic, shifting stage effects and transformation scenes. Like prose romance, dramatic romance presented female heroines or women in political power – but like the romance revival, dramatic romance replaced the narrative threat of female dominance with a great display of state pageantry. Overall, dramatic romances worked to resolve the ambivalence of the analogy between state and stage by projecting that ambivalence on to public women. The next few pages read Garrick's *Cymon* and Colman's *Blue Beard* as two exemplary romances: *Cymon* as the inauguration of the mode, and *Blue Beard* as its most popular representative. Within these two explicitly denominated "dramatic romances," the attractions of the nation are first embodied in the form of actresses on stage; the negative associations of spectacle and theatre are then abjected from the nation through a plotline which disciplines and subordinates these public women.

From its opening moments, *Cymon* insists on the (political) power of female attractions, and on the justice of punishing women who misuse their power. Merlin, a longtime suitor to Urganda, female ruler of

Arcadia, finds himself spurned in favor of a young prince (Cymon) whom Urganda has stolen from his father's court in order to win his affections. Her efforts predictably fail: her illicit desire for Cymon marks her moral and political fall. The play begins with Merlin demanding of Urganda "Have you not allured my affections by every female art?" and his denunciation of her actions:

MERLIN: False, prevaricating Urganda! . . . Were you not placed on this happy spot of Arcadia to be the guardian of its peace and innocence? And have not the Arcadians lived for ages the envy of less happy, because less virtuous, people?

URGANDA: Let me beseech you, Merlin, spare my shame.

MERLIN: And are they not at last, by your example, sunk from their state of happiness and tranquillity to that of care, vice, and folly? Their once happy lives are now embittered with envy, passion, vanity, selfishness and inconstancy. And who are they to curse for this change? Urganda, the lost Urganda. (6–7)

Established by others, the public woman rules through example rather than legislation: she embodies the morality of her people. Urganda falls from grace when she tries to choose her own consort, when she rejects the devoted advances of Merlin, a man of power who appreciates her "female attractions." But her fall matters remarkably little. Urganda may be lost, but she is also expendable: the nation recovers by abjecting her folly.

The play (or rather Merlin himself) repairs Urganda's negative example of national romance through the courtship of Cymon and Sylvia. Cymon begins the play as a handsome idiot, insensible to romance, incapable of conversation. Urganda believes her attractions will eventually bring his mind to life: the play proves her right in principle though not in practice. Immune to Urganda's charms, Cymon comes to mature intelligence (if it can be called that) in response to the beautiful Sylvia, a princess brought to Arcadia by Merlin in order to awaken the prince's affections. And while the play condemns Urganda for bringing Cymon to Arcadia, Merlin's transportation of Sylvia appears praiseworthy. By the end of the play, the virtuous Cymon and Sylvia have replaced the corrupt Urganda as rulers of Arcadia. Evidently it takes a man (Merlin) to bring national virtue (Cymon) to life, though he uses female attractions (Sylvia) to accomplish his ends.

Cymon disciplines its unruly women gently, or leaves them to discipline themselves. Urganda, for instance, participates in the reconstruction of the nation by condemning herself out of hand. Merlin stops scolding her when he sees her penitence: his "heart melts into pity." Urganda rejects his sympathy, however, and takes herself off stage with this final speech:

URGANDA: Pity me not. I am undeserving of it. I have been cruel and faithless and ought to be wretched. Thus I destroy the small remains of my sovereignty. [*Breaks her wand*] May power, basely exerted, be ever thus broken and dispersed. [*Throws away her wand*] (48)

Merlin's pity passes quickly: he announces that "[f]alsehood is punished, virtue rewarded, and Arcadia is restored to peace, pleasure and inno- cence!" (49). With this simple transition, the spectacle of the (male) state comes to fill Urganda's place: "Enter the procession of knights of the different orders of Chivalry, with Enchanters, &c., who range them- selves round the amphitheatre" (49). This procession grew with each passing year, until on January 3, 1792 the *Morning Post* described more than 100 persons involved in the spectacle: Anglo-Saxon knights, ancient British and Norman knights, Indians, Turks, Scythians, Romans, a dwarf, a giant, Hymen, piping fauns, bands of cupids, and so on.

Still, Garrick's dramatic romance does not simply replace its female ruler with a spectacularly male state apparatus: the reconstituted nation requires the on-going participation of reformed women. Perhaps for this reason, Merlin neither destroys nor banishes Urganda's talkative hench- woman Fatima: he merely disciplines her speech. Having caught her alone, Merlin charges Fatima to answer Urganda's questions with a simple "yes" or "no." "The moment another word escapes you, you are dumb" (40). For Fatima, no worse punishment exists. She succeeds in resisting the temptation to "babble" and is rewarded by being given a voice in the concluding "air" of the romance:

FATIMA: Let those who the sword and the balance must hold,
To int'rest be blind, and to beauty be cold.
When justice has eyes her integrity fails,
Her sword becomes blunted, and down drop her scales.

The play as a whole suggests the opposite, however. Indeed, when a corrupt magistrate's vulnerability to Sylvia's beauty saves her from unjust imprisonment, another character tells her not to whimper because "Justice has taken up the sword and scales again, and your rivals shall cry their eyes out" (34). And in delivering the epilogue to the play, Frances Abington, who played the role of Fatima, once again addressed the audience through her female attractions. She entered, equating the enchanted ground of romance with the power to discipline female speech: "Is the stage clear? Bless me, I've such a dread! / It seems

enchanted ground where'er I tread!" (2.52). The epilogue, written by
George Keate, then asks Abington to appeal to male chivalry: "I'm sure
there's no one here will do me harm. / Amongst you can't be found a
single knight / Who would not do an injured damsel right." Her injury,
the forced limit on her speech, is recalled to intensify the sexual implications of her appeal to the men in the audience:

> There's not a female here but shared my woe,
> Tied down to *yes*, or still more hateful *no*.
> *No* is expressive – but I must confess,
> If rightly questioned, I'd use only *yes*.

Abington threatens briefly to use Merlin's wand to limit the audience's
speech, then ends with a compromise: "If this fair circle smile and the
gods thunder, / I with this wand will keep the critics under" (2.53). The
thunder which marked Merlin's triumph over Urganda within the play
is translated here into the thunderous applause of the gods in the second
gallery, while Abington's return to speech was evidently designed to woo
women spectators back into humor.

Frances Abington's delivery of the epilogue shows the eighteenth-
century superimposition of a female star's persona upon a specific role.
While Fatima remains a minor character in a play that asks not to be
taken seriously, Abington's closing speech to the audience makes her role
one of central importance to the early success of the play. In speaking
the epilogue, Abington appears both as Fatima and as herself, an actress
with a social following, a public woman. Indeed, if *Cymon* shows that
Arcadia can be restored to peace and prosperity by banishing Urganda
(Sophia Baddeley) and disciplining the wayward tongue of Fatima
(Frances Abington), the reputation of these two actresses replicated their
roles in the romance and underscored the moral of the play.

Sophia Baddeley, for instance, was frequently scolded for "abusing"
her power as a famous actress: known for changing lovers rapidly, she
used them to pay off her ever-mounting debts and keep creditors at bay.
She also used her influence over men to break down the barriers excluding actresses from polite society. When the London Pantheon first
opened with the intention of excluding players, Baddeley challenged
that social authority with her sexualized power over influential men. She
arrived with a party of male admirers, many of them noblemen; when
the constables guarding the doors politely declined to admit her, the men
drew their swords and threatened to run the constables through.[27] Yet
Baddeley came to the predictable bad end, dying impoverished and

socially isolated. As Anthony Pasquin imagined the scene in his *Children of Thespis* (1787),

> Emaciate and squalid her body is laid,
> Her limbs lacking shelter, her muscles decay'd.
> An eminent instance of feminine terror,
> A public example to keep us from error.[28]

As we have seen, Frances Abington, while more sexually restrained, nonetheless used her beauty and her public position to determine social fashions. Abington was known for the sharpness of her tongue as well as her beauty; as the years went on, she and Garrick quarreled ever more fiercely about his casting decisions and management of the theatre (Richards, *Rise of the English Actress*, 53). In constructing his dramatic romance, Garrick wrote roles which typecast both of these public women: *Cymon* exploited their public reputations as it gestured toward disciplining both the actresses and the characters they played.

Blurring the boundaries between stage, society, and nation, Garrick's *Cymon* purged Arcadia of corrupt female power by exiling or largely silencing these influential public women. Of course, not all dramatic romances were quite so explicit in their logic. Plays leaning more heavily toward the gothic constrained women more simply through the threat of rape; Collier's orientalist *Selima and Azor* inverted the moral, restaging Beauty and the Beast in a setting reminiscent of the *Arabian Nights*, with a male hero disciplined for his disrespect to women. But Garrick's *Christmas Tale* again linked the power of theatre with that of female rulers, only to show both forces chastened and subdued. The heroine Camilla's virtuous magical powers, for instance, are often indistinguishable on stage from the evil forces of theatricality, in league with oriental despotism. By the end of the play, Camilla like Urganda surrenders her powers: "I resign my power, fortune, everything to love and be beloved by thee. [*Music is heard*]" (232; v.1.199–200).

Garrick's *Cymon* based the health of the nation on the character of the beauty who represents it: Urganda's fall corrupts the state; Sylvia's virtue restores it. The younger George Colman's *Blue Beard* similarly based the virtue of the nation on the character of its men – and on their responses to female beauty. Like *Cymon*, however, Colman's *Blue Beard* made no claims to *dramatic* quality. In his introduction to the published play, the dramatist insisted,

I am far from endeavouring the vitiate the taste of the Town, and to overrun the Stage with Romance, and Legends, but English Children, both old and young, are disappointed without a Pantomime, at Christmas; – and, a Pantomime not being forth-coming in Drury-Lane, I was prevailed upon to make out the subsequent Sketch, expressly for that season, to supply the place of Harlequinade.[29]

As chapbook romance unified readers old and young, a childlike delight in stage romance unifies the nation, at Christmas, at the level of the lowest common denominator.

Colman's idiosyncratic revisions of *Blue Beard* tell their own story of romance (inter)nationalism: the dramatist translated the basic plot of the Charles Perrault fairytale and the Grétry opera *Raoul Barbe Bleu* into a story of "Female Curiosity" and the punishment it received in Turkey. In Colman's dramatic romance, Raoul Barbe-bleu became Abomelique, the three-tailed bashaw; his chosen bride was renamed Fatima, and she and her sister Irene were rescued not by her brothers but by her true love Selim and *his* brother soldiers. In the process of translation, Colman also emphatically restaged the threat of violence against women upon which British sentiment as well as Turkish authority was based.

The moral of this romance, as I read it, fades into the (undeniably spectacular) background of the play, to be performed by the stage rather than its actors. At the center of the drama rests the Blue Chamber, which Fatima, Bluebeard's latest wife-to-be, is forbidden to enter. The audience, however, is allowed into the secret withheld from female curiosity. First we see the acceptable façade of the room, the image Fatima too is allowed to see:

A blue apartment. A winding staircase on one side. A large door in the middle of the flat. Over the door, a picture of ABOMELIQUE *kneeling in amorous supplication to a beautiful woman. Other pictures and devices on subjects of love decorate the apartment.*[30]

As Fatima's sister Irene later remarks, "I'm sure 'tis a very pretty room" (202); certainly it seems designed to appeal to women's vanity as it represents male power submitting to female beauty. But once the key to the door is inserted, the room is transformed:

The door instantly sinks, with a tremendous crash, and the Blue Chamber appears, streaked with vivid streams of blood. The figures in the picture over the door change their position, and ABOMELIQUE *is represented in the action of beheading the beauty he was before supplicating. The pictures and devices of love change to subjects of horror and death. The interior apartment – which the sinking of the door discovers – exhibits various tombs in a sepulchral building, in the midst of which ghastly and supernatural forms are seen, some in motion, some fixed. In the centre is a large skeleton seated on a tomb, with a dart in his hand, smiling, and, over his head, in characters of blood, is written:* "THE PUNISHMENT OF CURIOSITY." (192)

This all-too-emblematic image of sentiment's underside pulls out all the standard gothic stops. Colman's staging conflates sexuality and death: love turns to horror, supplication to severance. Yet the scene presents its specific threat to women's lives through an evocation of male sexual anxiety, in which women's bodies are figured as sepulchral and haunted interior spaces, running with blood. What kind of curiosity is to be punished here? One could read the scene as a gothic version of sexual consummation, the skeleton and his dart a crude and comic image of sexual penetration – in which case, death appears as a punishment for sexual curiosity, sexual experience.

Complementing rather than contradicting this symbolic reading of sexual curiosity is the play's own narrative of curiosity as a specific transgression, as the attainment of forbidden knowledge. Female curiosity in general is not banned but rather encouraged: Abomelique gives Fatima the keys to the castle and encourages her to sate her curiosity in all rooms but one. What makes that room inaccessible to her is its tale of male power, female helplessness, and the historical reality of corporal and corporeal punishment. The transformation of the Blue Chamber stages a primal scene of sentimental gender relations; a fantasy of the forms of sexual congress and gendered power relations which produce the figure of the sentimental heroine and her helpless reliance on male chivalry. Once the secret is out, romance seems somehow less appealing. Nothing guarantees Fatima that Selim's present support will not turn, like Abomelique's supplication of female beauty, into violence. Yet the play ends happily and sentimentally. As Abomelique forbids Fatima the knowledge inscribed within the Blue Chamber, so Colman's comic spectacle distracts its audience from the violent implications of this mode of sentiment: spectators learn the dangers of transgression, but without profiting more fully from the vision for which Fatima nearly pays with her life.

Two different but equally spectacular scenes at once draw attention away from and reinforce the central paradox of the romance. Abomelique's entrance on to the stage was perhaps the most celebrated moment of the play:

The sun rises gradually. A march is heard at a great distance. ABOMELIQUE *and a magnificent train appear at the top of the mountain. They descend through a winding path. Sometimes they are lost to the sight to mark the irregularities of the road. The music grows stronger as they approach. At length,* ABOMELIQUE'*s train range themselves on each side of the stage and sing the chorus as* ABOMELIQUE *marches through their ranks. The villagers come from their houses.* (186)

This magnificent march was presented on stage by an enormous piece of animated scenery, in which animals and human figures appeared and disappeared amid the irregularities of the road, and grew larger with every reappearance. The procession featured the mechanical ingenuity of the stage machinist Johnston – and the wonder evoked by his paste-board horses, elephants, and moving scenery fed into Abomelique's forceful stage presence. The bashaw's might could be portrayed through the power of stagecraft; scenery offered implicit and structural support to his claim of absolute and arbitrary power.

At the other end of the spectrum of staging possibilities, and of the plot, came the other unforgettable scene of this early production. Maria Theresa de Camp's portrayal of Irene was considered the finest perfor-mance of the play. As one contemporary remarked,

[t]he high achievement of the character was her interesting grief at the menaced woeful catastrophe; and in the quartette, where . . . the author places her at the top of a tower, to "look out if she can see anybody coming," her advance from infant hope to a full-grown assurance of aid, her progres-sive animation from the moment when she sees "a cloud of dust arise," to that when she sees "them galloping," her scream of joy, and the agitation of her whole frame when she "waves her handkerchief," – all these constituted the high perfection of the dramatic art; and there was not in the house an eye nor a hand which did not give signs of sensibility, and pay a tribute of applause.[31]

In this scene de Camp herself became the spectacle presented to the audience. With no help from ingenious machinery or staging (other than her placement at the top of the tower), the actress replayed the first pro-cession scene, the drama of a gradual approach, through her comments, her gestures, her exquisite (and exaggerated) sensibility. If the staging of Colman's drama underwrites the arbitrary power of Abomelique and (eventually) the valiant force of Selim and his troopers as they break through the walls of the castle and the sepulchre, the gothic background of the play can only threaten women – it offers them no support. Waving her handkerchief to call help, de Camp's Irene projected agitation throughout "her whole frame" – the only theatrical structure on which she could rely. The transformation scene shows Abomelique's male sub-mission to female beauty as a performance which barely covers his repeated acts of violence against them; the procession aligns his abso-lute power with the power of stagecraft; the tower scene displays women, bereft of structural support, forced to rely on performative extremity as a means of winning male protection. The "allurements of female attrac-

tion" call male chivalry into action to reform and reconstitute the apparatus of the state. Yet women are severely constrained by this demand
for their performance, as de Camp's acting career was restricted by the
fact that audiences continued to equate her with the role of Irene, and
resisted her "allure" in other roles.

Reforming the state through masculine virtue and chivalric action,
dramatic romances like *Blue Beard* and *Cymon* exiled women from political action: what Mary Robinson called "the participation of power."[32]
Yet these plays also suggested that on the stage of the nation, women's
bodies served the state in two ways. First, they represented the attractions of the state: embodying the image of the "lovely nation," they
allured men into patriotic defense, women into political passivity. [33] In
this idealized role, public women seemed to guarantee the sublimation
of material resources, the resolution of material conflict. Yet public
women could also be held to account for the inevitable failure of this
effort at resolution: this is the second way in which women's bodies
serve the state. Material resources remain material; public women can
always be reduced to their bodies, and in the most "common" of ways.
If an idealized female figure embodies the nation's spiritual victory
over economic and political conflict, the prostituted public woman
stands in for the unattractive elements of the nation's *mise-en-scène*, the
state apparatus.

The "imagined community" of the nation can also be seen in Slavoj
Žižek's terms as a social fantasy, "a scenario filling out the empty space
of a fundamental impossibility, a screen masking a void." Žižek argues
that "fantasy is, in the last resort, always a fantasy of the sexual relationship, a staging of it" – and while I remain unpersuaded of the eternal
truth of this statement, late eighteenth-century attempts to stage the
nation-state do seem to take shape repeatedly, even obsessively, around
women's bodies and sexual relations. Such fantasies of "female attractions" seem to me designed to displace or obscure the growing tension
of class divisions, fears that the nation might be coming apart rather
than coming together. As Žižek suggests, "social fantasy is therefore a
necessary counterpart to the concept of antagonism: fantasy is precisely
the way the antagonistic fissure is masked." The bodies of public women
stage the "allure" the nation needs to hold for public and private, upper-
and lower-class men alike; yet those bodies also represent the abjected
materiality of the nation. Fantasy allows the ideology of the nation to
"take its own failure into account in advance"[34] – public women embody
both the success of the nation's appeal to the people, and its inadequacy.

Exemplifying the tensions at work within any notion of romance nationalism, the scandalous careers of Emma Hamilton and Mary Robinson draw together multiple versions of late eighteenth-century romance. Emma Hamilton's affair with Horatio Nelson, exaggerating the histrionic tendencies of each partner, was replayed in contemporary caricatures both as romance and as farce. At the same time, the historical performances of these heroic lovers reenacted the gendered formal struggle between heroic prose romance and popular chapbook tale. Emma Hart's rise from unwed mother to the role of Lady Hamilton, her involvement in the revolutionary wars, and her relationships with the queen of Naples and Horatio Nelson came together to produce a narrative similar to the popular feminine form of the heroic prose romance. Southey's famous *Life of Nelson* (1813), on the other hand, abridged and reprinted throughout the nineteenth century, reads not unlike a chapbook tale, skipping from battle to battle, emphasizing uniformity of character along with geographical expanse. The chapter that follows argues that, in keeping with the norms of stage romance, public deification of Nelson as epic hero both denied and relied upon his relationship to Hamilton, that outrageous heroine of romance. Hamilton's representational strategies, adopted by Nelson, helped create public expectations of personal heroism and national agency, even as Hamilton herself became a by-word for vulgarity and sexual license.

Mary Robinson's career also underscored the connection between dramatic romance and stage farce. Her role as Perdita in *The Winter's Tale* – and her brief but highly publicized affairs with the Prince of Wales and opposition leader Charles Fox – brought her political influence *and* exposed her to public mockery. Entering the romance of the nation as a theatrical prop and struggling to become a participant, she eventually turned to writing as a means of claiming the conventions of chivalry, romance, *and* farce for her own purposes. Robinson's *Lyrical Tales* (a formal challenge to Wordsworth's *Lyrical Ballads*) and her haunting presence in and around the London book of Wordsworth's *Prelude* suggest some of the formal and political relations linking verse romance with women's role in popular theatre. Reading Wordsworth and Robinson together, the latter chapter again emphasizes the inseparability of verse and popular romance, as it explores the gendered and classed political conflicts resolved on the shifting terrain of romance nationalism.

CHAPTER THREE

Patriotic romance: Emma Hamilton and Horatio Nelson

The extravagantly public affair between Emma, Lady Hamilton and Horatio Nelson was both highly compelling and socially repulsive to contemporary observers. That Nelson, the "great naval hero – the greatest of our own, and of all former times" should publicly associate himself with the wife of a nobleman who had befriended him gave his admirers pause.[1] That Emma Hamilton should publicly betray the man who had raised her from the status of a kept woman to that of British "ambassadress" seemed indefensible. That Sir William Hamilton, the betrayed husband, should remain intimate with both Lady Hamilton and Nelson was simply incomprehensible. Still, the fascination generated by the Hamilton–Nelson affair greatly exceeded – and continues to exceed – the social scandal of this *ménage-à-trois*. Southey's *Life of Nelson*, first published in 1813, went through dozens of editions and abridgments over the course of the century, and other biographies both preceded and followed his canonical account. Lady Hamilton's life has been retold by multiple biographers and recounted in numerous fictional accounts.[2] Most relevant to a discussion of national romance, however, may be Alexander Korda's 1941 film, *That Hamilton Woman*, starring Laurence Olivier and Vivien Leigh. Korda reproduced the story of these star-crossed lovers partly as an attempt to drum up American support for the British side in World War Two, but the film appealed at least as much to the British war effort as to the American: Winston Churchill is said to have watched the film 300 times over the course of his life.[3] It is easy, of course, to imagine Churchill identifying with Nelson's heroic struggle against Napoleonic forces – what interests me is to see this identification taking place through the medium of *That Hamilton Woman*: both the film and the female figure herself.

As the figure of Emma Hamilton mediates between two of England's great national heroes, across a time gap of more than a century, so the appeal of the Hamilton–Nelson affair rests somewhere between real life (biography) and performance (film), in the confused and confusing terrain of national romance. In this chapter, I want to consider both Hamilton and Nelson as performers within different modes of romance.[4] The first part of the chapter emphasizes Hamilton's and Nelson's use of performance for political influence, and the different forms such performance seemed to take: Hamilton's career drew on the mobility, diversity, and expansiveness associated with feminized prose romance, while Nelson's performance as national hero was received in light of the moral consistency and unified stance of the chapbook hero. The second part of the chapter argues that Hamilton's and Nelson's joint dependence on performance developed out of economic vulnerability, even as the performance of each worked to deny or obscure economic constraints. The third section suggests that while Hamilton and Nelson each drew on the other's mode of performance at different times, public reception integrated these two forms of romance only in the public's mythical transfiguration of Nelson's death; during their affair, observers worked to abject the vulgarity of feminine prose romance and vulgar stage romance on to Hamilton, leaving Nelson free for the purposes of national idolatry. Indeed, while Hamilton's political performances may seem only tenuously connected to her more theatrical performance of "attitudes," *reception* of the Hamilton–Nelson affair harped on Hamilton's status as a (prostituted) performer. Overall, I hope to show how these real-life performances of national romance followed the path of formal struggle laid out in the introduction to this section: Nelson as chapbook hero and national idol appears at once inseparable from and inconceivable in relation to the romance heroine Emma, Lady Hamilton.

A brief outline of the Hamilton–Nelson affair may help contextualize these issues of romance performance. To begin with, a talent for performance helped a young woman known as Emma Hart rise from the position of unwed, abandoned mother to the role of Lady Hamilton, British "ambassadress" to Naples. Pregnant, and abandoned by one protector who doubted her sexual loyalties, Emma Hart threw herself on the mercies of one Charles Greville, who took her on, but made her earn her keep both as housekeeper and as artist's model for the promising young painter George Romney. When he decided to court heiresses as a means of gaining his fortune, Greville passed his mistress on to his uncle, Sir William Hamilton, the British ambassador to Naples, in the hopes that this amenable young woman would keep the widowed Sir William from a second marriage and the production of heirs. In Sir William's household, "Mrs. Hart" began to perform a series of antique "Attitudes": silent tableaux of figures drawn from classical mythology and Greek statuary. Her "Attitudes" were popular both with Neapolitan and English society, but Emma Hart's performance of domesticity was even more successful: in 1791, against the advice of almost all his family and friends, Sir William married his "pantomime mistress."[5]

The second stage of the story begins in 1798, when the young Commodore Nelson asked for assurances from Naples, officially a neutral country, that he would be able to water and provision his ships as he went chasing after Napoleon's fleet on its way to Egypt. Permission was ostensibly granted, but when Nelson first attempted to obtain provisions, local port authorities refused him. John Mitford, a retired navy man, later summarized the popular mythology surrounding this affair:

It is a well-confirmed fact, that French influence operated so powerfully at the Court of Naples, that [King] *Ferdinand* had written to the Governor of Syracuse to withhold all supplies from Nelson's ship, and compel him to leave that port. The *Queen*, at Lady Hamilton's instigation, took the dispatches from the *King's* pocket, opened them, inserting directions for supplies to be granted; and resealing them, deposited them again from whence they were taken. The *sagacious* monarch sent them off next *morning*. The fleet was promptly supplied with provisions, without which they could not have gone to Egypt, and the enemy's fleet would have escaped destruction . . . England never was better represented at a foreign Court than by this *Female Ambassador*.[6]

This account was much disputed and the truth presumably far more pedestrian – but Nelson and to a lesser extent Sir William consistently supported Hamilton's claim to have influenced the queen decisively in this affair. Properly provisioned, Nelson caught up with the French fleet off the coast of Alexandria and won a decisive victory. The conquering hero then returned to Naples (and the Hamilton home) to convalesce.

The king and queen of Naples, having forfeited even the appearance of neutrality, were at this point forced to decide whether to bow to French orders, or to fight against the French Republican forces despite the overwhelming odds against them. Urged on by both Hamilton and Nelson, the king and queen chose to fight, and sent their army to meet the Republican forces near Rome. Badly directed and organized, the Neapolitan army soon abandoned retreat for outright flight and desertion into the French camp. By December 1798, the royal family felt it necessary to flee to Sicily with Hamilton and Nelson easing their way:

Lady Hamilton, *like a heroine of modern romance*, explored, with no little danger, a subterraneous passage, leading from the palace to the sea-side; through this passage, the royal treasures, the choicest pieces of painting and sculpture, and other property, to the amount of two millions and a half, were conveyed to the shore, and stowed safely on board the English ships. (Southey, *Life of Nelson*, 186; my italics)

Nelson transported the Hamiltons and the royal family through a severe storm to Sicily: one of the royal princes died of convulsions in Hamilton's arms. From Sicily, Nelson and the Hamiltons sailed as envoys of the king and queen to retake Naples. They succeeded in this campaign, but in the process of quelling the city, produced scenes of legendary carnage, with body parts piled high on street corners and the Neapolitan Admiral Caracciola hung from a ship's yardarm in a grotesque and illegitimate enactment of a British naval court-martial. Once the king and queen were again installed in Naples, Nelson and the Hamiltons returned to England, their reputations sullied. Shortly after their return, Hamilton gave birth to Nelson's daughter, Horatia Nelson, without any social recognition of the birth: even Sir William appeared oblivious. Separated from his wife, Nelson invited both Hamiltons to live with him on an estate selected by Lady Hamilton and purchased by Nelson himself. Sir William died in 1803; Nelson died in 1805 at the battle of Trafalgar, leaving Lady Hamilton as a "legacy" to his king and country. The nation declined to accept this legacy: left without any reliable means of support and unable or unwilling to economize, Hamilton sank into poverty and alcoholism, dying eventually in Calais in 1815.

In this chapter, I am interested primarily in Hamilton's and Nelson's joint performance from 1798 to 1800 – the means by which they represented Britain in relation to Naples – and British reception of that performance. In order to reconstruct this theatre of national romance, I will be drawing on Hamilton's and Nelson's letters, the letters of their contemporaries, and political caricatures of the time. I will also be reading Nelson's performance as hero through its belated representation in Southey's *Life of Nelson*. Designed as a kind of chapbook romance for the navy, Southey's *Life* clearly selected and organized its material to produce a particular effect:

Many lives of Nelson have been written: one is yet wanting, clear and concise enough to become a manual for the young sailor, which he may carry about with him, till he has treasured up the example in his memory and his heart. In attempting such a work, I shall write the eulogy of our great naval Hero; for the best eulogy of NELSON is the faithful history of his actions and the best history must be that which shall relate them most perspicuously. (2)

Southey's equation of eulogy with history mimics the corruption or perversion of history performed by romance. Southey's chapbook approach
to Nelson's life – an approach exaggerated by the many abridgments of
his biography – further highlights the collaboration between performance and reception required to produce the national romance of patriotic heroism: Southey's encapsulation of Nelson's mystique carried
more weight than a rigorously accurate account could have done. This
collaboration between performance and reception in turn underscores
the heterogeneity of national agency, even in the heroic mode of
romance nationalism. Together, audience and actor constitute an imagined community, in which the performer acts on behalf of all, but only
by tacit permission, with the audience's vicarious participation. In
Naples, Hamilton and Nelson complicated the notion of national
agency by identifying themselves with a collaborative and self-replicat-
ing performance of British heroism – but British reception of their joint
performance worked to undo this collaborative display of national
heroics along the lines both of genre and of gender.

PERFORMING ROMANCE

The collaborative performance produced by Hamilton and Nelson on
the European stage of the Napoleonic wars presented a modified version
of stage romance. In Garrick's *Cymon*, as we have seen, the female ruler
Urganda embodied the attractions of the nation and the morality of her
people, while national agency seemed to reside in the figure of Merlin.
In Naples, however, Hamilton and Nelson together embodied not the
nation's morality but its political influence: representing their nation,
both figures acted for England by driving Naples to military action.
While the mobility of Hamilton's performance differed markedly from
the uniformity of Nelson's, these two "acts" shared a common goal and
a common effect. I want to consider Nelson's and Hamilton's joint performance of romance first by examining the ways they urged the
Neapolitan court to declare war on France, then by tracing the most
characteristic elements of each player's performance.

Both Nelson and Hamilton represented themselves as having urged
Naples to declare war on France. According to Southey, for instance,

Nelson told the king, in plain terms, that he had his choice: either to advance,
trusting God for his blessing on a just cause, and prepared to die sword in hand
– or to remain quiet, and be kicked out of his kingdom: one of these things must
happen. The king made answer, he would go on, and trust in God and Nelson;

and Nelson, who would else have returned to Egypt, for the purpose of destroying the French shipping in Alexandria, gave up his intention at the desire of the
Neapolitan court. (*Life*, 178)

It may seem overstated to call Nelson's action here a performance.
Southey stresses the "plain terms" of Nelson's speech, thus obscuring the
rhetorical extremity of Nelson's two options for the king. Yet that
extremity oddly echoes Saint-Just's justification of the Terror ("We will
have justice; or if not, Terror"): what Peter Brooks described as the "logic
of the excluded middle . . . the very logic of melodrama."[7] King
Ferdinand's response to Nelson, equating him with God, adopts this
extremity, but Southey's prose buries the hyperbole of the conversation
by linking short, simple phrases into a lengthy and rather pedestrian sentence. Southey's *Life of Nelson* preserves its subject's heroism partly by
downplaying its dramatic tendencies.

The element of performance stands out sharply, however, in
Hamilton's replaying of this scene. In a letter to Nelson, she wrote that

while the passions of the queen were up and agitated, I got up, put out my left
arm, like you, spoke the language of truth to her, painted the drooping situation of this fine country, her friends sacrificed, her husband, children, and
herself led to the Block, and eternal dishonner to her memory, after for once
being active, doing her duty in fighting bravely to the last to save her country,
her Religion from the hands of the rapacious murderers of her sister and the
royal Family . . . that she was sure to be lost if they were inactive, and their was
a chance of being saved if they made use of the day and struck now while all
minds are imprest with the Horrers their neighbours are suffering from these
Robbers.[8]

Like Nelson, Hamilton put out her *left* arm: the hero of the Nile had lost
his right arm in battle. Here, the "language of truth" and the physical
recollection of heroism seem to translate performance into policy. Yet
where Nelson's language as reported by Southey remained understated,
and condensed a whole range of possibilities into two simple options,
Hamilton's speech spins those two options out into imaginary scenes: the
queen's friends sacrificed, herself and her family led to the block. Even
Hamilton's account of resistance leads back to historical scenes of
"rapacious murder." Impressing the queen's mind with horrors,
Hamilton saw herself striking at a timely moment: "In short there was
a Council, and it was determined to march out and help themselves"
(Add. MS 34,989). Hamilton concluded this account of her performance with the claim, "If things take an unfortunate turn here and the
queen dies at her post, I will remain with her, if she goes, I follow her. I

feil I owe it to her friendship uncommon for me." Like Nelson, Hamilton modeled the heroism she wanted to see the queen perform – but Hamilton produced her own performance of heroism as an echo of the queen's, just as her speech purportedly echoed Nelson's "energick language" (Add. MS 34,989). In place of Nelson's heroic originality, Hamilton's performance represented itself in terms of romance replications.

Nelson's conversation with the king and Hamilton's scene with Maria Carolina, queen of Naples, were both highly characteristic of each figure's performance of romance: Nelson unified his role as hero around the fixed and repetitive logic of a forced choice; Hamilton, by contrast, took on multiple different personae, produced hyperbolic displays of patriotism, and blurred the boundary between performance and reception. In keeping with the conventions of the chapbook hero, Nelson was known for his steadfast devotion to heroic ideals. He himself insisted, "A uniform course of honour and integrity seldom fails of bringing a man to the goal of fame at last" (Southey, *Life*, 52–53). Southey's *Life* intensified Nelson's uniform course of honor by excluding from the biography information that might seem irrelevant to the hero's portrait: like a chapbook, the biography attempted to distill the action of romance while avoiding its narrative distractions and excess. Southey presents the essence of Nelson's childhood, for instance, in three short stories, juxtaposed without transitions to show the young hero in action. Two of the stories emphasized Nelson's courage ("'Fear! grandmama,' replied the future hero, 'I never saw fear: – what is it?'"); the other, his honor ("'We must go on,' said he: 'remember, brother, it was left to our honour!'") (5). Just as chapbooks were known for shifting from their hero's battle exploits in Egypt to his imprisonment in France with scarcely a breath wasted on transportation or transition, so Southey's heroic biography collapsed Nelson's childhood into three short scenes of heroic speech or action.

Nelson's devotion to heroic ideals was also repeatedly expressed through the either/or logic found in his address to the king of Naples. Writing to Sir William and Lady Hamilton to thank them for their help through the provisioning crisis, for instance, Nelson assured them he would return "either crowned with laurel, or covered with cypress" – to record either his victory or his death (Southey, *Life*, 141–42). Shortly before the momentous battle of the Nile, Nelson remarked to his officers, "Before this time tomorrow I shall have gained a peerage, or Westminster Abbey" (142–43). As the battle drew on, Nelson seems to have imagined the weight of this balance shifting toward victory. When one of his captains, overwhelmed by the ingenuity of Nelson's battle plan, exclaimed, "If we succeed, what will the world say!" Nelson replied, "[T]hat we shall succeed is certain: who may live to tell the story is a very different question" (145). Survival equals success, but death confers honor: Nelson's options repeatedly collapse into a prophecy of fame. During the middle years of the Napoleonic wars – the battle of Copenhagen, the search for the French fleet out of Toulon – this either/or logic seems to have lain dormant. Yet Southey shows Nelson returning to this construction shortly before the battle of Trafalgar:

"I verily believe," said Nelson (writing on the 6th of October), "that the country will soon be put to some expense on my account; either a monument, or some new pension and honours; for I have not the smallest doubt but that a very few days, almost hours, will put us in battle. The success no man can insure: but for the fighting them, if they can be got at, I pledge myself." (Southey, *Life*, 324)

Nelson's repeated contrast between death and victory served a function not unlike the late twentieth-century media soundbite, condensing his stance as hero into a memorable phrase; at the same time, Nelson's repetition of that heroic stance in a variety of situations replicated the constant courage of the chapbook hero within the geographical expanse of chapbook romance. Of course, the either/or logic of Nelson's address to the Neapolitan king inverted the logic of his own approach to action: he asked the king to choose between certain defeat and the uncertainties of devout honor. Once the terms of honor have been accepted, however, defeat vanishes, leaving only the options of victory or death. Like chapbook romances, Nelson's steadfast dedication to the pursuit of laurel or cypress, a peerage or Westminster Abbey, a pension or a monument, provided a model of heroic constancy amid geographical and historical diversity.

In her audience with the queen of Naples, meanwhile, Hamilton took on Nelson's heroic persona, but transformed that role in her hyperbolic display of heroic fervor: both the act of personal transformation and the hyperbole of her performance were common features of her earlier career as romance heroine.[9] Earning her keep with Charles Greville, Emma Hart had served as artist's model for the young painter George Romney, modeling a wide range of classic and heroic roles (Circe, Medea, Ariadne, Cassandra, Bacchantes, and so on) in over 300 sittings between 1782 and 1786. Acquainted with numerous actors and theatre buffs, Romney may have spoken to his model about contemporary theories of acting – theories which emphasized the importance of passion, and the modulation from one passion to another. Certainly Romney's biographer, William Hayley, noted that Hart-Hamilton's "features, like the language of Shakespeare, could exhibit all the gradations of every passion with a most fascinating truth and felicity of expression."[10]

Exiled to Naples, Hart drew on her theatrical experience of modeling in a markedly different context: her "Attitudes" presented a series of mute tableaux, each of which characterized a different figure from antiquity *and* a different passion.[11] Dressed in simple "Greek" garb, Hart used a shawl to define each character and to mark the transition from one scene or attitude to the next.[12] The Comtesse de Boigne, who as a child participated in these performances, recalled the dramatic intensity of two such "Attitudes":

she grabbed me by the hair with a movement so brusque that I came back to myself in surprise and even a little fear, which made me enter into the spirit of my role – for she brandished a poignard. The passionate applause of the artist-spectators made themselves heard with exclamations of: Bravo la Medea! Then pulling me toward her, she hugged me to her breast with the air of disputing against the fury of heaven for me, she tore from the same voices the cry of: Viva la Niobe![13]

Linking Medea and Niobe through the vulnerability of their children, Hart's "Attitudes" seem to have exploited metonymic associations along with a thematic of animation, a dialectic between statuesque fixity and graceful motion. While visual records of these "Attitudes" – most notably a series of prints by Frederick Rehberg – necessarily show Hart frozen in position, in practice observers were taken by her graceful and striking movements.[14] In an early description of the "Attitudes," Goethe insisted that

the spectator can hardly believe his eyes. He sees what thousands of artists would have liked to express realized before him in movements and surprising transformations – standing, kneeling, sitting, reclining, serious, sad, playful, ecstatic, contrite, alluring, threatening, anxious, one pose follows another without a break. She knows how to arrange the folds of her veil to match each mood, and has a hundred ways of turning it into a head-dress . . . [A]s a performance it's like nothing you ever saw before in your life.[15]

Beginning with postures and ending with passions, Goethe's account emphasized the element of emotional transformation, and the unbroken sequence of attitudes. Mrs. St. George, another contemporary observer normally critical of Hart, agreed that "[h]er arrangement of the turbans is absolute sleight of hand; she does it so quickly, so easily, and so well . . . It is remarkable that, though coarse and ungraceful in common life, she becomes highly graceful, and even beautiful, during this performance."[16] While Nelson's performance of heroism emphasized uniformity, a fixed dedication to fame and glory, Hamilton's performances relied on mobility, transformation, metonymic associations of mood, and situation.

Indeed, in producing a performance based on rapid, successive transformations, Hart's "Attitudes" embodied the pastiche element of prose romance: its mingling of historical periods and locales, its confusion of history and fiction. Two weeks before Hart's marriage to Hamilton, for instance, Horace Walpole remarked on "Sir W. Hamilton's pantomime mistress – or wife, who acts all the antique statues in an Indian shawl. I have not seen her yet, so am no judge, but people are mad about her wonderful expression, which I do not conceive, so few antique statues having any expression at all – nor being designed to have it."[17] Walpole's remark about the "Indian" shawl disputes any possible claim to authenticity in this portrayal of antiquity – even the "wonderful expression" acclaimed by spectators seem out of place in a reproduction of Greek statues. Walpole captured the problem with Hamilton's public and private attitudes alike: almost always, she had a little too much expression for the role. Acclaimed for bringing antique statues to life, this romance heroine was poorly suited to remaining stone: unmoved, cold, and to temptation slow.

With her 1791 marriage to Sir William, Hamilton entered a new social and political theatre: as the Napoleonic wars moved ever closer to Naples and the royal family, Sir William's health became increasingly uncertain, and Hamilton's political role increased correspondingly. She nursed her husband in his various illnesses, helped him in his diplomatic correspondence, and acted as an informal conduit between the queen and the British ambassador – a role of some importance given the limited capacities of the king and the political dominance of the queen.[18] Hamilton brought to this political role the mobility and passion developed in her attitudes: in her relationship to the queen of Naples, she moved across the boundaries of gender to take on the role of noble cavalier; in response to Nelson and his Nile victory, she turned reception itself into a performance, a hyperbolic display of patriotic fervor.

Reports of a lesbian relationship between Emma Hamilton and Maria Carolina, queen of Naples, have been dismissed by most of Lady Hamilton's biographers.[19] These reports may have originated with Napoleon; at the very least, they were supported by him and others in Republican France. Yet whether or not a physical relationship existed between Emma Hamilton and the queen, the terms of their friendship were at times unmistakably romantic, recalling older traditions of courtly love. Greville once remarked of Hamilton that "anything grand, masculine or feminine, she could take up, & if she took up the part of Scaevola, she would be as much offended if she was told she was a woman as she would be, if she assumed Lucretia, she was told she was masculine."[20] In 1795, Hamilton seemed to take on the masculine role of the queen's cavalier, commanding Greville, "Send me some news, political and private; for, against my will, owing to my situation here, I am got into politicks, and I wish to have news for our dear much-loved Queen, whom I adore. Nor can I live without her, for she is to me a mother friend and everything." Playing the role of devoted cavalier, Hamilton sought to answer all of her lady's needs and desires. Her letters idealized the queen in courtly and unrealistic language: "If you cou'd know her as I do, how you wou'd adore her! For she is the first woman in the world; her talents are superior to every woman's in the world; and her heart is most excellent and strictly good and upright" (Morrison, *Collection of Autograph Letters*, 1.263).

Hamilton had long presented English ladies to the queen; at times, she seems to have done the same for diplomatic gentlemen. In February 1796, for instance, she wrote to Lord Macartney,

I have been with the Queen this morning, and she desires so much to see you that I have appointed to carry you to her this evening at half past seven . . . You will be in love with her, as I am. Sir William is to go with us; shall we call on you or will you drink tea with us? – let me know . . . We will go to the opera to-morrow, but I would give up all operas for *my Queen of Hearts*. She expects you with impatience. (Morrison, *Collection of Autograph Letters*, 1.275)

Assurance and idolatry vie for the upper hand in this note: as in the tradition of courtly love, Hamilton's service to the queen seems to have increased her status in the court more generally. At the same time, Hamilton's adoration models for Macartney the proper (masculine?) response to the queen: "You will be in love with her, as I am." For her part, the queen seems to have accepted the devotion of this female cavalier within the conventions of courtly love. During the year(s) of crisis in Naples, the queen's frequent letters to Hamilton, written in awkward French, occasionally cast "the ambassadress" in a masculine role. In April 1798, she wrote to Hamilton: "Vous en étes le maître de mon cœur, ma chère milady, ni pour mes amis, comme vous, ni pour mes opinions ne change jamais."[21] And in June 1798, Maria Carolina proclaimed Emma "mon ministre plénipotencier."[22] Outside observers also seemed to see Hamilton as a gentil parfit knight: the emperor of Russia, acting on Nelson's advice, eventually awarded her the title of "Chanoiness of the Order of St. John of Jerusalem" for her intervention in the provisioning crisis, thus formally acknowledging her role as courtly cavalier. (Captain Ball, made a commander of the same order for his heroism in battle, subsequently addressed her as "her Excellency la Chevalière Hamilton" [II.478].)

In responding to Nelson's victory in the "Battle of the Nile," finally, Hamilton's performance turned reception itself into patriotic and hyperbolic display. On hearing of the British victory – and of Nelson's loss of an arm and an eye – Hamilton first fell to the ground in a faint, bruising herself badly. Next she draped herself, not in a shawl, but in Nelson himself. She wrote the "Hero of the Nile" to tell him, "My dress from head to foot is alla Nelson. Ask Hoste. Even my shawl is in Blue with gold anchors all over. My earrings are Nelson's anchors; in short, we are be-Nelsoned all over" (quoted in Sichel, *Emma Lady Hamilton*, 491). Hamilton responded to Nelson's victory by quite literally taking it on herself, dressing herself not only "alla Nelson," but also as Nelson, or in Nelson. For his part, the naval hero seems to have encouraged such a blending of identities: while Hamilton sent him sonnets, he sent her a remarkably un-ladylike listing of the results of battle, with table headings which read:

English. Number of: Guns. Men. Killed. Wounded.
French. Number of Guns. Men. How disposed of (Burnt, Taken, Sunk, Escaped)

The list ends with the laconic conclusion: "Kill'd, drown'd, burnt, and missing: 5,225" (Morrison, *Collection of Autograph Letters*, II.335). This stark listing of the results of battle adds a somber note to Hamilton's gala reception of the victory, revealing a darker underside to the patriotic sonnets and general display.

Hamilton ignored this side of the battle. After first responding to the victory as if she could take on the attributes of the naval hero, Hamilton received Nelson's performance as if it were a production of her own "Attitudes." Renowned for bringing statues to life, she visualized her hero preserved in a statue of gold: "What a day will it be to England when the glorious news arrives! Glad shou'd I be to be there for one moment. Your statue ought to be made of pure gold and placed in the middle of London" (quoted in Sichel, *Emma Lady Hamilton*, 499). Hamilton's hyperbole at once objectified and idealized Nelson: "If I was King of England I wou'd make you the most noble present, Duke

Nelson, Marquis Nile, Earl Aboukir, Vicount Pyramid, Baron Crocodile, and Prince Victory, that posterity might have you in all forms" (496). Even as these imagined honors memorialize and thus to some extent fix the form of victory, the multiplicity of forms imagined reproduce the kind of metamorphosis associated with Emma Hamilton's own attitudes.

Hamilton's hyperbolic response to Nelson's heroism influenced European affairs to a surprising degree: not only did her responsiveness increase her influence over the queen of Naples, her extravagant visual display of patriotic feeling also modeled for England's greatest naval hero a somewhat more extreme approach to heroic romance. Linda Colley has argued that Nelson's

calculated exhibitionism, this theatre, . . . embarrassed and appalled many of his more genuinely patrician contemporaries. For it seemed to caricature to a vulgar degree the very style and strategy that they themselves were increasingly adopting. Splendidly, unabashedly and utterly successfully, Nelson did what the majority of the men who dominated Great Britain sought to do more elegantly and discreetly: use patriotic display to impress the public and cement their own authority.[23]

I want to suggest that Nelson adopted this unabashed approach to patriotic display in part from Hamilton. Already in 1797, after the battle of St. Vincent, he had requested not a baronetcy, but the Order of the Bath, because of its visible splendor, its draped red ribbon. In November 1798, as a reward for his Egyptian victory, Nelson was licensed by royal authority to bear various augmentations to his armorial ensigns: palm trees, disabled ship, ruinous battery, and so on. Yet Gillray's caricature commemorating this event emphasized less the coat of arms than the oversized and over-the-top clothing of the hero (plate 8). Just as Hamilton's ludicrous dress "alla Nelson" was produced as patriotic flattery, however, so Nelson's "L'épée de l'Amiral de la grande Nation," with its appeal to national as well as personal vanity, turns the caricature's accusation of vanity back upon the Britons Nelson's costume was designed to impress.

Predictably, perhaps, contemporary observers blamed Hamilton for Nelson's attention to display, criticizing this as vanity and narcissism. The acerbic Mrs. St. George, for instance, noted with some acidity the reciprocal narcissism binding Nelson and Emma: "It is plain that Lord Nelson thinks of nothing but Lady Hamilton, who is totally occupied by the same object . . . Lady Hamilton takes possession of him and he is a willing captive, the most submissive and devoted I have seen . . . She puffs

Plate 8 James Gillray, "The Hero of the Nile." December 1, 1798.

the incense full in his face; but he receives it with pleasure and snuffs it up very cordially."[24] Nelson and Hamilton together *think* of nothing but Hamilton – yet their *actions* cohere around the cult of Nelson. Submission to one remains inseparable from devotion to the other. Yet as Hamilton and Nelson increasingly mirrored one another's roles and actions, their love affair became increasingly indistinguishable from self-love, and their social performances undercut their public influence rather than increasing it. A visitor to Merton, for instance, complained that Hamilton

goes on cramming Nelson with trowelfuls of flattery, which he goes on taking as quietly as a child does pap. The love she makes to him is not only ridiculous, but disgusting. Not only the rooms, but the whole house, staircase and all, are covered with nothing but pictures of her and him, of all sizes and sorts, and representations of his naval actions, coats of arms, pieces of plate in his honour, the flagstaff of *L'Orient*, etc., an excess of vanity which counteracts its own purpose. If it was Lady H.'s house, there might be a pretence for it. To make his own a mere looking-glass to view himself all day is bad taste.[25]

Her house, like her body, might with some excuse be "be-Nelsoned all over," but over time it became increasingly difficult to distinguish Hamilton's house from Nelson's, her ego from his. The more Nelson and Hamilton performed for one another, as opposed to an audience of the nation or their peers, the more it cost them in terms of public and political influence.

ECONOMIC VULNERABILITY, ROMANCE AGENCY

For Nelson and Hamilton alike, the performance of romance served a very specific purpose: the production of financial security or career advancement. Here it may be useful to recall the strictly limited, provisional agency available to actresses on the stage of romance. The dramatic romances of Garrick and Colman, for instance, divided their performers into those with power to act (Merlin, Selim) and those who lack such power (Urganda, Fatima). On the stage of the nation, similarly, public figures performing romance did so either from a position of strength, enacting the pageantry of the state and its established power, or from a position of weakness, in which case they were forced to rely on their own purely physical capacity for display. Regardless of gender, the extravagant posturing and physical display of romance provided a source of public influence to those otherwise excluded from the networks of national agency, the byways of power. Nelson, lacking well-placed friends, began his career from such a position of weakness; as a sixteen-year-old unwed mother, of course, Hart-Hamilton's economic disadvantages were far more extreme. And the performative conventions of romance predictably privileged male agency over female influence. With the institutional support of the navy, Nelson's performance as national hero won him not only ribbons and honors but also a substantial income. Within the social constraints of class and feminine propriety, by contrast, Hamilton's performance of romance was repeatedly harnessed to a confirmation of domestic restraint. As romance heroine, Hamilton only broke free of domesticity in the midst of the Neapolitan crisis, and her transgressive performance in that setting was publicly criticized upon her return to England. Nelson's and Hamilton's performances both denied the force of economic constraint, but only Nelson succeeded in overcoming the economic vulnerability with which he began his romance career.

Nelson's performance of heroism developed directly, at least in hindsight, from his economic constraints: returning from the East Indies early in his career and ill with malaria, he later claimed to have felt

impressed with a feeling that I should never rise in my profession. My mind was staggered with a view of the difficulties I had to surmount, and the little interest I possessed. I could discover no means of reaching the object of my ambition. After a long and gloomy reverie, in which I almost wished myself overboard, a sudden glow of patriotism was kindled within me, and presented my king and country as my patron. "Well, then," I exclaimed, "I will be a hero! and, confiding in Providence, I will brave every danger!" (Southey, *Life of Nelson*, 16–17)

The chapbook charm of this pronouncement should not distract from the fact that Nelson's patriotism developed to fill the void left by lack of patronage and family interest. While one might appeal quietly to a patron or family member for support, any appeal to king and country required a certain extravagance, display, or emotional charge, in order to capture the interest of this imaginary patron. Nelson's heroic persona balanced such extravagance with a canny grasp of institutions and the economic implications of war. Southey noted that after the battle of the Nile,

amidst his sufferings and exertions, Nelson could yet think of all the consequences of his victory; and that no advantage from it might be lost, he despatched an officer over land to India, with letters to the governor of Bombay, informing him of the arrival of the French in Egypt, the total destruction of their fleet, and the consequent preservation of India from any attempt against it on the part of this formidable armament. (Southey, *Life of Nelson*, 159)

One might wonder, rather more cynically, whose advantage was at stake here. Southey, like Nelson, noted that this prompt news of the victory saved the East India Company "the extraordinary expenses" of an enormous military defense; predictably, perhaps, the Company soon voted Nelson a grant of £10,000 (163). Nelson clearly knew both how and when to play the hero.

Yet Southey's chapbook romance defined Nelson's heroism through an on-going denial of economic interest. Nelson repeatedly appears putting the financial interests of his men before his own concerns: in 1783, for instance, "Nelson's first business, after he got to London, even before he went to see his relations, was to attempt to get the wages due to his men for the various ships in which they had served during the war"(Southey, *Life of Nelson*, 33). Southey also records that when the possibility was mentioned of excluding junior flag-officers from prize money, and thereby leaving more money for senior officers, Nelson asserted, "I desire that no such claim may be made: no, not if it were sixty times the sum, – and, poor as I am, I were never to see prize money" (223). Awarded a British pension of £2,000 per year and Sicilian property worth about £3,000 per year, Nelson claimed, "these presents, rich as they are, do not elevate me. My pride is, that, at Constantinople, from the grand seigneur to the lowest Turk, the name of Nelson is familiar in their mouths; and in this country I am everything which a grateful monarch and people can call me" (211). Finally, Southey cataloged Nelson's finances in some detail to show "that Nelson was comparatively a poor man; and though much of the pecuniary embarrassment which he endured was occasioned by the separation from his wife – even if that cause had not existed, his income would not have been sufficient for the rank which he held, and the claims which would necessarily be made upon his bounty" (286). The nation's debt to this great naval hero must be paid, Southey suggests, not in money but in honor. Romance heroism continually reproduced an imbalance in the nation's accounting – but the hero's own reduced means remained part of his performance of self-sacrifice. Indeed, the economic opposition Southey implicitly developed between financial self-interest and self-sacrifice replicates Nelson's repeated invocation of victory (with pensions) or death (self-sacrifice); Southey, writing after Nelson's death, emphasized the latter of the two options.

Hart's romance performances within the international theatre of the Napoleonic wars developed out of her training in the economically vulnerable role of female domesticity. As a kept woman, her early education in Greville's household followed two contradictory trends: on the one hand, she was asked to conform to a model of stable, reserved domestic femininity; on the other, she was asked to be a changeling, transforming herself into a vengeful Medea, a powerful Circe, an abandoned Ariadne. Greville reined in Hart's inclinations toward financial extravagance by putting her in charge of a stringent housekeeping budget: "Emma Hart's Day Books" of domestic accounts offered such a pretty performance of domesticity-in-training that they were preserved years later by both Greville and Hamilton.[26] At the same time, however, her modeling sessions with Romney called on her to embody the passionate extremities of various classical heroines. These two separate models of performance intersected most vividly in Romney's use of Hart as a model for his illustrations of William Hayley's *The Triumphs of Temper* – a "lady's poem" which suggests that late eighteenth-century models of femininity often combined the contradictory demands of mutability and domesticity. Written in six cantos and explicitly modeled on Pope's *Rape of the Lock*, Hayley's mock-heroic lady's epic used allegorical extravagance to promote domestic self-restraint: the cantos alternate between allegorical or dream sequences and more "realistic" episodes demonstrating the need for feminine self-control. While the mock-epic promises to reward good behavior with domestic bliss, however, the heroine Serena's marriage opportunities are repeatedly linked to the possibility of her attendance at a masquerade – and the masquerade is loosely equated in turn with the mutability of the female character or condition: "She's everything by starts and nothing long."[27] Serena's roving thoughts about the masquerade, flying through "all states of poverty and power," suggest a certain savvy about the marriage market, a grasp of how speculative her own financial situation might be. Yet within the poem, this speculative wisdom is disavowed: the allegorical cantos work to domesticate the mobility of masquerade costumes by using the trappings of costume and spectacle to preach the virtues of domestic self-restraint.

Hayley's *Triumphs of Temper* was written for and popular with a substantial female audience – which suggests that the tension between domestic self-restraint and the necessary mobility of financial and marital speculation was on some level a familiar one. Certainly Emma Hart, Lady Hamilton-to-be, took this fable very much to heart. Years later, she would write Romney to

[t]ell Hayly I am always reading his Triumphs of Temper; it was that that made me Lady H., for God knows I had for five years enough to try my temper, and I am afraid if it had not been for the good example Serena taught

me, my girdle wou'd have burst, and if it had I had been undone; for Sir W[illiam] minds more temper than beauty. (Morrison, *Collection of Autograph Letters*, 1.199)

Hart-Hamilton seems to have learned allegorical extravagance as well as domestic self-restraint from Hayley's *Triumphs of Temper*. When, as a long-awaited treat, Greville took her to Ranelagh Gardens, she was carried away by the favorable attention she was receiving, burst into song, and gave an impromptu performance. The spectators were delighted, Greville furious. Upon their return home, Hart used emblematic display to show that she had taken Greville's point. According to John Romney, the painter's brother, she dressed herself in the uniform of a lady's maid and tearfully begged Greville to take her in this fashion or to abandon her forever.[28]

Yet both the triumphs of temper and the performance of romance submission failed Emma Hart at this stage of her career. A few years after the scene at Ranelagh, enacting quite literally the traffic in women, Greville presented Hart to his uncle, Sir William Hamilton, as a ready-made mistress, better than a wife for Hamilton's needs. In a letter dated May 5, 1785 Greville articulated the economic terms of exchange he desired, invoking only the dim subterfuge of third-person reportage: "Your brother spoke openly to me, that he thought the wisest thing you could do would be to buy Love ready made, . . . & that he should be very glad to hear you declare openly your successor, & particularly so if you named me; I write without affectation or disguise" (Morrison, *Collection of Autograph Letters*, 1.137). In the person of Emma Hart, Greville had "Love ready made" conveniently and inexpensively for sale: he asked only that he be declared Hamilton's heir. Hawking this "Love ready made," Greville continued to invoke the ideas of value, profit, and economic interest as he outlined Hart's virtues and personal appeal. On December 3, he wrote:

She likes admiration, but merely that she may be valued, & not to profit by raising her price. I am sure there is not a more disinterested woman in the world, if she has a new gown or hat, &c. . . . as I consider you as my heir-aparent I must add that she is the only woman I ever slept with without having ever had any of my senses offended, & a cleanlier, sweeter bedfellow does not exist. (1.142)

The uninterested lover highlights Emma's "disinterestedness" at almost the same moment that his pimping becomes unmistakeable. In context, "disinterested" clearly means inexpensive, easily bought: rather than demanding marriage, she will settle for a new dress. Wishing to be declared Hamilton's "heir-apparent," Greville declares his uncle his own heir-apparent in Emma's favors. Hart's recognition of her economic vulnerability, her lack of security, developed only belatedly. In the spring of 1786, Greville sent Hart off to Sir William under false pretenses, suggesting to his uncle that Hart had accepted his protection, and telling Hart he would come to get her in a few months' time. Sir William was left to break the news of the exchange. Hart responded in a series of letters to Greville, first by negating the exchange as she understood it: "I belong to you, Greville, and to you only I will belong, and nobody shall be your heir apearant" (1.150). Hart's direct echo of Greville's proposal ("I consider you as my heir-aparent") suggests that Sir William showed her the letters, laid bare the terms of exchange. Certainly Hart went on to articulate clearly and logically the economic insecurity the deal represented for her:

I am poor, helpless and forlorn. I have lived with you 5 years, and you have sent me to a strange place, and no one prospect, but thinking you was coming to me. Instead of which, I was told I was to live, you know how, with Sir William. No, I respect him, but no never. Shall he peraps live with me for a little wile like you, and send me to England. Then what am I to do? What is to become of me? (1.152)

The proposed exchange made clear to Hart her own status as object and the cost of her willing subordination to men. Her struggle to submit to Greville's terms had brought no long-term benefits; it merely deprived her of the power to chart her own course.

In Naples, by contrast, Hart began to choose her own path. Her letters to Sir William during an early separation already contained the seeds of what would come to be known as "Emma Hart's Attitudes."[29] With Sir William's collaboration, she constructed those "Attitudes" around the dynamic of excess and restraint she had learned so clearly from Greville. Emma Hart's "Attitudes" were striking in part because of the limited materials she used: the performer seemed able to abstract an entire character and situation into a gesture, the fold of a shawl. At the same time, however, each gesture was overcharged with emotional connotations, with passion. The resulting "Attitudes" produced an aesthetic oddly combining excess and restraint – even as Hart's earlier career as artist's model and kept woman had emphasized the paradox of an idealized femininity composed of allegorical extravagance and domestic restraint. Her success in English society continued to depend upon a dynamic of restrained extravagance. Outdoing the art of portraiture, she could move, bringing statues to life, but she could not speak without destroying the illusion. Lady Holland recorded one such break in the performance: "Just as she was lying down, with her head reclining upon an

Etruscan vase to represent a water-nymph, she exclaimed in her provincial dialect: 'Doun't be afeard Sir Willum, I'll not crack your joug.' I turned away disgusted."[30] The restraint imposed by silence seems to have obscured the underlying economic relations of the spectacle (Sir William probably *was* worrying about the safety of his Etruscan vase, and Hart remained dependent on his generosity) and to have licensed Hart's emotional extravagance: what could not be spoken in upper-class society (at least not in a lower-class accent) could be silently performed.

Only in her role as royal cavalier and heroic companion did Hamilton finally break through the (economic) restraints of her earlier performances. After the flight from Naples to Sicily, she indulged in various modes of extravagance, gambling with the queen, cross-dressing to visit lowly taverns with Nelson. Returning to Naples with Nelson's fleet, Hamilton continued to act as the queen's cavalier, persuading Nelson to arm the Lazzaroni, the artisan-peasants of Naples, in order to form a "queen's party" and work against Maria Carolina's unfavorable image.[31] According to Emma's own account of July 19, 1799 (written, as ever, to Greville),

> The Queen is not yet come. She sent me as her Deputy; for I am very popular, speak the Neapolitan language, and [am] consider'd, with Sir William, the friend of the people . . . I had privately seen all the Loyal party, and having the head of the Lazeronys an old friend, he came in the night of our arrival, and told me he had 90 thousand Lazeronis ready, at the holding up of his finger, but only twenty with arms. Lord Nelson to whom I enterpreted, got a large supply of arms for the rest, and they were deposited with this man . . . I have thro' him [the head of the Lazzaroni] made "the Queen's party," and the people at large have pray'd for her to come back, and she is now very popular. (Morrison, *Collection of Autograph Letters*, II.411)

After her careful hoarding of domestic resources, Hamilton suddenly found thousands of men and weapons at her disposal. In helping determine national destiny, she remained as persistently devoted to Maria Carolina's cause as Nelson was to his ideals of honor. Still, the carnage these two heroes produced in Britain's name (though as Neapolitan *envois*) during the retaking of Naples required some public accounting. And with their return to England, Hamilton retreated from direct heroic action into a more conventional, feminine performance of heroic support and domestic dependence.

Hamilton's performances as romance heroine earned her public admiration and public disgust, but little in the way of cold hard cash: indeed, only her knack of mingling heroic performance with domestic restraint kept her consistently fed, clothed, and housed between 1780 and 1805. Nelson's heroism, by contrast, earned him pensions as well as titles, though he never achieved sufficient economic security to provide fully for Hamilton or their daughter Horatia. Southey's biography emphasized Nelson's self-sacrifices over his economic self-interest in order to stress the hero's claim on the nation's memory, but in his last will, written at sea shortly before the battle of Trafalgar, Nelson invited more concrete repayment than Southey had in mind, and thus united the opposing terms of victory and death, self-interest and self-sacrifice:

Whereas the eminent services of Emma Hamilton, widow of the Right Honourable Sir William Hamilton, have been of the very greatest service to my king and country, to my knowledge, without ever receiving any reward from either our king or country . . .

Could I have rewarded these services, I would not now call upon my country; but as that has not been in my power, I leave Emma Lady Hamilton therefore a legacy to my king and country, that they will give her an ample provision to maintain her rank in life.

I also leave to the beneficence of my country my adopted daughter, Horatia Nelson Thomson; and I desire she will use in future the name of Nelson only.

These are the only favours I ask of my king and country, at this moment when I am going to fight their battle. (Southey, *Life of Nelson*, 330–31)

This remarkable document is often read as a sign of Nelson's identification with Britain: certainly he asks king and country to care for his loved ones in exchange for his performance in battle, a battle fought for king and country. Most striking to me, however, is the notion of legacy at work in these lines. Unable to leave Hamilton a substantial legacy to support her after his death, Nelson left Hamilton herself as a legacy to the nation – not as a claim upon the nation, but as his legacy to his country. In this context, Hamilton becomes a national resource: perhaps a model of heroism and inspiration as she had been to Nelson – but perhaps a source of income through artistic speculation as she had been to Greville. Hamilton's status as unpropertied woman becomes indistinguishable from her status as female property. The hero's economic gains and the heroine's persistent economic vulnerability within this mode of patriotic romance determines both the range of performance open to each, and the public reception of those performances.

CARICATURING ROMANCE: THE FALL INTO FARCE

Emma Hamilton's "Attitudes," her allegorical modeling for Romney and others, and her political engagement – all were attuned to the conventions of heroic romance. But in returning to England, Hamilton lost control over the representation of her actions – her return inaugurated a generic shift in her career from the conventions of romance to those of farce. Caricatures by Isaac Cruikshank, Thomas Rowlandson, and James Gillray worked to reestablish the social divisions threatened by the Hamilton–Nelson ménage by separating the trio into a more acceptable though still scandalous sexual configuration of one couple plus the odd man out. They also worked to separate Nelson's self-consciously heroic performances in battle from his self-dramatizing affair with Emma Hamilton. In other words, the caricatures participated to some degree in the impossible task of creating a model of national patriotism purged of vulgarity. They did so by emphasizing Hamilton's status as a prostituted performer of sexualized attitudes. Focusing on Hamilton's body, the caricatures manage to ignore the importance of "attitude" in her career – and in the careers of the influential men and women whose lives and power she shared. In particular, caricatures repeatedly focused on Emma Hamilton's sexual exhibitionism in an attempt to limit the charges of political exhibitionism made against Nelson's heroic reputation: Hamilton's body could be used to exclude both her own and her lover's excesses from Nelson's claims to heroism.

Thomas Rowlandson's "Lady Hxxxxxxx's Attitudes" (November 1800), for instance, succeeded in separating Nelson and Hamilton – but only by looking back in time to Hamilton's early, disreputable career (plate 9). The print features a woman modeling nude for a young painter while an elderly bespectacled connoisseur peeps from behind a curtain. The two men are linked by their interest in the woman's belly and the glass (monocle and spectacles, respectively) through which they survey her.[32] The print traces a crude and somewhat questionable sublimation of sex into art: in the left front of the picture are two heads, Jupiter and a nymph kissing; back behind the artist on the right stands the statue of a nymph and a satyr embracing. The posture of Emma's upper body seems to echo that of the nymph: the model holds a bearded black satyr mask in roughly the same way as the nymph reaches up to touch her satyr's head. The *satyr* has been removed from the scene – the female model stands alone – but the *satire* on two men obsessed with a common woman's sexuality remains.[33] Yet Rowlandson, in leaving Nelson out of this scene, also revised the context, the kind of voyeurism Emma in her younger days endlessly inspired. The spectacle she presented most successfully to a minged company of artists and voyeurs was not nudity and sex, but rather an oscillation between

Plate 9 Thomas Rowlandson, "Lady Hxxxxxxx's Attitudes." November 1800.

domesticity and extravagance. Her later performances – both public and private – focused on questions of grandeur, heroism, and tragedy, while maintaining the vulgar excesses which marked her class origins. Reducing Hamilton's "Attitudes" and influence to sexual exhibitionism and manipulation, this print redomesticated the threat Hamilton posed by reinserting her into a world once again balanced between allegorical speculation and domestic restraint.

Gillray's first caricature on the Hamilton–Nelson ménage, published on February 6, 1801, tackled the problem of national romance more directly (plate 10). The print featured Emma as "Dido in Despair" and attributed to this modern Dido the following lines:

> Ah, where, & ah where, is my gallant Sailor gone?
> He's gone to fight the Frenchmen, for George upon the throne,
> He's gone to fight ye Frenchmen, t'loose t'other Arm & Eye,
> And left me with the old Antiques, to lay me down & Cry.

The antiques most immediately visible are those scattered on the floor in the bottom right corner of the scene, below Emma's dressing table – but there is another "antique" lying in the bed beside (or behind) her. Sir William's presence is overshadowed by Emma's histrionics, as his scandalously sexual antiquities remain a step below Emma's foreign makeup ("rouge à la Naples") and liqueur ("Maraschino"). Nelson appears only in the fleet seen through the open window on the left, sailing away. On the window seat – a liminal space that both separates and links Nelson and Emma – rests one of Emma's shawls, along with a book entitled "Studies of Academic Attitudes taken from the Life." Recalling Rowlandson's print, this open book emphasizes Hamilton's sexuality through her past performances. By far the most striking feature of this caricature, however, is Emma's ludicrous size. Her obesity, along with the vulgarity of her verses and the ubiquitous, rather tawdry insistence on sex, turns the whole affair into tasteless mock-heroics. Gillray used Emma's obesity to rewrite romance by representing her vulgarity in bodily form. Emma's physical condition at the time suggests a slightly different revision of romance: on January 18, 1801 she had given birth to the child eventually named Horatia Nelson: the child was promptly put out to nurse, and Emma Hamilton presented as godmother rather than biological mother.

Obscene and obese mock-heroics – or illicit reproduction on an ideological as well as a biological level? "Dido in Despair" focused the critical energies of caricature upon the self-dramatizing figure of "Dido" but

Plate 10 James Gillray, "Dido in Despair." February 6, 1801.

refrained from a parody of the absent Aeneas. Indeed, the caricature as a whole works to separate "arms and the man" from the *femme fatale* who might be viewed as a threat to the nation's glorious destiny. What embarrassed the patricians in Nelson, that element of unconscious and unintentional parody, could be displaced on to Emma Hamilton through the carefully designed caricatures of Gillray and others. But not even Hamilton could be ridiculed wholeheartedly: some of the posturing, the attitudes shared by Nelson and Hamilton must have seemed necessary to maintain the illusions and the new mythology of patriotic fervor. Richard Hurd claimed that without the admiration produced by romance, no epic poem could be long-lived. If Dido's abandonment helped define Aeneas' epic commitments, the Hamilton–Nelson affair contributed to the popular mythology of England's greatest naval hero in more collaborative ways. Southey, for instance, describes Hamilton urging Nelson to offer his services again to the nation, in the period leading up to Trafalgar: she assures him that those services

"will be accepted, and you will gain a quiet heart by it: you will have a glorious victory, and then you may return here, and be happy." He looked at her with tears in his eyes: " – Brave Emma! – Good Emma! – If there were more Emmas there would be more Nelsons." (Southey, *Life*, 319–20)

Hamilton's performances in Naples had transgressed both social and gender norms, but her subsequent life with Nelson, especially after Sir William's death, returned more or less to the norms of domesticity, while fulfilling the romance conventions by which women's bodies displayed the attractions of the nation and the rewards of patriotism. Nelson, in a letter to Hamilton, echoed the old cliché: "But, my dear friend, I know you are so true and loyal an Englishwoman, that you would hate those who would not stand forth in defence of our king, laws, religion, and all that is dear to us. – It is your sex that makes us go forth, and seem to tell us, 'None but the brave deserve the fair'; – and if we fall, we still live in the hearts of those females" (278). Both in the role of Dido and in that of heroic muse, Hamilton remained an integral albeit ambivalent part of the patriotic fantasies converging around the figure of Nelson.

Gillray's second caricature on the Nelson–Hamilton imbroglio, published on February 11, 1801, records more of this ambivalent public response (plate 11). Entitled "A Cognocenti contemplating ye Beauties of ye Antique," the caricature has at its center Sir William rather than Hamilton: on the wall above and behind the ambassador is a picture of

Plate 11 James Gillray, "A Cognoscenti contemplating ye Beauties of ye Antique."
February 11, 1801.

his beloved Vesuvius erupting. As in the previous print, Sir William seems to rule the right-hand side of the caricature: he figures there both as the portrait of Claudius (the Roman emperor known, like Sir William, in part for his enjoyment of food) and as the grotesque statue entitled "Midas" immediately below that painting. The portrait's frame is topped with a pair of horns which register Sir William's status as cuckold even as they might recall his frequent hunting parties with the king of Naples. Sir William thus appears as the cuckolded husband who nonetheless continues, in the role of Midas, to hold the purse strings.[34]

To the Claudius of Sir William, Nelson plays Mark Antony, while Hamilton is, inevitably, the Cleopatra figure. The portraits of Antony and Cleopatra are grouped together to the left of the volcano – again, Gillray seems to resist on a visual level the intermingling suggested by this scandalous *ménage à trois*. Nelson-Antony is quite a handsome figure in full naval regalia; on the other hand, Cleopatra's breasts are exposed and she holds a bottle labeled "Gin" in her right hand. Like the figure of Dido in the first caricature, Gillray's use of Antony and Cleopatra is clearly mock-heroic. Yet in this mythic recasting of the Hamilton–Nelson affair, Nelson appears almost as vulnerable as Hamilton. As Antony abandoned his flotilla in the midst of a sea battle to fly to Cleopatra's side, so Nelson was thought to have shirked his duties in order to remain with Hamilton in Naples and Sicily. Yet Antony and Cleopatra remain in cultural memory as legendary lovers, beyond any simplistic apportioning of blame. Gillray's caricature captures some of the ambivalence with which Hamilton's capacity for self-transformation was received – and the extent to which Nelson's own performance of heroic patriotism could be seen as tainted by the sensual temptations of this modern Cleopatra.

The most poignant element of this caricature, however, remains the confrontation between Sir William and the disfigured bust of an "antique beauty." The figure, boasting thick dark hair and large, wide-set eyes, seems an image of the young Emma Hamilton. Indeed, with the pearls around her throat and in her hair, this bust is strikingly similar to a portrait of Hamilton by Madame Vigée-Le Brun which Sir William sold to raise cash in 1801. Nelson, furious with Sir William, wrote to Hamilton, "I see clearly, my dearest friend, you are on SALE" (*Collection of Autograph Letters*, II.128) – by July 1802, he had purchased the portrait himself. Sir William had a miniature copy of the portrait made, and willed it to Nelson with the words, "The copy of Madame le Brun's picture of Emma, in enamel, by Bone, I give to my dearest friend Lord

Plate 12 Arthur William Devis, *The Death of Nelson*. 1805.

Nelson, Duke of Bronte; a very small token of the great regard I have for his Lordship, the most virtuous, loyal, and truly brave character I ever met with. God bless him, and shame fall on those who do not say 'Amen'" (II.424). The aggressiveness of this closing remark suggests some of the impact of Gillray's caricature. Here, the bust is disfigured, its nose and mouth broken off, perhaps in reference to Hamilton's adultery.[35] Sir William, hunched, gaunt, and hollow-eyed, peers intently at the bust, which despite its disfigurement, seems younger and livelier than he. The *cognoscenti* holds up to his eyes a pair of spectacles, as if to see more clearly, but he holds them up backwards. This reversal may be designed to suggest that Sir William now sees less clearly than ever, but it could also be read in terms of an uneasy reciprocity: Sir William trying to see things as if from Hamilton's perspective – or asking her to look at him more closely. Recalling yet again the indeterminacy of spectacle and spectator created by Hamilton's Neapolitan attitudes, I think the glasses could also be read as a visual pun: spectacles dominate the only relationship between Sir William and his wife that the caricaturist is able to envision. Yet the print also disavows Hamilton's intense physical appeal: the romance heroine appears in this print not in the flesh but only as a damaged statue and a damaging portrait. Gillray's caricature immobilized Hamilton's shifting performance of romance in a monument to flawed and broken beauty.

Nelson's monumental death at Trafalgar, by contrast, did much to reunite masculine and feminine modes of patriotic romance. I want to close this chapter with a brief look at two visual responses to his death: the painting by Arthur William Devis (plate 12), and a print by Gillray, ostensibly serious, submitted to the Lord Mayor of London as one possible model for a Nelson memorial (plate 13). Killed by a French sharp-shooter who knew him by the many ceremonial decorations he refused to remove, Nelson appears in Devis's painting denuded of his uniform and ribbons, yet bathed in a glow of almost holy light. The painting seems to suggest that patriotic display is no longer necessary: heroism shines most strongly unencumbered by such outward signs. At the same time, Devis's painting presents a feminized Nelson embodying the attractions of the nation and of patriotic romance, enclosed within an admiring, devoted circle of his men. In this strictly male portrayal of naval and national unity, Nelson's forced choices – laurel or cypress, victory or death – are themselves conflated. Yet Nelson here plays the role stage romances typically filled with a display of female bodies:

the Death of ADMIRAL-LORD-NELSON - in the moment of Victory!

Plate 13 James Gillray, "The Death of Admiral Lord Nelson in the moment of
Victory!" December 23, 1805.

Nelson's body, purified by death, monumentalizes the narcissistic attractions linking patriot to nation, while preserving patriotic romance from the unruliness of female bodies and female agency.

Gillray's design for a Nelson memorial has, perhaps, little to recommend it. An early editor of Gillray's work described this print only as "[a] rather feeble attempt at celebrating the great battle of Trafalgar."[36] Ronald Paulson, considering the print within Gillray's ridicule of other people's myths, remarked that even Gillray's own myth, "as his Death of Admiral Nelson must surely be, is ridiculous in the context of the convention established by his other pseudomyths."[37] Yet Gillray's print, unlike Devis's painting, acknowledged both the collaborative and the indisputably vulgar aspects of Nelson's heroic performance. In particular, the caricaturist presented not one but two tasteless blazons of Victory and Immortality in the background of Nelson's death scene. At the same time, Gillray imagined a weeping Britannia supporting Nelson at the moment of his death. But this Britannia's flowing locks and rather ample proportions bring Hamilton herself on to the scene to weep her partner's death. While Devis's painting used Nelson's wounded, vulnerable body to organize the centripetal appeal of national unity, Gillray's print equated Hamilton with the nation for which Nelson fought and which remained to mourn him. Vulgarity and self-parody play their part in this portrayal of Nelson's and Hamilton's collaborative national romance, but they remain in the backgound of this scene. Where Devis's famous painting erased the possibility of female agency within the norms of patriotic romance, Gillray's admittedly mawkish print records the exclusions structuring Devis's vision of patriotism – and its impact on nineteenth-century understandings of national agency. Moving through the postures of chapbook, prose, and stage romance, the Hamilton–Nelson affair embodied the conflicts of national romance: conflicts resolved only through Nelson's death and the male cult of heroism surrounding that death. In Gillray's monumental design, however, the performative excesses associated with Hamilton return to haunt viewers even in the mythically charged moment of Nelson's death. Hamilton's imagined participation in this scene underscores both the on-going impurity of performative romance and the power of collaboration in staging national agency.

CHAPTER FOUR

(Dis)embodied romance: "Perdita" Robinson and William Wordsworth

In "Varieties of Romance Nationalism," I argued that dramatic romances staged the attractions of the nation through the body of the public woman, then unified the nation through the act of disciplining or abjecting that public woman. With Mary "Perdita" Robinson, the drama of romance moved from the patent stages to the stage of the nation. On December 3, 1779, Robinson played the role of Perdita in *Florizel and Perdita* (Garrick's adaptation of *The Winter's Tale*) to an audience including the royal family. For the next two years, Robinson and the Prince of Wales played out the romance of "Perdita" and "Florizel" before the audience of the nation. Even after the royal affair had ended, however, "Perdita" Robinson's female attractions continued to fascinate men of national importance. Between 1781 and 1787, caricatures and pamphlets associated Robinson with three public men in particular: the Prince of Wales; Charles Fox, opposition Whig leader; and Banastre Tarleton, Tory hero of the American war. Robinson's performance on the stage of the nation seems to have been received at first according to the conventions of dramatic romance: prints and pamphlets presented her female attractions calling up (the performance of) male virility in the prince, Fox, and Tarleton alike. Yet her power to attract not one but a range of men raised concerns about political promiscuity and the ideological relations of public men and public women. These concerns were resolved largely by undercutting the power of women in romance: caricatures and pamphlets used the trope of prostitution to domesticate and degrade the figure of Mary Robinson as public woman.

Robinson responded to this public pillory only gradually, over the course of her second, literary, career. Barred from the stage through public disapproval of her affairs and after 1783 paralyzed from the waist down, Robinson turned to writing as a means of keeping herself near rather than in the style to which she had become accustomed. Driven in part by economic exigencies, she produced a remarkable body of writing between 1790 and her death in 1800, including seven novels, three volumes of collected verse, two political pamphlets, a series of news-paper essays, a tragedy, a farce, and an incomplete *Memoir*. Taken as a whole, her literary performances effectively undercut both the assump-tions of dramatic romance and the countervailing trope of prostitution. While Garrick's *Cymon* and Colman's *Blue Beard* relied on dramatic con-vention and stock characters to unify the nation, Robinson's writing invoked a wide range of literary forms to emphasize the empty conven-tionality of public and and private personae alike.

Robinson's *Thoughts on the Injustice of Mental Subordination* (1799) brings her revision of dramatic romance more sharply into focus: if Garrick's *Cymon* equated the public woman's access to material resources and political power with her morals, Robinson's *Thoughts* gave that equation a different spin. First, she argued that women should be allowed to defend their reputations to the death, since the "theft" of her reputation deprived a woman of all material resources. Second, she worked to reclaim women's communal reputation for mental acuity: demonstrat-ing female prowess in literature and history, she claimed for women as a group the right to "the participation of power." Insisting on the justice of female duelling, Robinson's *Thoughts* reframed romance as an equal-opportunity activity. The following year, Robinson staked a broad claim to literary participation and power with her *Lyrical Tales* (1800), which staged a literary and lyrical duel with the romance aesthetic of Wordsworth's *Lyrical Ballads* (1798/1800).

Wordsworth never responded directly to Robinson's poetic challenge: the *Lyrical Ballads* retained their original name and their author took no public notice of Robinson's attempt to usurp the title. But the London book of the 1805 *Prelude* responded to the combined challenge of Robinson's poetry and public persona in three ways. First, in the Belle of Buttermere, Wordsworth presented a revisionary Mary Robinson, a woman publicized despite herself, whose female attractions unite private men. Second, in the painted mother and lovely boy, Wordsworth attempted to abject the pros-tituted public woman from the public imaginations of private men. Finally, while the *Prelude* as a whole works to relocate the political power of romance away from the London stage and into the poetic imagination, book seven repeatedly emphasizes the figures of romance (and prostitution) as an uncanny link between the deadly power of London spectacle and the sur-vival of the poet's imagination. Even abjected as a prostitute, "Perdita" Robinson, like the lost women of romance, remains an integral part of Wordsworth's highly theatrical imagination.

Exploring the public personae of Emma Hamilton and Horatio

Nelson, the previous chapter charted the varieties of romance at work in their performances of nationalism and patriotism. Focusing on the work of Mary Robinson and William Wordsworth, this chapter traces a turn from performance to literature within the larger field of romance nationalism. The first part of the chapter addresses public reception of Robinson's "real life performance" of romance, highlighting the ease with which romance tropes could be degraded by imagining the nation as prostitute or prostituted. Various readers have suggested that Robinson's poems present literary performances: the second part of this chapter reads particular moments within Robinson's literary performance as a way for a fallen public woman to reclaim "the participation of power."[1] Examining Wordsworth's poetic responses to Robinson's performance of romance nationalism, the third part of this chapter suggests that anxiety and emulation together inform Wordsworth's romantic defense against theatre.[2] Robinson's writing, relying in part on her celebrity status, blurred the boundaries between literature and performance, just as dramatic romance blurred the boundaries between the stage and the nation, fantasy and reality. Working to conflate nationalism and romance in ways diametrically opposed to Robinson's public and literary performances, the 1805 version of Wordsworth's *Prelude* attempted, unsuccessfully, to exile performance from the harmonious realms of romance. Reading Wordsworth's invocations of romance through the lens of Robinson's performances highlights the Lake poet's reluctant reliance on a feminized staging of romance.

PERDITA AND FLORIZEL

Public scandal, like heroic romance, freely mingles fact and fiction: unbiased contemporary accounts of Robinson's career are hard to come by. Robinson and her detractors generally agree, however, that she married in 1773 at the age of fifteen and delivered a daughter in October 1774. Less than a year later, she accompanied her husband to debtor's prison – immediately after revising the proofs of her first volume of poetry. After her husband was discharged from prison, Robinson turned to the stage in search of income. Coached by Garrick and promoted by Sheridan, she made her début at Drury Lane under the protection of the theatre's leading men. Gaining celebrity status through her acting career, Robinson either exploited (according to her detractors) or was harassed by a variety of noblemen and commoners for the next several years. Then, on December 3, 1779, she played the role of Perdita in

Garrick's adapted *Winter's Tale* before the royal family. Robinson's enemies claim she made eyes at the Prince of Wales throughout the performance; she claimed to have been overwhelmed by confusion at his attention. A few days later the prince sent her a note signed "Florizel" and these two celebrity actors embarked on their own performance of romance. Robinson and her critics disagree both as to the start of the affair and its duration. Robinson's *Memoir*, for instance, suggests (for obvious reasons) that the romance became fully sexual only after her separation from her husband in June 1780. The lovers seem to have separated in December 1780, but Robinson's *Memoir* suggests that the prince blew hot and cold over the next several months. Certainly the finances of their separation were only agreed upon in September 1781.

Those finances were themselves a persistent source of scandal. During the affair, the prince had given Robinson a series of letters expressing politically dangerous sentiments as well as a bond for £20,000 payable upon his coming of age.[3] In the event, the prince's word (those dangerous letters) seems to have been worth more than his bond. George III wrote to Lord North in August 1781 that

My eldest son got last year into an improper connection with an actress and woman of indifferent character through the friendly assistance of Lord Malden. He sent her letters and very foolish promises, which undoubtedly by her conduct she has cancelled. Colonel Hotham has settled to pay the enormous sum of £5,000 for the letters, etc., being returned. You will therefore settle with him.[4]

The sum of £5,000 seems to have been accompanied by the promise of an annuity – a promise made good only in 1783 through the friendly offices of Charles Fox.

Separated both from her husband and her royal "protector" and granted at least some financial independence, in 1781 or 1782 "Perdita" Robinson abandoned the role of the lost princess for that of the fallen woman. M. J. Levy asserts that Robinson had affairs with Lords Malden and Cholmondeley among others through the spring of 1781, but these affairs remained remarkably quiet.[5] What caught the public attention was Robinson's 1782 affair with war hero Banastre Tarleton, followed by her brief liaison with Charles Fox and her rapid return to Tarleton. Robinson's affair with Fox was fleeting at best and her relationship with Tarleton lasted for sixteen years. In the public eye, however, Robinson remained infamous for several years as the overlapping mistress of the prince, Fox, and Tarleton – and, ironically, Fox is often shown as winning the lady's affections away from prince and soldier both.

From one perspective, Robinson's affairs simply dramatized in "real life" the romance power of the public woman: Robinson's female attractions called forth a virile response from prince, politician, and military hero alike. Early responses to Robinson's public career emphasized, tongue-in-cheek, the political power of this romance heroine. In 1781, toward the end of Robinson's royal liaison, J. Stockdale published the anonymous *Poetical Epistle from Florizel to Perdita: With Perdita's Answer. And a Preliminary Discourse upon the Education of Princes* – priced, rather tellingly, for half a crown. In the preliminary discourse, Perdita appears as the (oddly conservative) instructor of Britain's future king: "the politics of a great Prince's mistress are so far from being unworthy attention that it is very certain the true cause of all the royal smiles, which Perdita is well known to receive during her attendance upon the chace, are no compliments to the beauty of her person but merely meant as an approbation of her political system, which is intirely ministerial."[6] Her influence over the prince, while purely sexual, is not without political consequence:

When the connexion is broke between Florizel and Perdita the opposition have the Prince entire. The faction will then indeed have a right to boast. They already know his indignant spirit at conduct which has abridged his great inheritance. But while he is dissipated he is unsteady. Much less can they depend upon him, while Perdita attracts his youthful passions and with her enchanting discourse influences his mind. To break the bands of so complete an infatuation no engine is left unworkt. (18–19)

The pamphlet's on-going critique of princely dissipation relies both on romance (Robinson's "enchanting discourse") and on the physical degradation produced by loverly infatuation: Florizel's verse epistle to Perdita ends by complaining that she has passed the pox from her equally adulterous husband to him.

The range of Robinson's female attractions – her demonstrated allure for not one but three men of public importance – made her a visual, topical touchstone for anxieties over political promiscuity and the feminization of national politics, over the dubious union of public men and public women. Numerous prints link Robinson both with the prince and with Fox, visually and sexually recording the political alliance between these two public men. The anonymous print entitled "Florizel and Perdita" (October 16, 1783) already discussed in "Staging the Nation," for instance, suggests a kind of political promiscuity amongst the men linked through her. In the lower left of "Florizel and Perdita," the king mourns the prince's disgrace ("Oh! My Son My Son"), while on the right-hand side, the horns placed on *Mr.* Robinson's head support a shelf holding three of Perdita's reputed lovers: Colonel Tarleton, Fox, and Lord North.[7]

While certain prints and pamphlets worried publicly about the issue of "State Prostitution" (BM Sat 6242; June 12, 1783), others resolved the problematic power of Robinson's female attractions by recasting the public woman as a mere prostitute. This might be seen as the disciplinary movement of stage romance, implying that the prince, politician, and military hero were united but uninfluenced by their common use of a public whore. Yet while the trope of prostitution domesticated and degraded the power of the public woman, Robinson's ability to profit from her relationships with public men remained a source of some concern. An early pamphlet of 1781, for instance, showed Robinson translating her female attractions into cold hard cash – but insisted that her mercenary motives made her power over the prince all the more dangerous. *Letters from Perdita to a Certain Israelite and His Answers to Them* (priced at at a mere two shilllings) presents an ostensibly naïve response to the *Poetical Epistle* – but this naïveté serves only to highlight the vulgarity and commercial interests of the royal romance. Ignoring the earlier pamphlet's charges of sexual disease and illicit sources of power, the "editor" of these latter *Letters* claims to have read the *Poetical Epistle* as Robinson's own attempt at self-glorification. In response to "her" blatant attempt to "acquire that Notice and Popularity so requisite for the Prosecution of her Designs," this editor proffers a less poetical, less romantic collection of letters:

The general Object of this Publication is the same as was the *original* Intent of the *Society for checking and prosecuting Swindlers.* – This species of Imposture has long infested Trade; it is interwoven with legal Forms and Processes; it has furnished Parliament both with ministerial Tools and patriotick Declaimers; but it remained for Mr. and Mrs. R— to introduce it into the Traffick of Love.[8]

Claiming to "abhor the Thoughts of publishing the Frailties of the Sex," the editor systematically ab-whores Mary Robinson with allegations that she and her husband set out to profit by her sexual attractions, both from Lords like Lyttleton, Valencia, and Northington, and from moneylenders more directly. In this context, romance takes on financial power: the deluded "Israelite" associates Robinson's power over him with romance, claiming, "When I was a Stranger to Love, I smiled at the romantick Notions of my Associates; but ensnared in the same enchanting Net, my wild Fancy raves with all the Ardour of Juvenile Vehemence" (34). Yet the postscript to this same letter records his awakening from romance:

"You little Prodigal, you have spent 200£. in Six Weeks: I will not answer your Drafts" (34). The editor of the *Letters to a Certain Israelite* draws the obvious political moral, still ostensibly in response to the earlier pamphlet: "She arrogates too a Skill in Politicks, and declares, that the P— is entirely guided by the Sentiments he has imbibed from her: If he has really been so apt a Scholar, when he ascends the T— , we shall have a *prostituted* Government" (16). The actress's sexual and financial prodigality threatened to infect her lovers, royals and commoners alike.

Other prints and newspaper paragraphs worked to reclaim Robinson's sexual profits for her male lovers. When the *Morning Post*, for instance, announced on the 21st of September 1782 that Robinson had more or less settled down with Tarleton, the announcement represented sexual alliances as military encounters in which Robinson was repeatedly vanquished:

> Yesterday a messenger arrived in Town, with the very interesting and pleasing intelligence of the *Tarleton*, armed ship, having, after a chase of some months, captured the *Perdita* frigate, and brought her safe into Egham port. The *Perdita* is a prodigious fine clean-bottomed vessel, and had taken many prizes during her cruise, particularly the *Florizel*, a most valuable ship belonging to the Crown, but which was immediately released, after taking out the cargo. The *Perdita*, was captured by the *Fox*, but was afterwards re-taken by the *Malden*, and had a sumptuous suit of new rigging, when she fell in with the *Tarleton*. Her manoeuvering to escape was admirable; but the *Tarleton*, fully determined to take her or perish, would not give up the chase; and at length, coming alongside the *Perdita*, fully determined to board her, sword in hand, she surrendered at discretion.[9]

The nautical and military imagery tells the story from the perspective of Tarleton, a hero of the American wars, rather than that of Robinson. She is at once objectified and sexualized as "a prodigious fine clean-bottomed vessel," capable of conquering only the weaker vessel of the prince. The monetary gains attributed to her connection with Malden (a "sumptuous suit of new rigging") appear as Tarleton's profit from these multiple encounters. Tarleton's phallic "sword" appears as (almost) the last word in the passage, outlasted only by the lady's supposed "discretion."

Overall, however, the charge of prostitution, no matter how vulgarly put, failed to abolish the ideological scandal – and threat – of Robinson's sexual, financial, and implicitly political independence. James Gillray's "The Thunderer" (August 20, 1782), perhaps the most famous and most damning caricature of Robinson's career, captures the surprising ambiguity of her public position (plate 14). The title of the print focuses

Plate 14 James Gillray, "The Thunderer." August 20, 1782.

attention on Tarleton, and the foreground emphasizes the relationship
between this military man and the feckless Prince of Wales – but both of
these figures are upstaged by the degraded form of "Perdita" Robinson,
the woman who at once connects and distinguishes them. The caricature
presents Mary Darby Robinson as a tradesmen's sign, announcing an
(un)savory local "trade." Legs spread wide, and breasts uncovered, she is
"sexually impaled" above "The Whirligig," and raunchily redefines its
promise to serve "Alamode Beef, hot every Night."[10] The very post which
supports her is given eyes with which to look up her skirt. Foregrounded
by the print, the two male "rivals" of soldier and prince appear oblivious
to the female figure who defines their relative sexual prowess. Tarleton
looks dashing but sounds ridiculous in Gillray's adaptation of Jonson's
Captain Bobadil; the prince appears as the original featherhead, mum-
bling, "I'd as lief as twenty crowns I could Talk as fine as you." His
featherhead has little to say to Tarleton's plumed bragging – nor does the
droopy end of the prince's riding whip measure up to Tarleton's "poor
Toledo." Robinson's refusal to remain passively abandoned by her lover
leaves the prince looking vaguely envious and vastly impotent. Even as a
shop sign, Robinson is made to speak her preference for Tarleton: "This
is the Lad I'll kiss most sweet / Who'd not love a soldier."

The most vulgar verbal satire of Robinson's sexual career replicates the
political ambivalence of Gillray's print. In January 1783 the *Rambler's
Magazine* printed an extended allegorical lease of property from Perdita to
Florizel: "the said Perdita, for and in consideration of the rents, covenants,
and agreements herein-after mentioned, hath granted, demised, leased
and to farm let to the said Florizel, all that piece or parcel of arable land
called Bushy-Grove, situate, lying and being, between East-Ham and
West-Ham, in the county of — , together with the mansion thereon." The
exaggerated legalese draws attention to the crudity of Bushy grove, East
Ham and West Ham, while the lasciviousness supposedly motivating the
"lease" proliferates the number of orifices available for (sexual) use:

with all, and singular, the cellars, chambers, rooms, ways, paths, passages,
shrubberries, water courses, cascades, ponds, rivers, brooks, commodities, and
appurtenances thereunto belonging, or in any wise appertaining, and therewith
heretofore held, used, occupied, and enjoyed by Charles Reynard, late occupier
thereof; together with all and every the doors, windows, locks, keys, bolts,
staples, latches, hooks, hinges, cisterns, pipes, pumps, conduits, of and belonging to the same.

The topology of this satire shows the ease with which the enchanted
ground of romance could become the disenchanted ground of female

prostitution. The engraving which accompanies this "lease" shows Florizel, with his breeches loose, saying to Perdita, "Submit to my Royal Will." Holding him off with her right hand and with her left hand presenting the lease, Perdita responds, "Declare me Independant and then — ." A portrait on the wall behind the prince shows a nude Danae, half-reclined, receiving the shower of gold in her lap. In the disenchantment of romance, even the love of the gods appears in a sordid and mercenary light. At the same time, the issue of "independence" (reemphasized by the title of the engraving: "Florizel granting Independency to Perdita") brought yet another political hot spot to bear on this romance: the commercially motivated, newly declared and defended independence of the American colonies.

As these caricatures and satires suggest, Robinson's demonstration of sexual independence from the prince brought issues of political agency into focus for her contemporaries – and complicated the theatrical model of dramatic romance. Robinson's female attractions visibly linked prince to politician to military hero, providing one model of national unity – but her sexual independence seemed to set these men at odds, forcing them to compete against one another for her sexual favors. At the same time, Robinson's continued popularity with public men made her difficult to discipline publicly. Her fall from virtue barred her from the London stages, but Robinson was most effectively disciplined not by society but by "nature." In 1783 or 1784, as the result of a miscarriage (or, as her *Memoir* claims, a chill caught while traveling on Tarleton's business), Robinson at age twenty-five was paralyzed from the waist down. Forcing her into private life as her finances drove her into continental exile, Robinson's paralysis seems to have evened her score with society by diminishing the power of her female attractions. Contemporary prints and pamphlets could easily have invented for her a role of repentant humility; instead, they chose to prolong her (sexualized) popularity with public men well past its actual season.

DUELLING LYRICS

Wherefore are we
Born with high Souls, but to assert ourselves?
(epigraph to *Thoughts on the Condition of Women*, quoted from Nicholas Rowe)

After the political caricatures of the mid-1780s, Mary Robinson slipped out of the public eye for a number of years, only to reappear in 1788, publishing Della Cruscan poetry under the pseudonym of Laura Maria.

During the 1790s, her writings remained closely associated with shifting public personae and the notion of performance. Her daughter's remarks in the posthumous *Memoirs*, for instance, emphasize Robinson's skill as a poetic improvisatrice, and her poetry was often written in the voice of a poetic persona such as the Della Cruscan Laura, the noble Sappho, or the curmudgeonly Tabitha Bramble of the *Morning Post* verses. While Robinson's writing frequently made use of romance conventions – especially an appeal to male chivalry through female beauty – her later work also explicitly criticized and revised those same conventions. Most visible in the 1799 *Thoughts on the Condition of Women* and the 1800 *Lyrical Tales*, Robinson's revisions of romance repeatedly foregrounded economic relations as they questioned the social "law" of female passivity and male power. Robinson's *Thoughts on the Condition of Women* translated women's sexual honor into a material resource and presented political agency as self-defense; her *Tales* repeatedly unmasked cynical approaches to sexual politics. Together, these late works model for their readers a localized, embodied, cynically knowing participation in power.

Robinson's second political pamphlet, *Thoughts on the Condition of Women and on the Injustice of Mental Subordination* proposed a model of equal opportunity chivalry, open to both men and women.[11] Robinson's *Thoughts* begin with a tip of the hat to Mary Wollstonecraft, "an illustrious British female, (whose death has not been sufficiently lamented, but to whose genius posterity will render justice) [and who] has already written volumes in vindication of *"The Rights of Woman"* (1). Yet while Wollstonecraft and other women pamphleteers of the period denounce duelling as a relic of feudal manners, a clear example of the need for sentimental reform, Robinson proposes instead to open the practice of duelling to women as well as to men. She cites approvingly and at length the story of a young noblewoman abroad who when her fiancé suggests they "anticipate" their marriage vows by a few hours, challenges him to a duel and kills him. "This short story will prove that the mind of woman, when she feels a correct sense of honour, even though it is blended with the very excess of sensibility, can rise to the most intrepid defence of it" (7). Later in the pamphlet, Robinson compares the male seducer to the highway robber as a pest upon society:

If a man is stopped on the highway, he may shoot the depredator: and he will receive the thanks of society. If a WOMAN were to act upon the same principle, respecting the more atrocious robber who has deprived her of all that rendered life desirable, she would be punished as a *murderer*. Because the highwayman only takes that which the traveller can afford to lose, and the loss of which he will scarcely feel; and the woman is rendered a complete bankrupt of all that rendered life supportable. (22)

Robinson's rhetoric works to translate the loss of honor into a more "material" damage than the loss of wealth – but that rhetorical gesture is at once substantiated by the fact that women had so few material resources of their own and vitiated by her apparent narcissism through-out the pamphlet, the fact she seems so clearly to be universalizing her own experience of (dis)honor. Maria Edgeworth's portrait of the duel-ling feminist in *Belinda* offers not an exaggerated parody of Wollstonecraft, but an apt caricature of Robinson's pamphleting persona.

Robinson's *Thoughts on the Condition of Women* invites us to imagine women duelling against their "oppressors" as a last court of appeal: "What then is woman to do? Where is she to hope for justice? Man who *professes* himself her champion, her protector, is the most subtle and unre-lenting enemy she has to encounter" (8). In Robinson's view, "woman" confronts not only the enmity of individual men, but also "the force of prejudice, the law of custom" (23). And she echoes Shakespeare's Shylock in denouncing customs that forbid women to defend themselves in any way:

Let me ask this plain and rational question, – is not a woman a human being, gifted with all the feelings that inhabit the bosom of man? Has not woman affections, susceptibility, fortitude, and an acute sense of injuries received? Does she not shrink at the touch of persecution? Does not her bosom melt with sym-pathy, throb with pity, glow with resentment, ache with sensibility, and burn with indignation? Why then is she denied the exercise of the nobler feelings, and high consciousness of honour, a lively sense of what is due to dignity of character? Why may not woman resent and punish? Because the long estab-lished laws of custom, have decreed her *passive*! (3)

The "established laws of custom" work through petty insults to dissuade women from action: "Prejudice (or policy) has endeavoured, and indeed too successfully, to cast an odium on what is called a *masculine* woman; or, to explain the meaning of the word, a woman of enlightened under-standing" (21–22). The range of activity potentially open to women expands Robinson's challenge to male chivalry and social order to include mental activity, social status and political power: "Let woman once assert her proper sphere, unshackled by prejudice, and unsophisti-cated by vanity; and pride, (the noblest species of pride,) will establish her claims to the participation of power, both mentally and corporeally" (1).

As Robinson challenges the exclusion of women from "the participa-tion of power," she offers specific examples of women like herself who have participated in politics. A footnote asserts that "Lady Hamilton, and Helen Maria Williams, are existing proofs, that an English woman, like a prophet, is never valued in her own country. In Britain they were neglected, and scarcely *known*; on the continent, they have been nearly idolized!" (19). More often than not, however, Robinson's specific claims serve to reconstruct her own social position and public history. When, for instance, she claims that the "most argumentative theorists cannot pretend to estimate mental by corporeal powers," she offers the example of "Charles Fox, or William Pitt," either of whom, when "labouring under the debilitating ravages of a fever is a weaker animal than the thrice-essenced poppinjay, who mounts his feathered helmet, when he should be learning his Greek alphabet" (16). The renowned mistress of Charles Fox, Robinson may well have seen him ravaged by fever, physically debilitated. And as she challenges the "mental aristocracy" of contemporary politics, she bases that challenge upon her own, however dubious, claim to fame:

How comes it, that in this age of reason we do not see statesmen and orators selecting women of superior mental acquirements as their associates? . . . a British Demosthenes, a Pythagoras, a Loentius, a Eustathius, or a Brutus, would rather pass his hours in dalliance with an unlettered courtezan, than in the conversation of a Theano, a Themiste, a Cornelia, a Sosipatra, or a Portia. What is this display of mental aristocracy? what but the most inveterate jealousy; the most pernicious and refined species of envy and malevolence? (4)

Robinson's allusion to the stateswomen of Greek and Roman culture, while in keeping with her use of classical allusions throughout the pamphlet, reminds the reader of Robinson's own (corporeal) association with a wide range of contemporary British statesmen. The implicit analogy works to reframe the role of public woman from vulgar prostitute to cultured courtesan. Indeed, as she sketches the kinds of enmity women suffer, Robinson reproduces precisely the charges made against her own character in her days of public infamy:

If . . . she is wary, shrewd, thrifty, economical, and eager to procure and to preserve the advantages of independence; she is condemned as narrow-minded, mean, unfeeling, artful, mercenary, and base: in either case she is exposed to censure. If liberal, unpitied; if sordid, execrated! In a few words, a generous woman is termed a fool; a prudent one, a prodigal [miser]. (24; editor's correction in square brackets)

The odd alignment of prudence and prodigality here recalls the charges made by the *Letters to a Certain Israelite* – a pamphlet in which Robinson appeared both as a mercenary prostitute and a "little Prodigal."

Robinson's examples repeatedly reframe her own experience, working to clear her name or draw connections between her (still disreputable) public persona and the more illustrious women of antiquity.

If Robinson's *Thoughts on the Condition of Women* suffers from a certain egocentricity, however, the writer carefully articulates the political problem of identification, the consequences produced by a lack of appropriate role models for women. Robinson asserts that the modern woman "sees no resemblance of her own character in the Portias and Cornelias of antiquity; she is content to be the epitome of her celebrated archetype, the good woman of St. Giles's!" Another footnote brings the implications of such an identification sharply into view: "This elegant and estimable female, is represented headless; – and I believe almost the only female in the kingdom *universally* allowed to be a *good woman*" (26n). For her own part, Robinson insists on tracing resemblances of her own character in the Portias and Cornelias of antiquity, modeling one route to increased political agency. While her pamphlet speaks for "woman" in general, it represents much more effectively a single woman's individual attempt to position herself as a stateswoman, to achieve "participation in power."

Recent critics have emphasized the role of literature in the shaping of political hegemony during the Romantic period. Tellingly, perhaps, Robinson's attempt to overcome the mental subordination of women ends with a survey of literature produced by women. Once again, a footnote (or in this case, a postscript) points her argument:

I am well assured that [this Letter] will meet with little serious attention from the male disciples of modern philosophy. The critics, though they have liberally patronized the works of British women, will perhaps condemn that doctrine which inculcates mental equality; lest, by the intellectual labours of the sex, they should claim an equal portion of power in the tribunal of British literature." (28)

Robinson's next work, her *Lyrical Tales*, represented an attempt to claim this "equal portion" of literary power, as it offered a pointed literary challenge to the *Lyrical Ballads* of Wordsworth and Coleridge.

In publishing a collection of *Lyrical Tales*, Robinson directly challenged the literary power claimed by Wordsworth's *Ballads*. In September 1800, Wordsworth considered changing the title of *Lyrical Ballads* to "Poems by W. Wordsworth," since, as Dorothy Wordsworth put it, "Mrs. Robinson has claimed the title and is about publishing a volume of *Lyrical Tales*. This is a great objection to the former title, particularly as they are both printed at the same press and Longman is the publisher of both the works."[12] Staging a textual as well as a titular confrontation, the Robinson poems explicitly named "Tales" present a model of reading which challenges that provided by the *Lyrical Ballads*. Both Wordsworth's "Ballads" and Robinson's "Tales" asked readers to think actively about the process of reading, and of storytelling. Wordsworth's 1800 preface to the *Lyrical Ballads* asserted that "the human mind is capable of excitement without the application of gross and violent stimulants" and dedicates the poet's work to "produc[ing] or enlarg[ing] this capability."[13] He explicitly contrasted his work to the "frantic novels, sickly and stupid German Tragedies, and deluges of idle and extravagant stories in verse" which he saw overwhelming the discriminating powers of readers' minds: "When I think upon this degrading thirst after outrageous stimulation I am almost ashamed to have spoken of the feeble effort with which I have endeavoured to counteract it" (243). Wordsworth offered his readers a moral aesthetic, enabling individuals to respond more forcefully and thoughtfully to "great national events" and daily happenings alike. He asked readers to focus not on the sensational story of Martha Ray, but on the garrulous sea captain's attempt to retell that story, and in the process, come to terms with it himself. Not the moving accident, but the bystander's responses, comprise Wordsworth's trade.

Rather than contrasting an event with the response to that event, Robinson models for her readers two opposing stances: hypocritical innocence, and knowing cynicism. The tales repeatedly disrupt the naïveté they ostensibly support, to promulgate instead a mode of social cynicism, especially in cases of sexual impropriety. "The Mistletoe," for instance, tells the story of a young woman married to an old farmer. The tale opens by emphasizing her marriage vows – "That she a faithful mate would prove, / In meekness, duty, and in love" – and then casting doubt upon their value: "But, mark the sequel, – and attend!" At a Christmas party, a young admirer repeatedly urges her to accompany him beneath the mistletoe, and she betrays herself in trying to assert both her marital reserve and her power over him. "[R]esolved to make / An envious rival's bosom ache," Mistress Homespun

> Commanded Hodge to let her go,
> Nor lead her to the Mistletoe;
> "Why should you ask it o'er and o'er?"
> Cried she, "we've been there twice before!"

Yet the moral of the tale rebukes Mistress Homespun, not for kissing young Hodge, but rather for betraying herself to her husband:

> 'Tis thus, to check a rival's sway,
> That Women oft themselves betray;
> While Vanity, alone, pursuing,
> They rashly prove, their own undoing.

In criticizing the young woman's speech rather than the kisses themselves, the poem at once "undoes" its own ostensible morality, and urges
women readers to value the material good of reputation over the more
intangible indulgence of vanity. (Do not cut off your nose to spite your
rival.) Cheating on one's husband is taken for granted: the arena of
moral action restricts itself to the question of how a flirtation or affair is
to be managed.

While Wordsworth's "Ballads" look back to Percy's *Reliques of Ancient
English Poetry*, Robinson's "Tales" seem closer to the *Tales of the Minstrels*
of Pierre-Jean-Baptiste LeGrand D'Aussy, first translated in 1786 and
eventually (in part) adapted for the stage.[14] Full of "French" cynicism
and a farcical staginess, these "Norman Tales" offered a very different
view of romance than the nationalist model derived from ancient
English "reliques." Their relation to theatre presents one key point of
difference: the "drama" of the *Lyrical Ballads* resides in the narrator's
changing responses, that of the *Tales* in the situations presented.
Robinson's narrators pose few dramatic questions: the narrative voice
remains consistently knowing. The potential for change sketched within
the *Lyrical Tales* lies instead in the reader's response to a (repeated)
incommensurability of moral and story: to notice the mismatch is almost
inevitably to become a more cynical reader. In general, Robinson's
"Tales" portray an irreverence for social roles and sexual mores at odds
with Wordsworth's idealization of the figures of humble, rural life; they
also contradict the solemn and meditative reading process proposed by
Wordsworth's 1800 preface to the *Lyrical Ballads*. Indeed, if one accepts
Wordsworth's aesthetics as ennobling, Robinson's "Tales" must seem, by
contrast, corrupt and corrupting. The narrative voice of these "Tales"
speaks from beyond the social pale to redefine "virtue" – often, a
specifically sexualized female morality. Yet just as Wordsworth presents
his aesthetic as a partial response to "great national events," Robinson
uses her more equivocal position as discarded royal mistress to address
a (once and future) monarch. The "Old English Tale" of "The
Trumpeter" undertakes to teach a king how best to manage his business:
in the process, it disposes of a braggart who might have earned the nick-
name of "Thunderer" before that of "Trumpeter."

The "Monarch" of the "Old English Tale" is at first pleased to let dissolute men of birth and wealth determine his decisions and guide his rule, but when one particularly vile braggart claims the right to rule the banquet hall based on his military and sexual prowess – and his mistreatment of women – the king proclaims him a trumpeter instead, and promptly reforms his royal self, his court, and his kingdom. This story seems to me an uncanny replay of the Gillray caricature, with Robinson as poet removing herself from the position of "whirligig" and debasing the thundering, trumpeting figure of Tarleton to offer a different lesson to the Prince of Wales. To the bragging of a Captain Bobadil, Robinson adds a specifically sexual component:

> I have fought with all nations, and bled in the field,
> . . .
> And the Enemy fled – one and all!
> I have rescued a thousand fair Donnas, in Spain,
> I have left in gay France, every bosom in pain,
> I have conquer'd the Russian, the Prussian, the Dane,
> And will reign in the Banquetting Hall!

The monarch, hitherto oblivious to the injustices perpetrated by his realm, awakens after this speech to a proper sense of his own dignity and duty. The closing lines of the poem seem markedly unironic, and their promise is recalled by the final words of the collection:

> From that moment the Monarch grew sober and good,
> (And nestled with Birds of a different brood,)
> For he found that the pathway which wisdom pursu'd
> Was pleasant, safe, quiet and even!
> That by Temperance, Virtue and liberal deeds,
> By nursing the flowrets, and crushing the weeds,
> The loftiest Traveller always succeeds –
> For his journey will lead him to HEAV'N.

Yet irony remains in the fact that a fallen woman of dubious virtue, whose own path has hardly been "pleasant, safe, quiet and even" should presume thus to preach to a royal prince. Robinson's "Tales" are remarkable for an effrontery both political and aesthetic, and for their exploitation of what would seem a liability: the demimondaine status of their author. Robinson's late work – poetry and pamphlets alike – lays claim to a localized, embodied, and cynically knowing participation in power. Sexualized and commodified, reaching from kings to gypsies, Robinson's notions of power become tangible in her verse – more accessible through this vulgar, often comic embodiment.

REVISING MARY ROBINSON AND DRAMATIC ROMANCE

As I have already noted, Wordsworth offered no immediate public reaction to Robinson's literary challenge, though Dorothy's journal entry suggests some private vexation at Robinson's claiming of his title. But five years later, Wordsworth's "poem on my own life" – in particular, the seventh book, entitled "London" – developed an extended albeit indirect response to the aesthetic and political problems posed by Robinson's poetic challenge and public persona. Here I want to focus on two aspects of the London book – the poet's invocation of Mary (Robinson) of Buttermere; his recollection of the "alien boy" and his painted, theatrical mother in London – and the theatricality at work in the *Prelude* more generally. Close examination of these interwoven figures connects Wordsworth's response to Robinson with his more general attempt to rehabilitate the politics of dramatic romance while revising its aesthetics.

Wordsworth's portrait of the Belle of Buttermere counters the threat of "Perdita" Robinson with an image of pastoral simplicity. While the actress-turned-courtesan-turned-rival-poet never appears in the *Prelude*, another woman named Mary Robinson (the Belle of Buttermere) appears not once but twice: a figure of wronged rural innocence, she needs the poet's protection against the corruptions of the theatre and the commercialized city. The poet recounts the story of a woman from the Lake District who was tricked into marrying a bigamist, a forger, and an impersonator of the upper classes. The drama which represents *this* Mary Robinson is one of the topical plays, "recent things yet warm with life" (314), seen on the stage of Sadler's Wells. Wordsworth retells the romance of the "Maid of Buttermere" as if to rescue the "maid" (Mary Robinson) and her story from the contamination of the stage, for they seem to him "too holy theme for such a place, / And doubtless treated with irreverence, / Albeit with their [the players'] very best of skill" (318–20). Wordsworth melodramatizes the familiar outline of how Mary of Buttermere was seduced and betrayed; it seems unlikely that he ever saw the play he pretends to describe. In rewriting his own version of the melodrama, Wordsworth attempts to "save" Mary of Buttermere by "re-collecting" an image of a common past, the moment he and Coleridge first saw the "Maid," "then a name / By us unheard of" (329–30). In place of a woman's public fame, Wordsworth stresses her appearance in the eyes of private men:

> Not unfamiliarly we since that time
> Have seen her, her discretion have observed,
> Her just opinions, female modesty,
> Her patience, and retiredness of mind.   (335–38)

Mary's lack of speech in these passages – even her opinions are "observed," rather than heard – seems constitutive of her ability to survive the speech of others, to remain "Unsoiled by commendation and excess / Of public notice" (339–40).

Yet this description also abstracts her from flesh and blood, making her instead an allegorical figure for female purity in the Lake District. Wordsworth excludes from his account the economics of seduction that the historical Mary Robinson readily and publicly acknowledged. A newspaper notice of December 24, 1802 announced that

A letter has been received by Sir Richard Ford [the chief Bow-Street magistrate], from a Gentleman at Keswick, by which it appears, that Mary Robinson of Buttermere, declines prosecuting *Hatfield* for the Bigamy, as she is now very advanced in her pregnancy, although she expresses the greatest detestation of his actions. She says, she certainly married him, under an idea of his being Colonel Hope, brother to the Earl of Hopetoun, with a view of bettering herself; and, that she has been considerably injured by him in every way, as he left a very considerable bill for board, lodging, &c. at her father's house, unpaid, when he went off.[15]

Robinson's account of her rationale ("a view of bettering herself" materially) supports the analysis of marriage as legalized prostitution common in late eighteenth-century feminist tracts; her insistence on seduction as material injury also echoes Mary Darby Robinson's *Thoughts on the Condition of Women*. Wordsworth, however, never acknowledges Robinson's attempt to "better herself"; he continues to present her as passive victim to Hatfield's "cruel mockery / Of love and marriage vows." Removed from economic agency, this Mary of Buttermere becomes little more than an allegorical symbol, a blazoned name, like those that mark tradesmen's shops in London: "Shop after shop, with symbols, blazoned names, / And all the tradesman's honours overhead" (174–75). A figurehead of innocence, she remains stationed, Wordsworth's guardian saint, not "above the door," but on some imagined boundary between the corruption of commodified London and the refuge of the Lakes. Mary of Buttermere does for Wordsworth and the Lakes what Mary Robinson did for the "Whirligig."

Wordsworth's first pass at a "memorial verse" for the Belle of Buttermere remains inadequate, partly because the memorial implies, and to some extent performs, Mary's death. Constructed from memories, his version of her story also freezes "the maid" in past time: more specifically, in Wordsworth's past. Refusing to stay put, she comes back to haunt him: "thy image rose again, / Mary of Buttermere!" To calm this spectral image, the poet attempts to repair his story by relocating this Mary back in the Lakes. This revenant Belle of Buttermere differs emphatically from the public women of London: the Mary Robinson capable of being remembered in verse is neither a poet nor in any way a public woman.

> She lives in peace
> Upon the spot where she was born and reared;
> Without contamination does she live
> In quietness, without anxiety.
> Beside the mountain chapel sleeps in earth
> Her new-born infant, fearless as a lamb
> That thither comes from some unsheltered place
> To rest beneath the little rock-like pile
> When storms are blowing. Happy are they both,
> Mother and child! (351–60)

Wordsworth's characteristic repetition or redundance here seems designed to propitiate this living image, to compensate for the first, inappropriate memorial. In almost ritual fashion, the passage negates the ideas of contamination, anxiety, and fear, to replace them with peace, quiet, sleep, and happiness. Suffering is written out of the picture. Yet the figure of negation keeps the ideas of contamination, anxiety, and fear in play – and this story too misleads, in its odd resurrection of the stillborn or newly dead infant as a lamb who comes to seek shelter in burial. Avoidance of commerce and publicity leads to an idyll largely indistinguishable from death.

Turning away from this Belle of Buttermere and her still-life offspring, Wordsworth confronts the painted woman of the theatre – perhaps that other Mary Robinson which the Belle of Buttermere seemed designed to propitiate and erase:

> foremost I am crossed
> Here by remembrance of two figures: one
> A rosy babe . . .
> . . .
> The other was the parent of that babe –
> But on the mother's cheek the tints were false,

> A painted bloom. 'Twas at a theatre
> That I beheld this pair; the boy had been
> The pride and pleasure of all lookers-on
> In whatsoever place, but seemed in this
> A sort of alien scattered from the clouds. (7.366–78)

Just as Perdita Robinson – painted actress, mother, fallen woman, poet – provides the missing link between this theatrical family and the Belle of Buttermere, Wordsworth's image of the "alien boy" works to revise the relationship between theatricality and romance – and in the process, to answer the challenges posed by Robinson's poetry and theatrical persona. But the poet's attempt to defend childhood against the dangers of theatre presents its own dangers, especially for the adults that children may become.

Back in 1800, Robinson's *Lyrical Tales* had included a poem "The Alien Boy" which asserted the primacy and pathos of loss, as it insisted on society's failure to respond to individual needs. Her verse presented St. Hubert and his son Henry as émigrés in flight from the persecutions of the French revolution. They eventually settle "on a Mountain near the Western Main," and when St. Hubert perishes trying to save the life of a shipwrecked man, Henry loses his mind:

> From that hour
> A maniac wild, the Alien Boy has been;
> His garb with sea-weeds fring'd, and his wan cheek
> The tablet of his mind, disorder'd, chang'd,
> Fading, and worn with care.

Like Wordsworth's blind beggar, this young maniac offers a tablet to be read by others (though with increasing difficulty) – not by himself. Yet while Wordsworth uses the blind beggar to stress the common indecipherability of life and identity, Robinson fixes the meaning of the boy as tablet by making him a figure of social failure. Henry resists all "gen'rous" efforts to return him to society, remaining instead: "A melancholy proof that Man may bear / All the rude storms of Fate, and still suspire / By the wide world forgotten!"

As if feeding off this image, Wordsworth in book seven of the *Prelude* presents this "lovely boy" who seems "a sort of alien scattered from the clouds" (378) – a sharp contrast to the figure of the blind beggar or Robinson's broad notions of social alienation. This boy and his painted mother are introduced with a brief, perhaps coincidental, echo of the Robinson poem –

> 'Twas on a Mountain, near the Western Main
> An Alien dwelt . . .
>   'Twas at a theatre
> That I beheld this pair . . .

but the echo merely serves to underline more fundamental contrasts. Henry's noble, sainted, and deceased father brings into strong relief the fading, painted mother of the *Prelude*. While Wordsworth's boy occupies (with some danger) the center stage of a theatrical gathering, Robinson's suffers, isolated and uncared for; the former remains embalmed in poetic memory, the latter frozen in madness. Robinson's alien boy is a social outcast; outcast from heaven, Wordsworth's alien boy serves to emphasize the poet's premise that the most important alienation remains metaphysical rather than social.

Yet the poet continues to fear that theatre, instead of feeding childhood fantasies (or poetic power), will rather feed upon childhood itself. The boy first appears as a consumable spectacle, part of a moveable feast:

> Upon a board,
> Whence an attendant of the theatre
> Served out refreshments, had this child been placed,
> And there he sate environed with a ring
> Of chance spectators, chiefly dissolute men
> And shameless women – treated and caressed –
> Ate, drank, and with the fruit and glasses played,
> While oaths, indecent speech, and ribaldry
> Were rife about him as are songs of birds
> In springtime after showers.   (7.383–92)

As he eats, drinks, and plays, the child himself is metaphorically consumed by vision and by touch – and the fear remains that this consumption will reach a stage of more literal consumption. Though the poet repeatedly denies the possibility of the child's fall, he finally turns away from the boy with the suggestion that

> he perhaps,
> Mary, may now have lived till he could look
> With envy on thy nameless babe that sleeps
> Beside the mountain chapel undisturbed.   (7.409–12)

Embalming the boy cannot keep him safe: he may be better off dead. This seems to me a rather striking case of "Wordsworthian euphemism": the indirect suggestion of a "fate worse than death" for the boy is followed by a (displaced) reference to female prostitution.[16] Three years earlier, the poet remarks, he heard for the first time

> The voice of woman utter blasphemy –
> Saw woman as she is to open shame
> Abandoned, and the pride of public vice.   (7.417–19)

But of course prostitution has never been just a woman's profession: child prostitution, like child molestation, seems to have been a fairly common phenomenon at the turn of the century, while the sexuality of "dissolute men" in the theatre had been traditionally suspect.[17] Most readings of the painted mother and lovely boy emphasize that the fallen mother is sacrificed to maintain the purity of the boy child, with whom Wordsworth can then (in part) identify. Yet even within this passage, the sacrifice seems unable to keep fears of consumption and prostitution at a distance. Wordsworth's "alien scattered from the clouds" begins as a seeming refutation of Mary Darby Robinson's critique of solitude; yet the poet's account of the boy ends by turning to an uncanny approximation of her personal history – a woman "abandoned" to open shame and the pride of public vice.

These poetic anxieties about boyhood on the borders of the stage oddly refract Wordsworth's earlier strictures on motherhood, strictures delivered in relation to the constraints of education and the freedom of chapbook romance. The badly mothered "lovely boy" of the theatrical board seems both the opposite and the twin of the overmothered dwarf-man of book five. Debarred from the reading of chapbook romances, this earlier child becomes himself a figure out of romance: both an illusion, a formal deception, and a misbegotten revision of chivalry. A "monster birth / Engendered by these too industrious times," the dwarf-man is "a child, no child," but rather "[t]he noontide shadow of a man complete / A worshipper of worldly seemliness" (5.292–99). At the same time, he is "fenced round, nay armed, for ought we know, / In panoply complete" by the excess of his learning (5.314–15). While the poet presents the "lovely boy" of the theatrical board as "embalmed by Nature," this dwarf-man seems rather embalmed by artifice:

> Forth bring him to the air of common sense
> And, fresh and shewy as it is, the corps
> Slips from us into powder.   (5.352–54)

Protesting against contemporary theories of education and their illusory ideals of total mastery, the poet cries out for a return to chapbook romance. Counteracting the "vanity" and hollow self-love of the over-learned dwarf, chapbook tales "Of Fortunatus, and the invisible coat / Of Jack the Giant-killer, Robin Hood, / And Sabra in the forest with St.

George!" encourage children to lose themselves in wonder at the magic of romance.

As we have seen, throughout the eighteenth century chapbook romances were considered appropriate reading not only for children, but also for the working classes. Alan Richardson stresses the importance of reading Wordsworth's valorization of "fairy tales" in historical context, in light of "a period when the rapid and unforeseen growth of popular literacy, the mass distribution of radical political pamphlets, and the reaction of established interests in the form of censorship and mass propaganda of their own produced the literacy 'crisis' of the 1790s."[18] From this perspective, he suggests, the poet's advocacy of romance might even be seen as "yet another appropriation of the popular tale in the interests of returning the new mass readership to an apolitical, class-specific discourse" (123). "Apolitical" seems too mild a word for Wordsworth's treatment of romance: the lessons presented to Wordsworth's young or working-class readers are those of resignation and passivity, in exchange for imaginary participation in a disembodied power. Resignation is the first step. The poet claims that romance offers support and companionship during

> The time of trial ere we learn to live
> In reconcilement with our stinted powers,
> To endure this state of meagre vassalage,
> Unwilling to forego, confess, submit,
> Uneasy and unsettled, yoke-fellows
> To custom, mettlesome and not yet tamed
> And humbled down.   (5.540–46)

The poet turns the tropes of romance on their head in this passage: the trials and probations associated with romance questing here become a test not of power but of "reconcilement." The language of feudalism ("meagre vassalage") is invoked to account for the "stinted powers" of human maturity rather than the wonderfully impossible powers of romance heroes. Imaginatively empowered and practically consoled by romance, adults (specifically, adult men instructed by chapbook romance) can accept "stinted powers" in the realm of politics with better grace. They have learned to be willingly dazzled by their passive participation in a power at once immanent and nonexistent, "[h]ere, nowhere, there, and everywhere at once" (5.557).

The dwarf-man condemned and the chapbook romances celebrated in book five of the *Prelude* oddly refract the figure of the "lovely boy" on the edge of the theatre: this proposed return to romance leads back to

the consumption of childhood, as the poet urges his readers to feed on
their earlier belief in romance as a compensation for maturity, for an
adult disbelief in miraculous change. The motif of consumption
appears quite markedly, in terms that prefigure the lovely boy seated on
the theatre's makeshift table:

> Dumb yearnings, hidden appetites, are ours,
> And they must have their food. Our childhood sits,
> Our simple childhood, sits upon a throne
> That hath more power than all the elements. (5.530–53)

These yearnings are introduced to explain why "romances, legends,"
"fictions," "adventures" and so forth "will live till man shall be no more"
(5.521–29). And these "hidden appetites" aim not at childhood itself, but
at childhood's throne of power. Yet as with the alien boy of the theatre,
childhood seems to sit upon a throne which is also a table laid for eating.
In the sublimated cannibalism of this passage, childhood is simultaneously produced and consumed as a realm of imaginary power, a realm
described through the ambiguous language and temporality of
romance. While theatre seems to threaten childhood with sexualized
consumption, Wordsworth's poetic quest offers a more sublimated feast.
If theatrical romance (embodied in the painted and rival poetic figure of
Mary Robinson) appears in the *Prelude* as an unnatural mother,
Wordsworth himself seems unnaturally to consume the child he ostensibly wishes to preserve. Yet the nostalgic consumption of childhood
which links book five to book seven also enables the poet to move from
farce to romance, from stage to poetry, through a glorification of passivity and the practice of resignation. In Wordsworth's developmental
schema, boys mature by accepting romance both as a form of (masculine) consolation and as the shape of social constraint. And in the process
of poetic sublimation, the working-class associations of stage and chapbook romance vanish, consumed by the childhood nostalgia which fuels
the poet's internalized quest. The poet's romance of boyhood reading
leads to a vision of maturity as political passivity: chapbook readers
learn to enjoy being subsumed within and displaced by the disembodied
powers of romance.

If Robinson as poet represented a fallen figure of romance – her life,
Thoughts and *Lyrical Tales* various examples of romance gone wrong –
such waywardness remains "the issue" of romance, and the threat
against which book seven of the *Prelude* defines itself. But the doubled,

ambivalent figure of "Perdita" Robinson also points beyond the London book to a disavowed theatricality more generally at work in the *Prelude*.[19] In book seven, Wordsworth claims that the superficiality of stage romance serves to define by contrast the healing and creative powers of solitude and communion with nature.[20] Indeed, the "moral" of book seven, if such a thing exists, might be summarized in the poet's proposed antidote to the chaos of Bartholomew Fair:

> Attention comes,
> And comprehensiveness and memory,
> From early converse with the works of God
> Among all regions, chiefly where appear
> Most obviously simplicity and power.   (717–21)

Yet while earlier books of this figurative autobiography show the impact of early converse with nature, with simplicity and power, book seven explicitly links the exercise of attention to the feminized and feminizing world of stage romance. In describing his pleasure in Sadler's Wells, Wordsworth associates the world of theatre both with the exercise of mental power, and with feminine changeability:

> Through the night,
> Between the show, and many-headed mass
> Of the spectators, and each little nook
> That had its fray or brawl, how eagerly
> And with what flashes, as it were, the mind
> Turned this way, that way – sportive and alert
> And watchful, as a kitten when at play,
> While winds are blowing round her, among grass
> And rustling leaves.

Here, attention comes, not from early converse with the works of God, but from early commerce with the theatre. The mind as playful kitten: the image is so domesticated, so feminized, as to seem incompatible with more conventional versions of Wordsworthian psychology. Perhaps for this reason, the poet rapidly aligns this state of easy watchfulness with an "[e]nchanting age and sweet – / Romantic almost," and goes on to strengthen the network of associations already linking femininity, romance, pleasure, and the stage:

> Though surely no mean progress had been made
> In meditations holy and sublime,
> Yet something of a girlish childlike gloss
> Of novelty survived for scenes like these –
> Pleasure that had been handed down from times

> When at a country playhouse, having caught
> In summer through the fractured wall a glimpse
> Of daylight, at the thought of where I was
> I gladdened more than if I had beheld
> Before me some bright cavern of romance,
> Or than we do when on our beds we lie
> At night, in warmth, when rains are beating hard.   (466–88)

What remains of romance in the poet's young adulthood is "something of a girlish childlike gloss" – hardly comparable to the "meditations holy and sublime" which Wordsworth presents as his more honorable labor. Yet this passage, itself full of shifts and turns, at once replicates the larger structure of the London book and demonstrates the kinds of watchful, sportive motion required to profit fully from the world of popular entertainment.[21] Stage romance becomes visible as a structuring principle at the very moment it is most explicitly (and favorably) thematized – yet the structures of theatre pervade the Wordsworthian imagination throughout the *Prelude*.

Back in book five, the poet suggested that a love for romance leads to a love of the world and of language; maturity develops "[w]hen cravings for the marvellous relent, / And we begin to love what we have seen; / . . . and words themselves / Move us with conscious pleasure" (564–68). Yet the pleasure of those words points back toward the pleasures of the theatre. Wordsworth speaks of his sorrow at reading pages and poems which in his youth "Did never fail to entrance me, and are now / Dead in my eyes as is a theatre / Fresh emptied of spectators" (573–5). Aligning the pleasures of poetry with the pleasures of participating in a theatre audience, the poet's simile here suggests that poetic as well as theatrical "life" comes from the audience rather than the spectacle or poem itself. The penultimate shift of this fifth book, however, turns away from poetic theatre to Nature – at the same time, it also seeks to translate romance into an echo of Milton's spiritual epic, *Paradise Lost*. Wordsworth gestures at "the great Nature that exists in works / Of mighty poets" in order to claim that

> Visionary power
> Attends upon the motions of the winds
> Embodied in the mystery of words;
> There darkness makes abode, and all the host
> Of shadowy things do work their changes there
> As in a mansion like their proper home.
> Even forms and substances are circumfused
> By that transparent veil with light divine

> And through the turnings intricate of verse
> Present themselves as objects recognised
> In flashes, and with a glory scarce their own. (619–29)

As in book seven, the mind turns this way and that, through the intricacies of verse rather than the distractions of theatre, with "flashes" of recognition. The first book of *Paradise Lost* operates as the transparent veil here, lending these lines an ambiguous glory "scarce their own." For it is in hell that "darkness visible" makes abode, in hell that Satan's legions come together like Etrurian shades or locust flocks shadowing the plains of Egypt. Shortly after his famous claim that "the mind is its own place," Satan describes hell as "this unhappy mansion" and the latter part of book one is devoted to the creation of Pandemonium, a mighty palace or mansion for the "hosts" of "shadowy things."[22] Here the mind, far from a kitten playing in the grass, seems almost wholly disembodied, present only in the act of recognition, the reflection of glory. Yet certain ghostly continuities remain. Literature "dead in [the poet's] eyes" appears a theatre fresh emptied of spectators; living verse is like a mansion filled with shadowy beings. Both spaces seem haunted: the first by absence, the second by presence, and both by the relationship between words and performance.

Positioned midway between the glory of a Miltonic passage into verse and the "girlish childlike" pleasures of stage romance, Wordsworth's famous apostrophe to Imagination occludes theatre as it pays homage to Milton. Indeed, the apostrophe simply rewrites the "darkness" of the earlier passage as "greatness," while "we" take the place of "shadowy things":

> In such strength
> Of usurpation, in such visitings
> Of awful promise, when the light of sense
> Goes out in flashes that have shewn to us
> The invisible world, doth greatness make abode,
> There harbours whether we be young or old.
> Our destiny, our nature, and our home,
> Is with infinitude – and only there. (6.532–39)

Satan, the would-be usurper of heaven's throne, remains dimly present in these lines, raising questions about the nature of greatness as well as the kind of infinitude constituting "our" destiny, nature, and home. For the most part, however, the Satanic undertones of the power Wordsworth claims for poetry are allowed to go unquestioned in books five and six – perhaps because in these two books that power is grounded in Nature as well as Imagination. But yet another flash of light brings the "delusion bold" of the fallen angels into sharp relief. In the latter part of book ten, describing the entrancing delusions of Godwin's revolutionary rationalism, the poet more clearly invokes Satanic pride as a corruption of the mind's visionary powers:

> The freedom of the individual mind,
> Which, to the blind restraint of general laws
> Superior, magisterially adopts
> One guide – the light of circumstance, flashed
> Upon an independent intellect.　　　　　　　　　(825–29)

Believing itself superior to "the accidents of nature, time and place," such a mind remains dependent on the accidents of circumstance. The result is "a work / Of false imagination" (10.846–47), a delusion of romance.

The Wordsworthian imagination simultaneously derives from and disavows the theatre of romance. While the false imagination of politics offers a clear contrast to the true Imagination of poetry and nature, the theatre of romance remains a more ambiguous influence. In the playhouse of romance, flashes of light return the viewer to himself, and the return to self-presence gradually strengthens the poet's independence from the imaginative force of stage romance: theatre exercises the poet's attention through his resistance to its domination. Yet while this struggle privileges the poet's mental theatre over the literal theatre which surrounds him, it also makes the internalization of romance a theatrical production. In reclaiming romance, Wordsworth disembodies power by moving beyond the popular theatres in which romance was, however crudely, performed. Yet at the same time, the motifs of stage romance – and the anxieties they provoke – move beyond the boundaries of the London book to reflect (in flashes) on the structure of the Wordsworthian imagination itself. The flashing structure of imagination culminates in the poet's "meditation" at the top of Snowdon, a vision focused on "The perfect image of a mighty mind, / Of one that feeds upon infinity." But the theatricality of the Wordsworthian imagination and the poet's earlier concerns about consumption raise the question of what, beside infinity, that mighty mind might feed upon. Between the "flash" of light upon the turf and the "universal spectacle" rests a "gloomy breathing-place," filled with "innumerable" streams and torrents "roaring with one voice" (7.40–60). Wordsworth, ostensibly following

Nature, "lodge[s]" the "imagination of the whole" in "that breach /
Through which the homeless voice of waters rose" (7.62–63). Moving
slowly from the popular theatres of London to the mountains of
North Wales, the disembodied power of the poet's verse displaces, as
it claims to speak for, the "innumerable" masses who might otherwise
drown out the roar of a single voice.

CONCLUSION: ROMANCING THE CITY

Mary Robinson's challenge to Wordsworth's project of gentrifying and
internalizing stage romance remains visible throughout the lineaments
of Wordsworth's London: a city at once popular, theatrical, conflicted,
feminized, commercialized, prostituted, and irrepressibly romantic.
That city of romance gathers itself into spectacular form at
Bartholomew Fair: in order to meet the popular and populous challenge
of the city, the poet finds himself forced to call upon the female figure of
the Muse – and his reluctant invocation once again reinstates and reem-
bodies the lost women of romance.

At the close of book seven, Wordsworth claims that the power of the
mind determines reality: "things that are, are not, / Even as we give
them welcome, or assist – / Are prompt, or are remiss" (643–45). Yet the
mind's mental power and control are promptly challenged as
Wordsworth imagines the city "break[ing] out" as it does at Bartholomew
Fair:

> What say you then
> To times when half the city shall break out
> Full of one passion – vengeance, rage, or fear –
> To executions, to a street on fire,
> Mobs, riots, or rejoicings?   (645–49)

No time is given for any response. The social unrest figured by "Mobs,
riots or rejoicings" is promptly translated back into an aesthetic problem:
the explosion of the city at Bartholomew Fair becomes

> A work that's finished to our hands, that lays,
> If any spectacle on earth can do,
> The whole creative powers of man asleep   (653–55)

But this sleepwalking movement from social unrest to aesthetic incapacity is hardly a lasting solution. To move through the creative impasse of
spectacle – and the city's potential for mob violence – the poet turns to
the female Muse:

> For once the Muse's help will we implore
> And she shall lodge us – wafted on her wings
> Above the press and danger of the crowd –
> Upon some showman's platform.   (656–59)

Deposited on this showman's platform, however, Wordsworth becomes largely indistinguishable from the other hawkers of the fair. And the catalog of carnival images that follows seems closer in many ways to the work of Mary Darby Robinson (a prostituted muse if ever there was one) than to Wordsworth's own standard ware.

I want to suggest that Robinson herself is the prostituted *and* politicized Muse invoked here, and that Wordsworth found the help he needed not in a sketch of Bartholomew Fair or even of a "London Morning" but in an account of a military camp pitched on "Winkfield Plain":[23]

> Tents, marquees, and baggage-waggons;
> Suttling-houses, beer in flagons;
> Drums and trumpets, singing, firing,
> Girls seducing, beaux admiring;
> . . .
> Tax'd carts full of farmers' daughters;
> Brutes condemn'd, and man who slaughters!
> Public-houses, booths, and castles,
> Belles of fashion, serving vassals;
> . . .
> Tradesmen leaving shops, and seeming
> More of war than profit dreaming:
> Martial sounds and braying asses,
> Noise, that ev'ry noise surpasses!
> All confusion, din, and riot,
> Nothing clean – and nothing quiet.

Robinson's rhyming couplets highlight the pattern of differences operating – without syntax or significance – within the chaos of a war camp. The woman poet speaks from a place beyond even fallen romance: her verse shows the apparent contradictions of the war camp already resolved, through self-delusion and cultural complicity – people's willingness to live out the contradictions of a gendered national and commercial ideology.

Wordsworth produces a similar chaos through his aesthetic horror at Bartholomew Fair's commercialization of culture:

> the midway region and above
> Is thronged with staring pictures and huge scrolls,

Dumb proclamations of the prodigies;
And chattering monkeys dangling from their poles,
And children whirling in their roundabouts;
With those that stretch the neck, and strain the eyes,
And crack the voice in rivalship, the crowd
Inviting; with buffoons against buffoons
Grimacing, writhing, screaming. (7.665–73)

The two passages share a general sense of chaos, din, and riot – as well as a proliferation of gerunds. We might imagine Wordsworth's own voice cracking a bit in rivalship here, straining out of blank verse toward Robinson's string of gerunds and rhyming couplets (scrolls/poles). Stuart Curran remarks of "Winkfield Plain" that "no man could have written this poem so conscious of the place of women within the economy of war and no woman in English society but an inhabitant of the demi-monde like Robinson, would have dared to."[24] Obviously, the same could not be said of Wordsworth's portrayal of Bartholomew Fair. Even the difference in form seems suggestive: Mary Robinson offers a formal recognition of the coupling of commerce and war, while Wordsworth's contorted blank verse sketches the "blank confusion" he finds in London and the Fair. Wordsworth, unlike Robinson, displays a general horror of the market: a reluctant fall into the grotesquerie of commercial transactions.

Wordsworth's insistence on chaos in this closing portrait of London serves to maintain the possibility of unraveling its contortions into "[c]omposure and ennobling harmony" (741) – the romance promise of resolution, to be produced by the overcoming of romance. First, however, the poet translates the popular forms of the Fair into a pervasive cultural slavery:

An undistinguishable world to men,
The slaves unrespited of low pursuits,
Living amid the same perpetual flow
Of trivial objects, melted and reduced
To one identity by differences
That have no law, no meaning, and no end –
Oppression under which even highest minds
Must labor, whence the strongest are not free. (7.700–7)

This cultural slavery is notably difficult to distinguish from romance: in book five, the poet blessed romance writers as "forgers of lawless tales"; the tales of the *Arabian Nights* – another central example of romance for the *Prelude* poet – were known for their lack of explicit meaning;[25] and the unending nature of the prose romance was one of its most notable features for eighteenth-century readers.

Wordsworth claims to overcome the senseless variations of romance by "steady vision, attention, comprehensiveness and memory" – mental features developed through early converse with the works of God. In practice, however, he seems to overcome the perilous forms of feminized romance by embodying them. "Attention . . . and comprehensiveness and memory" produce the poet as the (feminized, prostituted) city even as they recreate the city along the sight lines of poetic memory. While these three aspects of interpretation or analysis may well come from "early converse with the works of God," book seven also shows them developing in response to the romance of the stage. And the far side of romance repeatedly appears in the figure of the prostitute, a figure defined by Samuel Johnson as "a woman who converses unlawfully with men." Mary Darby Robinson remains the closest historical and lyrical prototype for such an unlawfully voluble woman – a figure of and yet beyond romance, in response to which the reluctant poet of London perversely and romantically takes shape.

The chequered careers of Emma Hamilton and Mary Robinson show the generic struggle which accompanied the formation of gender roles within romance nationalism. Both Hamilton and Robinson played out, at times, a role of romance heroine drawn from the feminized tradition of prose romance. Their counterparts, Horatio Nelson and William Wordsworth respectively, relied on a model of romance nationalism drawn instead from the highly accessible, highly compressed form of chapbook romance. Hamilton and Nelson saw themselves as partners, as opposed to Robinson's and Wordsworth's more competitive relationship – but public reception of the Hamilton–Nelson affair set one partner against the other, degrading Hamilton in order to elevate Nelson. In this imaginary struggle between public men and public women, manly chapbooks and feminized prose romance, dramatic romance sided with the former. And in keeping with the theatrical logic of dramatic romance, public women like Hamilton and Robinson were alternately idealized as Britannia herself (or in Robinson's case, as Perdita, the lost princess of romance) and reviled as prostitutes, bodies devoid of spirit and health. A source of inspiration, a source of infection: public women at once revitalized and threatened the nation's body politic, as their performances of romance nationalism threatened to dominate the men with whom their names were linked.

PART III

Mixed drama, imperial farce

CHAPTER FIVE

Mimicry, politics, and playwrighting

In the autumn of 1789, Astley's Ampitheatre and the Hughes's Royal Circus in St. George's Fields presented competing versions of the fall of the Bastille. Astley, advertising the closing days of his show in the *Morning Post* on October 28, 1789, offered for the delectation of the public six scenes, including the portrayal of "[t]he Bastille and the head of the Governor together with that of the Prevot des Marchands" and "the real military proceedings of the armed citizens during the three hours siege of the Bastille." Such performances laid no claim to the status of legitimate theatre: banned from performing spoken drama, circuses and minor theatres presented purely visual spectacles leavened only by songs and written legends. Yet such lowly shows nonetheless staged contemporary political upheaval for "the masses" when Covent Garden and Drury Lane kept silence. According to Frederick Reynolds, a play he had written in 1789 and entitled *The Bastille* was banned at Covent Garden; John Philip Kemble withdrew his politicized production of *Coriolanus* from the repertoire for fear it would spark public disturbances – yet the dangerous spectacle of revolution was nonetheless promptly commodified, offered up for consumption by the lower classes, those most immediately concerned in the events of the revolution across the channel. In 1790, Edmund Burke would characterize the French National Assembly as a political farce; in 1789, the conventions of farce and spectacle already mediated popular British perceptions of the French revolution.

A caricature published on November 1, 1789 emphasized the dramatic crudity of this kind of "Amphitheatrical Attack of the Bastile" – in part, I think, as a means of undercutting its impact and appeal (plate 15). In the print, the stage scenery seems flimsy, undersized, and insubstantial. Play-acting is the theme of the day: in the foreground of the stage, a man fires at a toy cannon with his cane. Written legends clarify possible sources of confusion (e.g., "This is a Drawbridge"), thus

An Amphitheatrical Attack of the Bastile.

Plate 15 Anonymous, "An Ampitheatrical Attack of the Bastile." November 1, 1789

mocking the intelligence of the spectators, the quality of the staging, or both. The flag inscribed "France" helps to identify the governor of the Bastille, on whose shoulder it is carried, but the surliness of his response to the armed citizens ("D—n You what do you want") serves as an even clearer badge of identity, while his vulgar lack of eloquence also serves to suggest bad acting. The major event of the show, the fall of the prison, is recorded only in legend: a man on the far left of the stage holds up a cloth which reads, "No Bastille." Even this purely legendary triumph is upstaged by theatrical and commercial competition: a far more substantial sign asserts, "Mr. Centaur can assure the publick since his return from ~~Dublin~~ Paris that this here Bastile is the most exactest of any of the Bastiles existin." This caricature, like the amphitheatrical attacks on the Bastille it represents, worked to keep the prison "existin" – in addition to representing its fall, these comic performances kept the symbol of authoritarian repression visually at the forefront of popular attention.

What would it mean to read the early years of British Romanticism as an amphitheatrical as well as an antitheatrical age? As in the chapters on romance, we might have to acknowledge a reliance *on* spectacle – working both with and within a resistance *to* spectacle – shaping the spirit of the age. And we might find the center of the period shifting out of London toward England's colonies. Here, for instance, Dublin rather than Paris becomes the (in)authentic site and source of multiple Bastilles: the allusion reminds viewers of Dublin's role in producing pirated editions of plays and texts, but it also records Dublin's status as the capital of a colony oppressed by British "Bastilles." More generally, we might find the lowly form of stage farce, like the political caricatures considered here and in previous chapters, marking an important intersection between Romantic theatre and Romantic politics.

The previous section of this book focused on female actresses, arguing that dramatic romance staged the attractions of the nation through the bodies of these public women, then purged the nation of negative theatricality by subordinating those women or by expelling them from the stage and the nation. Yet some women performers used their narrow window of influence to broaden the range of action available to women within romance conventions. The next chapters focus on the figure of the female dramatist, arguing that woman-authored farce – or the combination of farce and sentiment frequently deployed by late eighteenth-century women dramatists – registered both the intersections of and the contradictions among empire, nation, and gender. Mingling the agency of performers with the structuring constraints of dramatic form, women playwrights used farce to unsettle the reigning, systematic assumptions of sentimental imperialism.

In order to appreciate the work of playwrights like Hannah Cowley and Elizabeth Inchbald, however, we must first understand the traditions of eighteenth-century farce and sentiment upon which they drew. By the latter part of the century, farce was often (though not always) a term used to designate the afterpiece of an evening's program: afterpieces might include elements of burlesque or pantomime; others invoked sentimental moralizing.[1] Yet mainpiece sentimental comedies often included scenes full of the more physical humor of farce. Rather than attempting to define farce as a form distinct from comedy and pantomime, then, I will be addressing elements of farce – especially materiality and mimicry – at work within both shorter and longer plays. The first part of this introduction tracks the development of eighteenth-century farce as political mimicry through the work of Henry Fielding and Samuel Foote; the second explores the associations between farce and caricature at the close of the century; the third briefly summarizes the reasons women writers might have been drawn to farce or the form of mixed (sentimental) drama. Farce has been and continues to be a seriously undertheorized form, but in exploring historical connections among women dramatists, imperial critique and the forms of farce, two models of cultural criticism seem highly relevant: Luce Irigaray's reading of femininity as mimicry, and Homi Bhabha's model of colonial mimicry (which I would describe as colonial *sentiment*). The final part of this introduction reads the broader systematic claims of Irigaray's and Bhabha's theories in light of the history sketched through the previous sections.

FARCE, POLITICS, AND MIMICRY

The early history of eighteenth-century farce emphasizes the form's subversive relationship to authority, be that authority theatrical, critical, or governmental. Attempts to define farce repeatedly set the form in conflict with critical judgment, though this conflict was often framed in terms of farce's "license" to present impossibilities on stage. Dryden, in a preface to his own farce, *An Evening's Love, or the Mock-Astrologer* (1671), aligned farce with "forc'd humours, and unnatural events," with extravagance, fancy, and a general lack of judgment on the part of the audience.[2] Some twenty years later, Poet Laureate Nahum Tate agreed with Dryden that farce evaded judgment and critical standards, even as he defended the abused form by emphasizing its writerly challenges: "the business of Farce extends beyond Nature and Probability . . . [T]here are no Rules to be prescribed for that sort of Wit, no Patterns to Copy, 'tis altogether the Creature of Imagination."[3] By 1735 Henry Fielding was using this absence of patterns and rules to mock critical precepts. A playwright-character in Fielding's short "comedy" *Don Quixote in England* explained that a particular prologue could not be used to introduce his work because the prologue attacked the form it was meant to praise: "The author never read my play: and taking it for a regular Comedy of five acts, hath fallen very severely on Farce."[4] More conservative in his aesthetics if not in his theatre practice, Samuel Foote in 1752 echoed Dryden's earlier views of farce: "No unnatural assemblages, no creatures of the fancy can procure the protection of the Comic Muse; men and things must appear as they are. To *Farce* greater liberties are permitted."[5]

By the end of the century, some critics were willing to abdicate all claim to judgment while granting the liberties permitted to farce. In 1789, for instance, the theatre critic of the *St. James Chronicle* asserted that "Aristotle has defined Tragedy and Comedy . . . But in Farce we are left to our own Imaginations and Feelings, if we should happen to have any. Farce is an unlimited Region of happy Absurdities, Antitheses, Puns, and Repartees. These should be brought together by a Fable as improbable and Characters as extravagant as possible."[6] By contrast, Coleridge, in his *Lectures on Shakespeare* (1808), attempted to articulate farce's extravagance more precisely, according to its "philosophical principles and character." He claimed that "A proper farce is mainly distinguished from comedy by the license allowed, and even required, in the fable, in order to produce strange and laughable situations. The story need not be probable, it is enough that it is possible . . . [F]arces commence in a postulate, which must be granted."[7] By the end of the long eighteenth century, the "forc'd humours" once associated with farce had become a model of narrative license, paradoxically required of the form, to which the audience, granting the postulate from which the plot began, was likewise required to submit.

Henry Fielding, the most important farceur of the first half of the century, exploited farce's perceived subversion of judgment by turning the form to political critique. From the start of his dramatic career, Fielding had used the stage as a platform from which to criticize the government; in 1736 and 1737, he applied his dramatic talents wholeheartedly to the task of political satire. *Pasquin; a dramatic satire on the times* (1736) presented two plays within a play: the comedy *The Election*, which sketched the corrupt electioneering practices of the time, emphasizing bribery both direct and indirect; and the tragedy *The Death of Common*

Sense, which took more general aim at the social and cultural effects of governmental corruption. *The Historical Register for the Year 1736* (1737) sharpened Fielding's political attack by emphasizing the connections between theatre and politics: "When my politics come to a farce, they very naturally lead to the playhouse where, let me tell you, there are some politicians too, where there is lying, flattering, dissembling, deceiving, and undermining, as well as in any court in Christendom" (16). In the farce *Eurydice; or the Devil Hen-Pecked* (February 1737), Fielding played up popular complaints of an improper alliance between queen and prime minister, and the queen's excessive power. When *Eurydice* folded, "damned" by the town, Fielding promptly staged another farce, *Eurydice hiss'd; or, a word to the wise* (April 1737), aggressively exploiting his own apparent failure, and pursuing his satirical attack on the ministry of Sir Robert Walpole by equating government with farce. In each of these plays, Fielding mocked political corruption by equating politics with the vulgarity, materiality, and excess that defined farce. Rather than expanding farce's claim to serious consideration, Fielding attacked politicians by applying to them the limitations associated with farce.

In the end, of course, Fielding's attempt to broaden the political license of farce turned into a literal dispute over theatrical licenses, as prime minister Sir Robert Walpole, the butt of Fielding's satires, pushed the Licensing Act of 1737 through parliament. Arguing that "theatrical entertainments . . . from their excess, fill both town and country with idleness and debauchery; and, from being under no restraint, exhibit to the publick encomiums on vice and laugh away the sober principles of modesty and virtue," the act was first introduced in the House of Commons on May 24, 1737 and passed into law on June 21st.[8] The Licensing Act, as it came to be known, distinguished between legitimate (spoken) drama and spectacular or musical performances (including opera); limited the number of legitimate theatres in London to those operating under royal patents (Covent Garden and Drury Lane); and instituted state censorship, requiring all plays commercially performed to be "licensed" by the Lord Chamberlain's office. The Little Theatre in the Haymarket promptly closed, and on November 1, 1737, Fielding enrolled in the Middle Temple to study law.

While the Licensing Act reestablished the limitations of farce, however, it failed to destroy the form or its political interests. By 1747, Samuel Foote, a gifted mimic, had begun evading the Licensing Act, first by putting on "The Diversions of the Morning," then by charging "friends" for a morning "Dish of Chocolate" or an evening "Cup of

Tea" and providing free entertainment along with that purely virtual beverage. During the first half of Foote's career, from 1747 to roughly 1766, his dramatic productions were largely occasions for his mimicry of actors, actresses, social taste, and private reputations. Charles Churchill's description of Foote in *The Rosciad* (1771), for instance, emphasized the vicious personal nature of Foote's dramatic caricatures:

> His strokes of humour, and his bursts of sport,
> Are all contained in this one word – distort.
> Doth a man stutter, look asquint, or halt,
> Mimics draw humour out of Nature's fault,
> With personal defects their mirth adorn,
> And hang misfortune out to public scorn.   (399–404)[9]

Only after he had gained a lifetime license to perform at the Haymarket during the summer season did Foote launch out into more political farces, attacking public men in relation to colonial affairs.[10] His *Nabob* (1772) ridiculed Englishmen grown wealthy from Indian exploitation; *The Bankrupt* (1773) linked his own fortunes to the trial of Robert Clive, "Conqueror of India," for imperial corruption; and *The Cozeners* (1774) burlesqued a Mrs. Grieves famous for selling brides and jobs by having her match the son of a wealthy social climber to a black heiress from Jamaica. Yet even the broader imperial perspective of these later plays failed to balance Foote's endless attacks on personal idiosyncrasies and public reputations. His political critique remained largely incidental to his more limited brief: the public exposure of private persons.

Launching into public satire, Foote's personal attacks and Fielding's political interests nonetheless shared a common approach to humor: each was accused of abandoning comic mimesis for political mimicry. Eighteenth-century distinctions between comedy and farce, mimesis and mimicry, were often linked to distinctions between public and private issues: ironically, farcical mimicry of politics was thought to constitute a "private" abuse of theatrical mimesis. In the *Daily Gazetteer* of May 7th, 1737, for instance, the "Adventurer in Politicks" attacked Fielding's political farce by complaining that

To encourage then Politicks on the Stage, is not only *unjust* in itself, and *improper*, but of a most pernicious Tendency to the Stage itself, which instead of being a general Mirrour, where the Beauties and Deformities of human Nature are represented Impartially; whence we either *copy* or *reject*, as we find our Resemblance *good* or *bad*, becomes a private Looking-Glass, where Spleen, Resentment, and inconsiderate levity, displays Objects without any Regard to Truth, Decency, Good Manners, or true Judgment.[11]

The public stage should be a general and impartial mirror to society but farce as a "private Looking-Glass" presents a partial and distorted view. From this perspective, general mimesis legitimates comedy; mimicry marks farce a bastardized social form. We might compare the strictures of this "Adventurer in Politicks" with Samuel Johnson's strictures on Samuel Foote. When Boswell praised Foote's "singular talent of exhibiting character," Johnson responded, "Sir, it is not a talent; it is a vice; it is what others abstain from. It is not comedy, which exhibits the character of a species, as that of a miser gathered from many misers; it is a farce, which exhibits individuals."[12] Yet Johnson's great friend and protégé David Garrick followed Foote's lead while disavowing his practice. Mary Granville, for instance, remarked of Garrick's *Miss in her Teens* that "nothing can be lower, but the part [Garrick] acts in it himself (Mr. Fribble) he makes so very ridiculous that it is really entertaining. It is said he mimics eleven men of fashion."[13] Farce as a private looking-glass presents an individual's view of the world: personal bias or even malice produces the distortions of mimicry. So too where comedy presents a social whole, mimicry fragments social identity into distinct and divergent parts.

Mimicry as practiced by Fielding and Foote relied primarily on audience response. In different ways, each farceur presented a simple yet degrading analogy, one which contaminated public perceptions of the original person or object mimicked. Fielding's most powerful critique of Walpole, for instance, lay less in his portrayal of government as farce than in his portrayal of Walpole as the minor farceur, Pillage:

> PILLAGE. Who'd wish to be the author of a farce
> Surrounded daily by a crowd of actors,
> Gaping for parts, and never to be satisfied?
> . . .
> [Yet] Wolsey's self, that mighty minister,
> In the full height and zenith of his power,
> Amid a crowd of sycophants and slaves,
> Was but perhaps the author of a farce,
> Perhaps a damned one too. 'Tis all a cheat,
> Some men play little farces, and some great.   (II.298)

Once the two figures of Walpole and Pillage have been successfully superimposed on the spectator's vision, it becomes very difficult indeed to disentangle them. In *Euridyce hiss'd*, Fielding succeeded only too well in cutting Walpole down to size: the Licensing Act became a radical face-saving maneuver for a man unwilling to be seen as a little farceur.

Mimic humor lives in the spark produced by forcing together an antag-onistic pair of terms or characters, such as prime minister and minor farceur. Successful mimicry thus produces a split perspective and a split relationship to time. Mimic entertainment is the work of a moment: the audience laughs only for the instant in which the degrading recognition is forced upon their judgment. The degradation, however, may well linger, altering the public reception of a person or idea. Mimicry creates an environment in which to be oneself is to betray oneself to the mockery of others: once a degrading resemblance has been recognized, recogni-tion itself becomes judgment, or rather, condemnation. Emphasizing (and distorting) the characteristic features of a person or concept, mimicry suggests those features will never change, but the successful mimic ensures that the original's performance itself will henceforth be received as something distorted, distorting and unnatural.

A topical, ephemeral art, mimicry survives, extends itself, only by con-stantly shifting the base of its comparisons, altering the antagonisms off which it plays. Churchill's verbal portrait of Foote thus stressed the farceur's mobility as well as his knack for distortion:

> By turns transformed into all kinds of shapes,
> Constant to none, Foote laughs, cries, struts and scrapes:
> Now in the centre, now in van or rear,
> The Proteus shifts, bawd, parson, auctioneer.   (394–97)

Still more radically shifting the ground and framework of their mockery, the most successful mimics were always ready to turn the joke back upon themselves. When Foote proposed to mimic a Dublin printer named George Faulkner in a Dublin performance of *The Orators*, for instance, Faulkner threatened to bring legal action against him. The mimic responded by appearing belatedly on stage in the character meant for Faulkner, assuring the audience "that he had been detained at his lawyer's, in giving instructions to bring an action against a rascally fellow, one Foote, who, by a *vile* imitation of his voice and figure, had brought him on the public stage."[14] Mimicking the victim's denunciation of his own performance, Foote deformed legal process as he disrupted social representation. Fielding's political burlesques produced a similar dou-bling or division of critical perspectives, using the dramatic form of the rehearsal (popularized by the perennial success of Buckingham's *Rehearsal*) to promote a mocking self-critique of the play-within-the-play. In *Eurydice hiss'd*, for instance, the author Spatter and the critic Sourwit discuss the author's "cunning" choice of subject:

SPATTER. [A]s the town have damned my play, for their own sakes they will
    not damn the damnation of it.
SOURWIT. Faith, I must confess, there is something of a singular modesty in
    the instance.
SPATTER. And of singular prudence too. (II.297)

Spatter–Fielding's shifting authorial perspective produces mimicry as an
unstable doubling of critical positions. Proclaiming the public's antagonism toward his last play in his new title, Spatter mimics the town and
through his mimicry undermines that public hostility: his simple logic
neutralizes the rejection of *Eurydice* by turning that rejection to his own
account.

Ironically, perhaps, mimicry's unending transgression of the judgment it evokes becomes most clear as farce is interpellated within larger
systems of law and order. On April 30, 1748, the Court of Criticism in
Fielding's *Jacobite's Journal* indicted Foote for personal mimicry in terms
which emphasized, through their own mimicry, the material or literaliz-
ing aspects of Foote's theatrical performances – and which drastically
undercut the judgment they ostensibly demanded. Stressing the indis-
criminacy of the mimic's personal attacks and his lack of dramatic skill,
the court attacked Foote for replacing the fictions of ridicule with the
physiological peculiarities of the mimic or his victim. Yet in the conclusion to this scene of sentencing, Fielding blended his own allegorical
mode of mimicry with Foote's more material, physical strategies of ridicule:

I shall proceed therefore to pronounce the Judgment of the Court; which is, that
you Samuel Fut be p—ssed upon, with Scorn and Contempt, as a low Buffoon;
and I do, with the utmost Scorn and Contempt, p—ss upon you accordingly.
    The Prisoner was then removed from the Bar, mimicking and pulling a Chew
of Tobacco from his Mouth, while the P—ss ran plentifully down his Face.[15]

Fielding imagines Foote, in the midst of his sentencing, busily mimicking Fielding himself, by reference to Fielding's familiar chew of tobacco.
And as the court's judgment is performed through an act of low
buffoonery, the magistrate sinks to the moral level of the prisoner: not
even justice remains secure from the contagious, degrading appeal of
material mimicry.

What does all this history mean for Romantic women dramatists?
Nothing like the crude physicality of these bodily fluids appears in the
work of Romantic farceuses – and yet the split perspective and subversive mobility of Fielding's and Foote's mimicry remained a characteris-

tic feature of Romantic farce and mixed drama. Hannah Cowley's comedies and mixed dramas, for instance, often featured characters who act like mimics: in *A Day in Turkey; or the Russian Slaves* (1791), the Frenchman A la Greque constantly shifts political positions and invites scornful laughter in the hope of achieving a temporary personal advantage. A subtler mimic, the heroine of Cowley's *The Belle's Stratagem* (1782) performs both the English femininity her fiancé despises and the continental mystery he thinks he desires: in the process, she inverts his assumptions and unmasks his deeper desires. Elizabeth Inchbald blended the role of mimic with that of dramatist: in *Such Things Are* (1787), for instance, she parodied the public figure of Lord Chesterfield through the burlesque character Twineall and the more ominous Lord Flint. Inchbald's *Wives as They Were, Maids as They Are* (1797) more subtly mimics Cowley's *Belle's Stratagem* by staging the consequences of the earlier play: in Inchbald's comedy, the *wife's* stratagem relies on a hidden yet versatile mimic duplicity. Indeed, the play's power depends in part on its surprise revelation: a "straight" minor character like Lady Priory turns out to be a mimic after all, encompassing the opposite roles of excessively obedient wife and masculine, masterful woman. Moving from personal mimicry to the broader outlines of social caricature, farceuses like Charlotte Smith and Mary Robinson exposed the gap between material conditions and social fictions, producing mimic humor from their forced juxtapositions. In general, as the next section suggests, the close of the century seemed to mark the disappearance of mimicry's personal, partial looking-glass in a return to comedy's more "general mirrour," yet the distortions of farce remained, refocused on the defining features of national and social identity.

FARCE AS CARICATURE

Indeed, frequent comparisons between comedy and caricature attest to the on-going presence of farcical distortion in English Romantic theatre: at the end of the eighteenth century, foreign visitors to London repeatedly complained that English comedy had degenerated into mere caricature. After seeing a performance of Sheridan's *The Critic* in 1792, for instance, Friedrich Wilhelm von Hassell complained that the whole play was "exaggerated even to the extent of the most ghastly caricature."[16] In 1794, Jacob Christian Gottlieb Schaeffer preferred English tragedy to comedy because "in the latter the actors exaggerate their rôles and everything is turned into caricature."[17] In 1795, Jacques Henri Meister

felt that English comedy relied upon "very complicated plots, very positive characters, very lively, original repartee" – all of which produced
"a comedy bordering more or less on caricature."[18] Finally, in 1801, a
German resident of London remarked, "Our new comedies are for the
most part nothing but caricatures and would be hissed off the German
stage."[19] Some of this comic extremity could be blamed on the size of
the patent theatres and the visual exaggerations they demanded; other
kinds of dramatic excess bore social implications that made foreign visitors uncomfortable. Von Schütz, for instance, complained of one play
that

> The chambermaid in making her exit passed the burning candle under the
> lackey's nose, so that the light was extinguished. I am sure that the director of
> a good German theatre would punish such insolence. But in Drury Lane
> general applause betokened approval. The natural consequence was that the
> actress in question sought to exaggerate her playing even more in the next act,
> whirled around on one leg for joy over a new dress and threw herself to the floor
> in a position not in keeping with female propriety.[20]

While a German theatre manager might punish the actress's insolence,
the London audience rewards her for finding such a vivid way of displaying her character's impertinence. What disappears in this collaborative relationship between actress and audience, however, is obedience to
models of female and dramatic propriety alike.

Beyond this level of social discomfort, foreigners' complaints of
comedy as caricature operated largely on a formal level, emphasizing
the performative exaggerations of actors and actresses alike. Even on a
purely formal level, however, the link between comedy and caricature
was seen as having national implications. The charge of caricature had
been leveled at English comedy as early as 1747 by Abbé Jean Bernard
le Blanc, who claimed,

> You find at this time more pitiful buffoons on the stage at London, than toler-
> able actors; which seems to me the effects of the national state. The English, if
> you'll permit me to use a term of painting, which can alone express my idea,
> love caricaturas; they are more struck with a large face and a great nose,
> designed by Callot, than with a noble and graceful countenance, trac'd by
> Correggio's pencil . . . the more he [the actor] finds the caricatura in his part,
> the more he thinks there ought to be of it, in his action; and thus, he endeavours
> to express the humour of it, more by the grimaces of his face than the proper
> modulation of his voice.[21]

If the English could be characterized by their love of caricatures,
English farce had a long tradition of caricaturing other nationalities.

Dryden had attributed the (limited) art of the grimace to the French, urging his countrymen to "forbear the translation of French Plays: for their Poets wanting judgement to make, or to maintain true characters, strive to cover their defects with ridiculous Figures and Grimaces" (preface to *An Evening's Love*, 204). Farceurs such as Foote and Cowley had followed this hint by turning national identities into rigid caricatures. Doricourt, the hero of Cowley's *Belle's Stratagem*, for instance, in returning from continental travels, brought with him a corrupt set of foreign servants, to his friend Saville's dismay:

SAVILLE. I prepared my mind, as I came up stairs, for a *bon jour*, a grimace, and an *adieu* . . . [C]an't an Englishman stand behind your carriage, buckle your shoe, or brush your coat?

DORICOURT. . . . Englishmen make the best Soldiers, Citizens, Artizans, and Philosophers in the world; but the very worst Footmen. I keep French fellows and Germans, as the Romans kept slaves; because their own countrymen had minds too enlarged and haughty to descend with a grace to the duties of such a station. (7)

Cowley's drama degrades the French and Germans through references to their stock mannerisms – that tell-tale grimace – as well as their obedience to absolute government. Conversely, the English are characterized by their set insistence on exercising the civil liberties of critique and debate: "A Frenchman['s] . . . whole system of conduct is compris'd in one short word, *Obedience*! An Englishman reasons, forms opinions, cogitates, and disputes; . . . and is therefore your judge, whilst he wears your livery, and decides on your actions with the freedom of a censor" (8). The farcical image of the groom as judge and censor may caricature the English, but in this context ennobles rather than degrades the national character. So too the figure of John Bull, that representative of England featured prominently in the war-time caricatures of James Gillray, might be endlessly abused, but in his thick-headed goodwill, he remains surprisingly admirable. One German visitor to the London theatres complained about this uneven distribution of farcical effects: "Why have most dramatic poets this mania for seeking only among a neighboring people errors, absurdities and vices which are abundant enough at home? If comedy is to correct our faults by making us laugh at them, how can it fulfill its purpose whilst aiming all its arrows at foreign countries?"[22]

Romantic farces did in fact mock native social extravagance as well as foreign folly, but the link between comedy and caricature also recorded an important shift in farcical sensibilities. During the first half of the eighteenth century, farce had been associated with the lower classes: Dryden aligned farce with the vitiated tastes of "the people," and toward the middle of the century, the form was linked with vulgarity in both the middle and lower classes. Henry Fielding's prologue to *The Lottery; A Farce* (1732), for instance, asserted that

> As Tragedy prescribes to passion rules,
> So Comedy delights to punish fools;
> And while at nobler games she boldly flies,
> Farce challenges the vulgar as her prize.

The author of *City Farce* (1737) likewise suggested making "a new Essay toward reviving the Spirit of our English Farce, which was designed to yield some Benefit as well as Diversion, by exposing those Follies which affect chiefly the Middle Station of Life, and are therefore beneath the Province of Comedy, which is principally confined to the Genteel Part of Mankind."[23]

In 1747, however, Samuel Foote differentiated English humor from that of the French by grounding comedy in social equality:

In *France*, one Coxcomb is the Representation of the whole Kingdom. In *England*, scarce any two are Alike. I don't know but this Variety of Humour may, in a great Measure, derive its source from Vanity. Property, with us, is so equally diffused, that the Distinctions arising from it are very trifling. In order then to procure a Pre-eminence, we have recourse to particular singularities, which, though at first affected, are at last by Habit so closely rivited to the Mind, as to make it impossible for the Possessor ever to divest himself of it.[24]

Foote's remark, stressing the equality of property and by implication the irrelevance of class, was anomalous or at least anachronistic. Yet Foote's insistence on English equality pointed toward a more generalized social critique: by 1771, the still-derogatory term *farce* could be applied to the social order as a whole. According to "Honestus," author of a sketch entitled "The Universal Farce display'd,"

The world is a theatre; mankind are the comedians; chance composes the piece, and fortune distributes the parts; theologists and politicians govern the machines; and philosophers are the spectators. The rich take their places in the pit and upper boxes, the powerful in the front and sides, and the galleries are for the poor. The women distribute fruit and refreshments, and the unfortunate snuff the candles. Folly composes the overture, and time draws the curtain.[25]

"Honestus" – a name drawn from Henry Fielding's political burlesque *Eurydice hiss'd* – presented allegorically what dramatists such as Fielding and Samuel Foote had already staged more literally: the machinations of politicians and those with social power. Yet this particular description resisted any impetus toward social critique by attributing the outer bounds of the farce primarily to time and folly.

Social caricatures – in print and on stage – likewise tended to sketch comic relationships without the sharper political edge of satire. George Colman's prologue to Garrick's farce *Bon Ton* (1775) explicitly compared the events of the farce to contemporary social caricatures – the Macaroni prints produced by Matthew and Mary Darly: "Tonight our *Bayes*, with bold, but careless tints, / Hits off a sketch or two, like Darly's prints" (2.255). Darly's prints mocked the distortions of fashion, recording variations in clothing, gesture, and activities. So too later eighteenth-century farces emphasized the materiality of social life. Even in *Miss in her Teens*, Garrick had contrasted "The vap'ring bully and the frib'ling beau," defining the latter through the tenderness of "the silk he wears."[26] Objects stand in for characters, manifesting identity as materiality. Indeed, one of the hallmarks of eighteenth-century farce was its emphasis on materiality: both the "thingness" of bodies and commodities, and the material motives underlying nobly articulated ideals. Opponents of the form invoked materiality to demonstrate farce's failure to engage human affairs in a serious or considered way: where comedy sketched character, farce remained focused on dress and demeanor. Yet this reliance on material props could also be used to mock society through its commodities.

Romantic farceuses built on and extended the relationship between farce and the materiality of caricature. In *Le Rire* (1900), Henri Bergson explicitly linked caricature to an underlying perception of materiality: according to Bergson, the caricaturist "makes his models grimace, as they would do themselves if they went to the end of their tether. Beneath the skin-deep harmony of form, he divines the deep-seated recalcitrance of matter."[27] This "recalcitrance of matter" suggests both the resilience of material objects within the forms of farce, and farce's stubborn potential for political and social critique. Women-authored farces of the 1780s and 1790s emphasized this "recalcitrance of matter": the materiality underlying language, personal mannerisms, and social conventions repeatedly overwhelmed and threatened to erase individual character. Indeed, in these farces, as Daniel Gerould has suggested of the "well-made play," "objects dominate and become the organizing principle of life" – but the extent of this domination varied with individual farceuses.[28] Cowley's *Who's the Dupe?* (1777), for instance, literalized language itself, so that the scholar Gradus stood "reeling between two characters like a Substantive between two adjectives" (18). In Mary Robinson's *Nobody* (1794), a naïve reader of newspapers effectively deconstructed society into its material base and component parts by reading across rather than down the columns: "Theatre Royal Drury Lane – Just imported a large Quantity of Excellent Spirits – A certain Lady of the Beau Monde – Stray'd from a Field near Hackney – with twelve waggon loads of Flannel Shirts – for our gallant Troops on the Continent."[29] Theatre, alcohol, society, scandal, and military movements: this improvised narrative covered all the bases. Yet as the listener's personal beauty vanishes into its material components, this deconstructive reading is brought to a halt:

NELLY. The lovely Lady Languid is remarkable for a large quantity of Pearl,
    Powder, French Rouge, Shaving Soap – Blacking –
LADY. Put down the Paper, and give me some tea. (11–12)

Even Lady Languid's resistance to this itemizing of beauty aids relies on the social prop of tea: Robinson's farce emphasized the materiality not only of public news but also of any private refuge from that publicity. Playwrights like Hannah Cowley and Elizabeth Inchbald would retain this kind of farcical emphasis on social props even in their longer comedies.

Offering a still more cynical view of social machinery, Charlotte Smith's *What is She?* (1799) linked the material relations of social convention to the economic and political relations of the British empire. In Smith's mixed drama, the minor character Jargon explicitly defines fashion as the arbitrary (and ridiculous) production of convention. He improvises, not in strictly verbal form, but rather in conjunction with a group of coconspirators, the order of ridicules:

Our business is to push fashions, oaths, phrases, shrugs, and gestures. Let a mode be ever so ridiculous, stamp it with the name of one of our order, and it passes current. Absurdity, absurdity is the grand secret to which we owe our success. – The first three weeks we sport a thing, it's laughed at; the fourth it's abused, and the fifth becomes general.[30]

Indeed, Jargon measures his success by the wide-ranging adoption of social habits as rigid as they are fleeting. At the same time, his reference to financial instruments ("passing [as] current") in the midst of this description of social convention links social structures to the financial bases of commodity culture. Jargon's effectiveness as a swindler and gambler operating in high society depends on his success in passing himself off as valid social currency.

The apparent arbitrariness of social fashion not only reflects the conventionality of cash; as social fashions aim at an ideal of cosmopolitan sophistication, they also encode the ambitions of imperial expansion. Jargon's protégé Lady Zephryine describes her "systemizing" of women's "summer costume" in this way: "Oh, yes! – As soon as the dog-days began, I took care to introduce the Kamschatka robe, the Siberian wrapper, and the Lapland scratch." The discussion of fashion ends with an account of Mrs. Parchment freezing at the opera ("when the cold drew tears from her eyes she pretended it was the effect of music on her sensibility") and Lady Lovemode catching "a quinzy by going to see the skaters in Hyde-Park in an Otaheite chemise" (240–41). While the naming of markedly ethnic costumes is meant to highlight an impractical disregard of English weather, it also suggests a certain vulnerability of these ex-centric cultures to the expansion of the British and the Russian empires. The wife of Zephyrine's guardian remarks, "your ladyship has the most elegant imagination; though it is sometimes a little at variance with our climate," but of course that variance is exactly the point: fashion exploits the exotic and struggles to surmount the limits of locale as colonial power works to overcome geographical distance and exploit cultural difference.

Romantic farceuses delighted in farce's ability to expose the recalcitrance of matter underlying social forms; they also understood the popular appeal of nationalistic stereotypes. Emphasizing the materiality of social life and social distinctions, farce dehumanized its targets by equating them with specific social props; within this perception of society and individuals, the whole is somehow less than the sum of its parts. Zoffany's portrait of Foote, for instance, showed the farceur swamped in the jackboots which had defined his role as the Mayor of Garrat: the farceur, like his victim, can be captured only through allusion to his wardrobe. Nationalities were reduced to national stereotypes by a similar process: the French people grimace, while livery defines a more general continental slavishness. Farceuses like Cowley, Robinson, Inchbald, and Smith drew on this stereotyping, caricaturing aspect of farce to mock the extremities of fashion both through dress and through grimacing gesture – but they also insisted that such fashionable extremities had national and international implications.

WOMEN, FARCE, AND SENTIMENT

In 1777, when Hannah Cowley had trouble getting her tragedy *Albina* produced, she cannily brought out a farce, *Who's the Dupe?*, which was promptly accepted both by Thomas Harris at Covent Garden and by

Sheridan at Drury Lane. Cowley's prologue to the latter play – printed but notably *not* performed – linked farce to romance, and genre to gender. The prologue begins by imagining "days of yore" filled with "doughty Knights, / Enchanters, Squires, and valiant Wights," all pledged to the protection of women and the service of beauty: "No Ravisher dar'd stalk the earth; / No faithless Lover turn'd to mirth / The oaths his fondness once had swore – / Is he inconstant? – He's *no more*."[31] Cowley here replays the fall of romance into farce from the perspective of a woman and a farceuse; she goes on to associate genre with gender. Even in the "rare times" of romance, Cowley points to those who "Could shew their teeth, and vent their spite" against women:

> These were your Learned Men – your *Writers*,
> Whom no age ever mark'd for Fighters;
> But war with *Women* they could wage,
> And fill their bold, satyric page
> With petty foibles – *Ladies* faults –
> Who still endure their rude assaults.

In this battle of the sexes, Cowley proposes to fight fire with fire, satire with farce: she claims for women a literary weapon more generally associated with men. Finally, implying that such ridicule must be licensed, not by the Lord Chamberlain's official censor, but by the audience, Cowley applies for permission to laugh on the basis of justice and fair play: "Sure then 'tis fair *one* hour to give – / 'Tis all she asks – a Woman leave / To laugh at those same learned *Men*!" The audience licenses this woman's mockery, the prologue implies, partly because of the paucity of her request: a single hour is pitched against centuries of abuse. In Cowley's framing of her play, farce constitutes a woman's all-too-limited weapon of self-defense against misogynist mockery – and against social constraints more generally.

Theatrical demand for farces and afterpieces, along with the low literary status of farce, made it a form that was particularly accessible to women and working-class writers. During the 1780s and 1790s, the decades under consideration here, far more new afterpieces were produced than mainpieces: afterpieces created opportunities for spectacular staging and let theatre managers offer the public a more varied, often topical, playbill with little expense. For dramatists, conversely, farce offered little profit, so male writers had little reason to defend the form. Indeed, throughout the long eighteenth century, farce had been denigrated by its practitioners. According to John Dryden, for instance, success with farce only emphasized a playwright's incapacity: "a true

Poet often misses of applause, because he cannot debase himself to write so ill as to please his Audience."[32] Dryden even criticized his own success with *An Evening's Love*: "I confess I have given too much to the people in it, and am asham'd for them as well as for my self, that I have pleas'd them at so cheap a rate" (204). To succeed with a farce might bring popular applause, but it meant failing before an imaginary tribunal assessing literary value. Thus a reviewer of one of Inchbald's early farces mixed measured praise with resounding dismissiveness: "If this little *bag-atelle* was of the importance to challenge criticism, we should put the author in mind, that Nature may be copied too closely."[33] Farce offered no challenge to criticism – nor much profit to dramatists.

Still, the lack of seriousness and literary value associated with farce made the form accessible to women struggling to gain a foothold in the tightly woven systematicity of London theatre. Actress Catherine Clive's *Rehearsal; or, Bays in Petticoats* (1750), for instance, was a farce written for her own benefit-night performance; it burlesqued the difficulties facing a female dramatist – difficulties which notably included an arrogant actress by the name of Clive. Yet the *Rehearsal*'s self-reflexive mockery only sugar-coated the unpalatable difficulties facing female dramatists at the time: Ellen Donkin speculates that Clive's farce may have sparked Garrick's mentorship of female playwrights in the later years of the century.[34] After Garrick's retirement, farce again seemed the surest path to production for women dramatists. As we have seen, Hannah Cowley turned to farce when balked in the production of her tragedy *Albina*. So too Elizabeth Inchbald, trying to move from acting to playwrighting, first applied her efforts to the farce *A Mogul Tale* (1784); her success in that form, despite the cavilling review quoted above, licensed Inchbald's move to more regular comedies. Indeed, Inchbald made a good living as a playwright largely by oscillating between comedy and farce, translation and original writing, throughout her career.

Farce provided an entry point, but not a final resting place in the theatrical market: both finance and status would have urged successful dramatists such as Cowley and Inchbald to move beyond farce to longer comedies. Cowley, for instance, earned over £500 on her comedy *The Runaway*, and a mere £70 from *Who's the Dupe?* Yet in moving from farce into comedy, writers such as Cowley, Inchbald, and Charlotte Smith nec-essarily engaged the reigning fashion of sentiment – and sentiment itself constituted a complicated form for women writers to tackle. On the one hand, the ideology of sentiment or sensibility was associated with colo-nialism and its inequities: sentimental drama thus encouraged writers to tackle issues of contemporary political importance. On the other hand, sensibility was also associated in ambivalent ways with femininity: elevating women's claim to moral and emotional authority, sentiment also stressed female frailty and reliance on male gallantry. Combining farce and sentiment in the form of the "mixed drama," writers like Cowley and Inchbald set one form against the other, using the mobility of farce to disrupt sentiment's subordination of women, while nonetheless attempting to retain the moral authority sentiment had attributed to femininity.

In the final decades of the eighteenth century, sentimental ideology both relied upon colonialism and criticized its structures. Reading women poets of sensibility, Julie Ellison argued that

Sensibility . . . is almost by definition the culture of a colonial, mercantile empire. It is an international style, both in the sense of being adopted elsewhere than in England, often by creole literati, and also in the sense of being *about* what we would now call multicultural experience. The literature of sensibility is inconceivable without victims and its victims are typically foreign, low, or otherwise alien and estranged.[35]

Addressing the inequities produced by colonialism, sentimental drama sometimes criticized British imperialism – but often it served as an uneasy apologia for the empire.[36] Sentimental fiction might criticize patriarchal family structures, but sentimental drama, whether comic or tragic, tended to underwrite the authority of the benevolent patriarch. In Cowley's *Belle's Stratagem*, Colman's *Inkle and Yarico* (1787), Holcroft's *The Road to Ruin* (1792), or Inchbald's *Wives as they Were, Maids as they Are* – to take just a few examples – fathers appear almost uniformly well-intentioned and supportive of moral action. They may be flawed or mistaken – indeed, they may not take a strong enough hand with their willful offspring – but these fathers remain fundamentally good parents. Structurally, then, sentimental drama tended to support England's imperial projects more consistently and emphatically than other genres of sentimental writing. Such drama also tended to relegate women to supportive if not supporting roles. Clarissa herself, model of the justly rebellious daughter, if assigned a loving and sympathetic father, would have been a rebel without a cause, cheated of her moral martyrdom. Despite the conflicts predictably arising within the plot, sentimental drama implies that the good father will eventually provide for his offspring; the burden of the drama is to reconcile and reunite this good father with his alienated or oppressed children – and sometimes with his own better self.

Of course sentimental drama, like other forms of sentimental litera-ture, tended to duck the very questions it raised. Raymond Williams defined this tendency as the failure of the form:

Sentimental comedy failed, and continues to fail, because it never works through, to any point of intensity, the conflict between the belief that certain social virtues are paramount and yet that good men can offend against them. Its history is an evasion of this conflict by artificial solutions or "a sprinkling of tender melancholy."[37]

What Williams saw as the failure of sentimental comedy, I take as its structuring principle: the determined refusal to follow a single line of argument. Translating money into morality and back again, oscillating between intense physical suffering and abstract systems of global exchange, sensibility shifts among different registers of discourse, deflecting the attention it has summoned, making it nearly impossible to imagine a sustained movement from conflict to resolution.[38] Sentimental works often take as their starting point a material conflict and the suffering it produces; their end point may be "a sprinkling of tender mel-ancholy" or a happy ending which utterly ignores the material conflict from which they started. Yet sentimental drama does not "fail" to resolve the conflict; its *raison d'être*, I would argue, is to acknowledge the conflict while obscuring or obviating any real need for change.

Indeed, sentimental drama develops an emotional resolution to material conflict through characters espousing willing subordination. As we have seen, farce offers an antagonistic double vision of public figures: it superimposes a deformed, degraded image over the recognizable public persona. Sentiment, by contrast, presents social identities through a complementary pairing of father and child, husband and wife, actor and spectator, master and slave. Familial pairs – father and child, husband and wife – may be at odds throughout the play, but they are united by its end. Both onstage plotting and the overall effect of senti-mental comedy rely on a partnership of actor and spectator: those self-consciously performing, and those often conscious of responding to sentiment's dramatic effects. Finally, the sentimental figure of the benev-olent master remains incomplete without a subordinate to receive benevolence and (crudely) articulate its power. At its most extreme, this pairing produces the paradox of the willing, even eager, slave: a paradox that in the plays of Elizabeth Inchbald at least appears to encapsulate sentiment's imperial ideology.

As I am defining them, then, sentiment and farce constitute almost perfectly antagonistic forms. Sentimental drama begins with material conflict – the real oppression of a person or a people by others who may themselves be well intentioned – only to obscure that conflict over the course of the drama, or provide an artificial or irrelevant solution. Farce, by contrast, insists on "the recalcitrance of matter": the impossibility of moving beyond the material conditions underlying social relations. Sentiment's typical motion, shifting with all the weight of moral concern from one register of discourse to another (e.g., from threatened female virtue to accounts of international relations or social mores), perversely mimics farce's amoral shiftiness, the farceur's necessary willingness to abandon one framework of mockery for another. Finally, sentiment's benevolent pairing of characters stands in direct contradiction to farce's antagonistic superimposition of opposing figures. Thus farce potentially resists sensibility's strategies of translation, its idealizing abstractions, in three ways: first, by refusing to let go of material issues; second, by mocking sentiment's own moral shiftiness; and third, by undercutting high-minded cooperation with antagonism and malice.

As they wove mimicry's double vision into a sentimental plotline, women dramatists effectively based sensibility's already dubious performance of benevolence and gallantry upon farce's canny opportunism and self-interest. In this context, farce's reflexive mimicry repeatedly joined two or more divergent registers of discourse and analysis, and could be used to capture in midflight sensibility's characteristic movement from one register to another. At the same time, however, the gap between sentiment and farce in these mixed dramas offered yet another means of deflecting social conflict – and the possibility of resolution. Cowley's *Day in Turkey*, for instance, translates a political battle of the sexes out of farce and into sentiment: as a result, it is easy to forget that the resolution of her sentimental plot depends on the machinations of her farcical, nationalist characters. Inchbald's *Wives/Maids* does more to integrate the mimicry of farce within a sentimental plotline – but in the process it produces sensibility as a self-divided, destabilized model of domestic government. In Cowley's and Inchbald's "mixed dramas," sentimental ideology itself becomes a farce, a hollow self-mockery. In the chapters that follow, I try to show Hannah Cowley and Elizabeth Inchbald using farcical episodes to mimic or contradict sensibility's most characteristic motions, as the materiality of farce and its political allusiveness work together to expose sentiment's structural hypocrisies. Undercutting sensibility, these women dramatists used the mimicry and materiality of farce to denature sexual politics and thereby disrupt the sentimental basis of imperial policy – yet, as we shall see, their plays also attempted to maintain the moral authority sentiment had associated with femininity. Their comedies played off the double-edged politics of farce: in particular, its ability to expose the coercive power of social convention and its often malicious complicity with the powers that be.

THEORIZING FARCE AND COLONIAL RELATIONS

Hannah Cowley's and Elizabeth Inchbald's mixed dramas roughly equate the situation of European women with that of colonized and enslaved peoples: such an equation raises political and ethical questions about the "use" of the Orient (both enslaved and enslaving) in their work. In a reading of nineteenth-century women's prose, for instance, Joyce Zonana uncovered a pattern of "feminist orientalism," which she described as "a rhetorical strategy (and a form of thought) by which a speaker or writer neutralizes the threat inherent in feminist demands and makes them palatable to an audience that wishes to affirm its occidental superiority."[39] Zonana shows how women writers such as Mary Wollstonecraft, Mary Shelley and Charlotte Brontë used analogies with eastern culture and epithets such as "Mahometan" to dissuade Englishmen from controlling Englishwomen or denigrating their capacities. In the plays of Inchbald and Cowley, "feminist demands" are moderated by the humor of farce and complexities of context, but orientalism undoubtedly contributes to audience complacence in the reception of these dramas.

Analyzing Elizabeth Inchbald's *A Mogul Tale* and Hannah Cowley's *A Day in Turkey*, Mita Choudhury described a more general appropriation of existing modes of orientalism. Choudhury's reading of these plays focuses on their comic inversion of roles, in which the master is eastern, the slave western. Yet Choudhury argues that "the myth of Western enslavement is a playful paradox, constructed, in part, by an eastward authorial gaze that perceives chaos beyond the boundaries and – as a palimpsestic gesture – seeks to appropriate a long tradition of Orientalism."[40] Choudhury's working definition of orientalism emphasizes the attribution of chaos, perverse sexuality, and savagism to the East. I would argue by contrast that the orientalist plays of Inchbald and Cowley show the East ordered according to the same categories as western civilization. In *A Day in Turkey; or the Russian Slaves*, sentimental chastity is aptly described as "exotic" and eroticized, modes more often associated with "oriental" sexuality; in *Such Things Are*, western benevolence is shown to be inextricable from eastern despotism. Indeed, in the chapters that follow, I want to suggest that these mixed dramas record a larger cultural gesture by which absolute dominion, exiled from the public sphere, is simultaneously abjected on to the East and internalized within western gender relations and the sentimental family.

What role do farce and sentiment play in sketching these larger imperial relations? Choudhury quite rightly emphasizes the way in which theatrical jokes confirm rather than undermine the complacence of the audience, yet as a result, she seems to see farce and comedy almost wholly allied with dominant culture. Her essay thus provides a useful corrective to other writers, such as Luce Irigaray and Homi Bhabha, who have tended to attribute to farce a subversive power beyond its means. Still, I would argue that farce and sentiment operate in complicated and oppositional ways. For my purposes, Homi Bhabha's discussion of narcissism and paranoia as inseparable responses to cultural *difference* articulates a feature of sentiment rather than of farce: it helps foreground the ways Cowley and Inchbald used sentiment to underscore uncomfortable political *similarities* between East and West. In this context, as Choudhury's argument suggests, farce and humor distract from and undermine the possibilities for political subversion: but *only* when possibilities for political subversion rely on sentiment. Conversely, Luce Irigaray's model of femininity as mimicry helps delineate the ways Cowley and Inchbald used the mimicry of farce to counter the more oppressive aspects of sentimental ideology. Farce may circumscribe and undercut the liberal tendencies of imperial sentiment, but it also mocks and destabilizes sentimental drama's conservative view of domestic government.

Before using Homi Bhabha's account of narcissism and paranoia to describe sentimental drama's engagement with colonial affairs, I should explain why I distinguish this account from eighteenth-century traditions of mimicry. Bhabha's invocation of mimicry in "Of Mimicry and Man" (1987; see *The Location of Culture*, 1994) largely elides its theatrical and feminist history and displaces its theatrical relations on to the act of historical or cultural criticism. Bhabha claims that "[i]f colonialism takes power in the name of history, it repeatedly exercises its authority through the figures of farce" and "produces a text rich in the traditions of *trompe-l'oeil*, irony, mimicry and repetition" (85). Farce and mimicry are both theatrical forms, but in Bhabha's essay, they lose their theatrical connotations, becoming largely indistinguishable from ironic repetition. In the theatre, mimicry involves three parties: a mimic parodying a public figure for a canny audience. In Bhabha's theory, these three parties become blurred, confused, and confusing: one might argue that colonialism mimics and deforms Enlightenment thought, but even in this formulation (which Bhabha avoids) questions of intentionality and audience remain. In his reading of Charles Grant's "Observations on the state of society among the Asiatic subjects of Great Britain" (1792), however, Bhabha himself acts as a mimic, "taking off" Charles Grant to a twentieth-century audience. Likewise, in pointing to the two meanings of "slavery" in Locke (a legitimate form of colonial ownership *versus* an intolerable abuse of power in an imagined "original" state of Nature), Bhabha creates an antagonistic pairing of terms, as an eighteenth-century mimic might do. The critical power of Bhabha's superimposition, however, relies on his readers' recognition of the ways "legitimate" slavery degrades Enlightenment claims of liberty and rationality.

In eliding the theatrical contexts of farce and mimicry, Bhabha also obscures questions of agency, and thus creates precisely the kind of disembodied power (and subversion) he attributes to colonialism. Such elision also leads to errors in historical attribution. Implicit in Bhabha's linking of history and farce, for instance, is an assumption of farce's power to debunk the sentimental claims of history – a power which seems to remain merely potential until the critic invokes its force. Attention to Romantic political theatre and the literal production of farce, however, suggests a slightly different historical trajectory: farcical displays of colonial abuse *preceded* sentimental claims for the divine reasoning behind imperial rule. Samuel Foote's *The Nabob* (1772), for instance, represented the return of colonial power – English "Nabobs" grown rich in their exploitation of India – through the figures of stage farce. Foote's characters are as rigid, bigoted, and stereotypical as their names: the Nabob Sir Mathew Mite, for instance, uses the "Christian" middleman of bribery (Touchit) to negotiate with the mayor of the borough of "Bribe-em" for parliamentary seats. Touchit shamelessly articulates the process by which English commerce turned to English conquest, excusing what the mayor calls "incivility" on the grounds that "these people are but a little better than Tartars or Turks." The mayor corrects him: "No, no, Mr. Touchit; just the reverse; it is they have caught the Tartars in us."[41] Foote's colonial burlesque, played out over the course of a five-act comedy, provided a licensed critique of the open secret, the uncontested scandal.

Only belatedly did colonialism cover its tracks, taking power in the name of history. Supporting Charles Fox's 1783 East India Reform Bill, Edmund Burke acknowledged that the circumstances structuring

colonial relations "are not . . . very favourable to the idea of our attempting to govern India at all. But there we are; there we are placed by the
Sovereign Disposer: and we must do the best we can in our situation.
The situation of man is the preceptor of his duty."[42] The distance separating this chivalric view of history from farce is slight indeed. Half a
page earlier, Burke had echoed the commonplaces cited in Foote's earlier
farce: "The Tartar invasion was mischievous; but it is our protection that
destroys India. It was their enmity, but it is our friendship" (v.402).
Burke's ironic turn of phrase moves away from farce by insisting on the
importance of sentiment: England's ruinous "friendship" for India
results from the fact that "[y]oung men (boys almost) govern there,
without society, and without sympathy with the natives" (v.402). Taking
power in the name of history coincides with a turn from farce toward
sentiment and romance: the white man's burden is yet another variation
on the knight's quest to save the forms of civilization for humanity.
Reversing the sequence implied by Bhabha's argument, these two texts
suggest that the debunking form of farce could do little to prevent a subsequent turn to sentimental imperial rhetoric.

In fact, while Bhabha takes on the role of critical mimic, the subject
matter he analyzes seems to me eminently sentimental: his focus on narcissism and paranoia as interwoven responses to difference highlights
Romantic anxieties over the borders of sentimental subjectivity. The
psychoanalytic concepts of narcissism and paranoia are of course
anachronistic for the Romantic period, and I do not mean to propose
their precise application here. I would argue, however, that a number of
social movements, issues, and events had disrupted conventional understandings of social roles and identities, while simultaneously focusing
attention on the disputed borders of identity; attempts to resolve this
sense of disruption ranged from the narcissistic to the paranoid. The
1790s debates over women's rights, for instance, raised questions about
the "identity" of husband-and-wife or father-and-daughter as debates
over East Indian reform raised questions about imperial identity, about
the relationship between colonial and national subjects. In the domestic
realm, Blackstone's formulation of marriage – that man and wife
become one person and that person is the man – had social implications
far beyond its legal weight. Theoretically, husbands and wives were a
single social unit: in practice, they were often divided, at odds with one
another. In late eighteenth-century theatre, the tension at work in familial relations was often staged in terms of polarities. Fears of unruly
women could be assuaged by showing such women transformed into

obedient subjects – even as such performances raised the specter of duplicity, the fear that obedience itself might be no more than an act, a mimic response to authority. Cowley's and Inchbald's plays present men narcissistically eager to believe in women's willing subordination, even as they find their paranoia confirmed, their strictures ridiculed or disempowered by those apparently compliant subordinates.

The confusing legal status of the East India Company – its blend of political and commercial functions – similarly acted as a lightning rod for anxieties about imperial identity. Edmund Burke's indictment of Warren Hastings, functionary of the Company and Governor of English India, for High Crimes and Misdemeanours, held Hastings himself accountable for the uncontrollable, uncontainable crimes of colonialism. Yet in opening the Hastings impeachment, Burke attributed the execution and even production of those crimes to the East India Company's mixed-race system of governance. Insisting that a class of Indians epitomized by the "Black Banyan" held sway over Englishmen arriving in India, Burke asserted that "the Master is no longer a Master; he is the tool in the hands of this man."[43] The unstable identities of master and slave reverse one another here: at other moments in Burke's speeches, they become indistinguishable.

For Bhabha, colonial relations produce an uncontrollable oscillation between narcissism, perception of "a difference that is almost nothing but not quite" and paranoia, perception of "a difference that is almost total but not quite" (*Location of Culture*, 91). Inchbald and Cowley repeatedly replace perceptions of difference with an underlying recognition of similarity – yet the evaporation of difference does little to soothe orientalist anxieties. While Mita Choudhury points to sexual extravagance and savagism as features of Romantic orientalism, for example, Cowley's characters repeatedly, jokingly, equate eastern and western sexuality, and Inchbald's sentimental plotlines stress the similarites between eastern despotism and western benevolence. As Choudhury's reading implies, however, both playwrights use sexualized or gendered humor to deflect attention from the political moral at work within their use of sentiment. The self-divided humor of farce allows spectators to choose a flattering rather than a critical interpretation of particular jokes and more general narrative events.

On the other hand, the duplicity of farce can also undercut the complacence of sentimental ideology – and Luce Irigaray's model of feminine mimicry may help us to see how Cowley and Inchbald use elements of farce to complicate the politics of female subordination. Irigaray's model of mimicry precedes Bhabha's account of "Mimicry and Man" and retains a theatrical perspective in the midst of philosophical inquiry. Both in *Speculum of the Other Woman* (1974/85) and *This Sex Which Is Not One* (1977/85), Luce Irigaray addressed herself to "'reopening' the figures of philosophical discourse . . . to make them 'render up' and give back what they owe the feminine."[44] As a part of this reopening, Irigaray urged an interrogation of "*the conditions under which systematicity itself is possible*" and drew attention to the theatricality inherent in systems: "the scenography that makes representation feasible . . . the architectonics of its theatre . . . its props, its actors, their respective positions, their dialogues" (75; original italics). Irigaray's critical methodology works to point out "how the break with material contiguity is made, how the system is put together, how the specular economy works" (75). But when it comes to women introducing themselves into the "tightly-woven systematicity" of philosophical thought, Irigaray suggests that mimicry may be the only available alternative: "One must assume the feminine role deliberately. Which means already to convert a form of subordination into an affirmation, and thus to begin to thwart it" (76). For Irigaray, mimicry means entering into existing systems, but preserving the differences that those systems erase.

Within the more specifically theatrical terms of this book, Irigaray's theory links the systems proposed by sentimental theatre to the mimicry performed within stage farce. The political theatre of sensibility broke with "material contiguity" by translating suffering into system. As Irigaray's model might have predicted, eighteenth-century women spectators and dramatists consistently maintained sentimental systems and conventions, even as they worked to debunk and critique those systems. Especially in the mixed dramas of Cowley and Inchbald, sentimental plotlines continued to link family politics with national affairs and imperial policies, while elements of farce presented a radically different perspective on the workings of those systems. While the political mimicry developed by Fielding and Foote forced a degrading comparison of unequal terms, meanwhile, Irigaray's view of mimicry superimposes conscious choice upon forced subordination, producing an enabling model of resistance for women. Like Irigaray's model, the mimicry practiced by Cowley's and Inchbald's female characters tends to extend the options open to them rather than degrading public men. Yet the potential force of this feminist mimicry remains constrained by the caricatures of nation, gender, and class also operating within these mixed dramas.

Returning to Cowley's *Belle's Stratagem*, for instance, we find a heroine driven to mimic femininity for personal reasons which rapidly become indistinguishable from national roles. Letitia Hardy's first adult meeting with her promised husband having been marred by her "English reserve," she proposes to exaggerate this trait before displaying her social command in a slightly different role: "it may seem a little paradoxical; but, as he does not like me enough, I want him to like me still less, and will at our next interview endeavour to heighten his indifference into dislike" (18). Letitia produces this heightening of her character and his response by exaggerating and vulgarizing her present role, slipping from comedy into outright farce. Doricourt had longed for "that something, that nothing, which every body feels, and which no body can describe, in the resistless charmers of Italy and France" (9); he finds himself confronted instead with an English country bumpkin. Letitia's companion Mrs. Rachet sketches to Doricourt "the poor girl's defects" (36), but the worldly young man doubts Racket's character sketch until he sees his fiancée's self-mimicry:

MRS. RACKET. What think you of my painting, now?
DORICOURT. Oh, mere water-colours, Madam! The Lady has caricatured your picture. (39)

If Letitia's first self-caricature emphasizes everything Doricourt dislikes, however, her second performance of mimic femininity provides him with everything he claims to want. Appearing before her beloved at a masquerade, Letitia dances, sings, and speaks in veiled terms of personal mysteries. Predictably, this performance enchants Doricourt – until he is told, and believes, that his charmer has been the mistress of a series of men.

Letitia's mimicry "make[s] "visible," by an effect of playful repetition, what was supposed to remain invisible" – but this exposure operates on different levels and in contradictory ways.[45] In the revelation scene the following day, Letitia explains:

The timidity of the English character threw a veil over me, you could not penetrate. You have forced me to emerge in some measure from my natural reserve, and to throw off the veil that hid me . . . You see I can be any thing; chuse then my character – your Taste shall fix it. Shall I be an *English* Wife? – or, breaking from the bonds of Nature and Education, step forth to the world in all the captivating glare of Foreign Manners? (81)

As it reveals her personal charms, her performance also exposes to Doricourt the moral flaws of continental femininity; Doricourt promptly recants his earlier desires, swearing instead that "cursed be the hour – should it ever arrive – in which *British* Ladies shall sacrifice to *foreign Graces* the Grace of Modesty!" (82). More generally, however, Letitia's performances suggest an unsuspected degree of volition under-lying *any* performance of femininity, even though her closing explana-tion works hard to reobscure that sense of agency and choice. Her claim "I can be any thing" is buried within references to Doricourt's vision and choice; his taste, she insists, will "fix" her character – mend it by demanding a return to the moral fixity attributed to English modesty and reserve. On a third level, then, Cowley's *Belle's Stratagem* makes visible the impossibility of mimicking feminine identity without simulta-neously engaging issues of class and national identity: Letitia's perfor-mance as country bumpkin destroys English modesty by translating English reserve into a hoydenish disregard of polite (upper-class) behav-ior; her performance of "Foreign Manners" captivates, but in glaringly sexual ways; proper femininity can only be equated with English upper-class behavior.

In rewarding the "belle's strategem" with marital success, Cowley's comedy also promoted enduring stereotypes of national and feminine character. Letitia mimicked ever more extreme versions of her role in order to establish an acceptable middle ground for British femininity: Cowley's play reified both the foreign and lower-class stereotypes even-tually rejected and the native models finally accepted as social norms. Elizabeth Inchbald's comedies, mixed dramas, and translations also linked questions of national character to those of feminine propriety, but in somewhat more controversial ways. Inchbald's introduction to the infamous *Lover's Vows* (1798), her translation of Kotzebue's *Das Kind der Liebe* (1788), for instance, distinguished the performance of femininity permissible on the German stage from that acceptable to the English, insisting in particular that the young heroine Amelia's behavior when "she announces her affection to her lover . . . would have been revolting to an English audience."[46] Inchbald's revised Amelia supposedly appears "with manners conforming to the English, rather than the German taste" (XXIII.6), but Austen's *Mansfield Park* (1814) followed theatre critics such as William Cobbett in doubting that Inchbald's trans-lation had revised German femininity quite enough.[47] Inchbald's earlier mixed drama *Such Things Are*, by contrast, presents European femininity translated to the colonies and prisons of India (or Sumatra) in the figure of Arabella, a European woman mistakenly imprisoned for years. The translation is so perfect that at first neither English nor Indian charac-ters can distinguish the national and racial differences supposedly fixed by Arabella's European origins. In Inchbald's drama, gender and nationality do not delimit a character's performance; rather, performance (re)defines or casts into question a character's gendered nationality. For both Inchbald and Cowley, however, the mimic affirmation of women's subordination carries national as well as domestic implications, and this connection begins to reverse a more general historical propensity to map nationalism on to gender. George Santayana once remarked, "Our nationality is like our relations to women: too implicated in our moral nature to be changed honourably, and too accidental to be worth changing" [48] – but the "accidents" of sex and morality inflect nationalism more deeply than this apparently casual analogy implies.

In the chapters that follow, I mean to use Homi Bhabha's attention to the shifting borders of colonial identity to focus on Cowley's and Inchbald's largely sentimental rewriting of oriental difference as disturbing similarity; conversely, Irigaray's model of mimicry as a performative undoing of forced subordination suggests some of the ways Cowley and Inchbald use farce to disrupt the sentimental status quo. Cowley's and Inchbald's mixed dramas oscillate between sexual and imperial conflicts: they sketch international discord on to a plot of sexual strife, and then vacillate between these two levels of discourse. Mixed dramas evade the resolution of material conflict by alternating between imperialism and sexual domination – or they use one level of dispute to resolve the other artificially: in Cowley's *Day in Turkey*, for instance, the bashaw's marriage becomes an excuse for freeing the Russian slaves. Relying on crude stereotypes of the Sultan and Bashaw, their eunuchs and their harem women, Inchbald and Cowley both invoke prevailing traditions of orientalism. At the same time, however, their peculiar blending of farce and sentiment makes visible "what was supposed to remain invisible": the theatrical gestures by which absolute domination was exiled from the public sphere of rational critical debate by being at once projected on to the East as despotism and internalized within the family as sentimental morality.

PREVIEW

The next chapter, "The Balance of Power," reads Hannah Cowley's mixed drama *A Day in Turkey; or the Russian Slaves* (1792) as a commentary on the 1791 parliamentary debates over whether or not to side with Turkey against Russia in the Oczakow dispute. The first section of the chapter emphasizes the role played by gender in parliamentary debates over the wisdom and justice of attacking the empress of Russia – and in the political caricatures which reconfigured those debates as pure farce. The second section links these caricatured male anxieties about female military and sexual power to Cowley's inversion of harem "slavery" through a sentimental love plot – a translation into sentiment that preserves the power relations of farce. Gender roles remain inseparable from nationality: while the gender politics of the play ostensibly favor sentimental femininity, the drama's national politics at once degrade French and Italian licentiousness and depend upon that license to produce a happy ending.

The final chapter, "The Farce of Subjection: Elizabeth Inchbald," focuses on three of Inchbald's most popular plays: the short farce, *A Mogul Tale*, and two full-length sentimental comedies, *Such Things Are* (set in Sumatra) and *Wives as They Were, Maids as They Are* (set in London). Her farce, written in 1784, poses a stringent critique of early British imperialism: it does so by parodying even as it produces the paranoia and narcissism that Homi Bhabha aligns with the construction of colonial identity. Inchbald's farce pokes fun at colonial paranoia: British fears of eastern power structures reappear as comedy; menace turns back to the mimicry of farce. Three years later, the sentimental comedy *Such Things Are* (1787) attempts to move beyond critique to a resolution of the problems inherent in colonialism. Yet while the play presents an apparently naïve reliance on the powers of sentimental benevolence, it nonetheless exposes willing slavery and female subjection as preconditions for resolving the contradictions of empire. Finally, the late comedy *Wives as They Were, Maids as They Are* (1797) brings the gendered lessons of colonialism home to London, as a father returns in disguise from the East Indies to discipline a wayward daughter. Reading *Wives/Maids* against the background of Inchbald's orientalist drama shows the extent to which late eighteenth-century gender disputes and notions of national identity were worked out through the nexus of imperial connections. The pervasive irony of *Wives/Maids* also raises the question of how women's doubled speech might undermine the assumptions which define the public sphere and private domestic control alike.

CHAPTER SIX

The balance of power: Hannah Cowley's Day in Turkey

On the third of December 1791, Hannah Cowley's eleventh play, a mixed drama entitled *A Day in Turkey; or the Russian Slaves,* was first produced at Covent Garden. The piece did reasonably well, receiving fourteen performances between December 3rd, 1791 and May 25th, 1792; it was published early in 1792. Yet the advertisement to the printed play begins by complaining of a public injustice:

[ADVERTISEMENT]
HINTS have been thrown out, and the idea industriously circulated, that the following comedy is tainted with POLITICS. I protest I know nothing about politics; – will Miss Wollstonecraft forgive me – whose book contains <u>such a body of mind</u> as I hardly ever met with – if I say that politics are *unfeminine?* I never in my life could attend to their discussion.[1]

Rife with contradictions, this advertisement mingles (dis)ingenuousness with commercial ingenuity. Cowley records the social and economic forces demanding a disavowal of political interest on the same page that provides that disavowal: "The illiberal and *false* suggestions concerning the politics of the comedy I could frankly forgive, had they not deprived it of the honour of a COMMAND." She distinguishes herself from the political Mary Wollstonecraft by asserting her inability to "attend" to political discussion – yet she has read Wollstonecraft's *Vindication of the Rights of Woman* closely enough to remark somewhat ambiguously on its "body of mind."[2] On the face of it, Cowley's remark rebuts Wollstonecraft's claim that women's intellect should not be constrained by "sexual prejudices": the dramatist reinserts the pamphleteer's mind back into her scandalously female body. Yet the remark could also be read – out of the context of this advertisement – as a compliment to Wollstonecraft's persistent articulation of those prejudices which limit women's development and power: the prejudices which constrain other women's bodies *and* minds. The drama which follows this ambiguous advertisement will seem at different times to underwrite each of these two contradictory readings. Overall, however, the

contradictions of the advertisement present the female playwright as
slightly too knowing: she understands enough of politics to know it is supposed to be unfeminine, *and* to know that an apolitical female has no business reading Wollstonecraft's *Vindication of the Rights of Woman*.

Cowley's public (and political) disavowal of politics in the advertisement to *A Day in Turkey* seems in retrospect to have been simultaneously
unbelievable and unexceptionable. Parliamentary debates in the spring
of 1791 had argued at length over the dubious political wisdom of supporting Turkey against Russia in their hotly contested claims to
Oczakow, a barren but important military base. Portraying the tribula-
tions of Russian captives under the power of a Turkish Bassa (or pasha),
Cowley's play seems to side with the Russians. Yet Cowley also contextualized the questions of slavery and of European politics by invoking
related events: debates over the slave trade in Britain, and the early after-
math of the French revolution. The most immediately objectionable
politics in the play seem to have been those expressed by A la Greque, a
French *valet de chambre* to a noble Russian prisoner. Cowley claimed
poetic license as a means of distancing herself from the views he
expressed:

How then could I, pretending to be a comic poet, bring an emigrant Frenchman
before the public at this day, and not make him hint at the events which had just
passed, or were then passing in his native country? A character so written would
have been anomalous – the critics ought to have had no mercy on me. It is A
LA GREQUE who speaks, not *I*; nor can I be accountable for *his* sentiments. *Such*
is my idea of tracing CHARACTER; and were I to continue to write for the stage,
I should always govern myself by it.

Cowley could, however, be held accountable for choosing to introduce a
French character in a drama concerning Russians and Turks – yet her
contemporaries seem to have been willing to let her rather aggressive
claim to political innocence pass without challenge.

In fact, Cowley's insistence on her political innocence worked to distract attention from other flaws within the play. The reviewer "Aesopus,"
for instance, gave the dramatist a good drubbing, but politics was the last
and apparently least of his concerns:

From the pen of Mrs. COWLEY, judging from her other performances, we had
to expect something less fearful of criticism, and more deserving of praise than
the present Operatical Tragi-Comedy. Without entering into an invidious
recital of defects, we shall only say, that the language is in parts inflated, in
others it is replete with trite sayings, strained witticisms, and broad vulgarity.
The similes are ill selected, and worse applied. The songs are unconnected with

the drama, and absurdly introduced for the amusement of a parcel of unfeel-ing eunuchs. The poetry of the songs, of which we subjoin a specimen, has not a single recommendation – are only admissible on a comparison with the *music*! The Authoress has hazarded the introduction of numberless political allusions, many of which were violently resisted by the audience.[3]

Vigorously engaging the charge of political meddling, Cowley ignored the literary and dramatic complaints of her critics, as if a disavowal of politics would also protect the play from charges of farcical vulgarity and insignificance. If by the end of the eighteenth century the form of farce suggested political commentary, the converse might be made to seem true: freedom from politics would mean eschewing the degraded theatre of farce.

The gender politics of female innocence and purity which mark out the borders of the play operate within the dramatic narrative as well. Cowley shows the arbitrary power of a Turkish bashaw overcome by the sentimental force of romantic love and the ideal of female chastity; this exploration of gendered power can be seen as a response both to Wollstonecraft's *Vindication* and to the gendering of politics which accompanied political discussion and popular representations of the Russian empress, Catherine II. While Cowley's support for Russian slaves rather than Turkish barbarity seems clear and somewhat conven-tional, her gender politics remain distinctly ambivalent – and persis-tently disruptive. In parliamentary debates and the mixed drama alike, gender norms were invoked to stabilize an uncomfortable indetermi-nacy of political relations – yet in practice the performance of gender repeatedly restaged the indeterminacy it was meant to resolve.

"THE TAMING OF THE SHREW"

In "Frame-Up: Feminism, Psychoanalysis, Theatre," Barbara Freedman argues that "traditional Western theatre offers us only two stages, comic and tragic, upon which are always playing some version of *Oedipus* or its sister play, *The Taming of the Shrew*." With such limited choices, Freedman argues, "a set-up is therefore always being staged as well," since the spec-tators of these plays "'cannot choose' but accept the interpellation or hailing that indoctrinates the subject into a confusing and limiting iden-tity, a *méconnaissance*, a delusion." That delusion is specifically gendered: *The Taming of the Shrew* identifies civilization "with male control over a dis-ordered female sexuality" and thus "not only record[s] but promulgate[s] the values of a repressive patriarchal culture."[4] In 1791, however, James

Gillray invoked this old comedy of patriarchal power to register a perceived threat to the basis of that power: the Russian empress's threat to Turkish sovereignty and thus to the balance of power in Europe.

On March 28, 1791, William Pitt read to the House of Commons a message from the king announcing that attempts to persuade Russia to negotiate a favorable settlement with Turkey had failed, and that armament was felt to be necessary as a further step of persuasion and possible force. The message was an implicit request for funding: when members of the Whig opposition suggested that time was required to deliberate the issue, Pitt invoked parliamentary precedent, arguing that it was standard procedure to wait no more than one day to respond to a message from the king. The prime minister managed to push through a vote of support and funding the next day – only to have the opposition return to the issue repeatedly over the next few weeks, gathering strength in the process. The threat of war, and opposition resistance to that threat, brought together a complicated set of issues. Pitt presented the funding for arms as a necessary step to maintain the balance of power in Europe – but the armament was also seen by the opposition as an example of the imbalance of power in British government. Discussions of the armament presented parliamentary politics mirroring European politics, but in partial, confusing, and contradictory ways. Gender seems to have been invoked by parliamentary debates and caricatures alike as a means of stabilizing the cross-patterns of identification, of providing a basis for critique or action. At least half the time, however, the question of gender further complicated the issue at hand.

Gillray's caricature, "Taming of the Shrew: Katharine & Petruchio; The Modern Quixotte, or what you will" (April 20, 1791) called up (at least) two contradictory plots to capture some of the doubled (or multiple) vision at work in the parliamentary debates (plate 16). *The Taming of the Shrew* plot, for instance, seems to show Russia as the empress easily vanquished. Confronted with Pitt as Petruchio and his allies (Prussia and Holland) mounted on good King George, she surrenders in the terms of Kate's final speech:

> I see my Lances are but straws;
> My strength is weak, my weakness past compare;
> And am asham'd that Women are so simple
> To offer War when they should kneel for Peace.

Brought to her senses with a little show of force, Russia as the tamed shrew suggests the wisdom of Pitt's policy – or at least, she embodies the

Plate 16 James Gillray, "Taming of the Shrew: Katharine & Petruchio; The Modern Quixotte, or what you will." April 20, 1791.

narrative of Russian repentance and submission that Pitt and his ministers were hoping to see develop. Yet Petruchio in the *Shrew* is known for his arbitrary, whimsical, and often abusive assertion of authority over Kate: his command that she throw off her cap is presented explicitly as a mark of his absolute authority over her, and her performance of complete submission. Casting Pitt as Petruchio thus offered a double-edged reading of the former's international strategies. So too reference to Shakespeare's Katherine revised parliamentary portraits of Russia's Catherine: where the former emphasizes the generic frailty of all women ("*our* lances are but straws"), Gillray's Catherine II applied specifically to herself the lesson of an earlier shrew. Gillray took his lines out of context and out of sequence, ostensibly or perhaps ostentatiously avoiding the specifically contractual relationship that Katherine invokes:

> I am ashamed that women are so simple
> To offer war, where they should kneel for peace;
> Or seek for rule, supremacy, and sway,
> When they are bound to serve, love, and obey. (5.2.161–65)

In the *Shrew*, Katherine's acceptance of female subordination is based on a contract whereby the woman's husband serves both as sovereign and protector, one who "commits his body / To painful labour both by sea and land" (5.2.148–49) to support and protect her. Yet as Burke had noted, no such contract existed between England and Russia, nor was one proposed. Rather, "England had declared that Russia shall be dependent, and still unprotected."[5]

Gillray represented Pitt not only as Petruchio but also as Don Quixote, for whom King George is but a scrawny Rosinante: in this version of the story, Pitt's authority over the king of England became a central issue. By forcing armament on parliament in the king's name, Pitt was seen as having usurped the royal prerogative: from this perspective, George III served merely as the minister's beast of burden. But Don Quixote is also an infamous dreamer, consistently misreading reality. Dreaming of Catherine's subservience, he may well have chosen to apply the wrong plot (i.e., *The Taming of the Shrew*) to the current political situation. Part of the inspiration for this print seems to have come from Grey's long speech on April 11 attacking the military build-up. Grey claimed that "the balance of power" had been originally a Whig concern, linked to the defensive strategy of making war only in cases of self-defense. Pointing out that the Tories had applied "the epithets of wild and romantic" to this general system, Grey thought that those who had been so loud in talking of the romantic idea of the balance of power, would have explained their own system. He had watched them closely, and he believed that he had seen some of the workings of conviction in their minds. They had changed their sentiments, and had now confessed that the balance of power in Europe was no longer a romance. (106)

Yet Gillray's caricature suggested that the balance of power in Europe remained a romance, a fantasy which only the knight of La Mancha would engage to defend – and that a drubbing may await Pitt and his allies outside the imaginary boundaries of a plot in which the shrew is tamed. A Major Maitland posed this perspective on the ministers' position most succinctly: "Why, then, did they enter into the war? . . . It was to support a balance of power never before heard of; an ideal balance of power, which was never before entertained, and which was never supposed to have any relation to the politics of Europe, nor any connection with its political safety or existence" (112). Gillray's final title for the print, however, refuses to settle for either of these readings, suggesting that any version of the political story underway might have equal validity: call it "what you will." Fox's objection to a Tory speaker on the 29th of March invoked theatre to emphasize a similar indeterminacy: "His [Steele's] speech resembled the specimen of the paragraph writer in the play about Russia, Prussia, Turkey, and what not, of which the person to whom it was shewn pronounced that it was well done, for it was finely confused, and very alarming" (42).

The same complaint might be made of the debates more generally, though Gillray's doubled plot of *Don Quixote* and *The Taming of the Shrew* roughly encapsulates (while inverting) the antagonistic histories of the armament presented by opposition members and ministerial supporters. The opposition's portrait of a patient, civilized, and long-suffering Russia might well be compared (cynically) to Don Quixote's vision of Dulcinea as a fine court lady – though of course this comparison undercuts the realism of that portrait. Supporters of the ministry for their part painted Russia as the shrew, inclined beyond the call of reason to act against Britain and British interests – yet in supporting the armament these speakers sketch a shrew almost impossible to tame.

For the opposition, Russia rather than Turkey seemed Britain's natural ally: an important trading partner provoked to war by Turkey, but nonetheless willing to return many of the lands it had conquered; a Christian nation and imperial power.[6] Indeed, the opposition repeatedly cast Russia not only as a trading partner but as a sister empire, mirroring Britain's rapid imperial growth. Various speakers mentioned their discomfort with Britain presuming to dictate to Russia which imperial conquests "she" might keep and which "she" must resign; several drew the analogy to Britain's Indian empire quite explicitly. Of course, for the Tories, Russia's imperial expansion constituted much of her threat to Britain's welfare – the Whigs, looking back to recent British history, applied the imperial analogy in another direction. In 1791, the loss of America remained a vivid memory; the Whig Whitbread suggested that Russia's "empire, by extension, became more unwieldy, and less to be dreaded" and that the best course of action was "to suffer her to pursue her schemes to the South; to suffer her to fight, and weaken herself" (137). The Oczakow debates show imperial rather than colonial narcissism at work: it seems to have been impossible for members of parliament to speak of Russia's imperial fortunes without seeing their own reflected back to them. Yet once again narcissism and paranoia are intermingled: if Russia appears to the Whigs as a sister empire, worthy of respect and support, to the Tories she appears a ravaging, voracious monster, threatening to destroy Britain's power and very way of life.

Dulcinea or Katherine the Shrew? Gillray's doubled vision cut to the heart of the parliamentary debates, as gender – and a gendered definition of political roles – became a touchstone of the discussion. The convention of using the female pronoun for nations contributes to the feminizing of Russia, yet Turkey's actions are rarely discussed in feminine terms, and it may be worth noting that the female figure of Britannia does *not* appear in the armament debates or associated caricatures. Within the gendered terms of the debate, ministerial supporters concentrated on destroying the image of Russia as a mirror to Britain, or as a trading partner with claims on British gallantry, by emphasizing "her" barbarism and rapacity. A Mr. Pybus, for instance, worked to redefine Russia's national character through "her obvious schemes of conquest and dominion" (119) and through the bloody fall of Ismael, a city on the banks of the Danube: "the capture of that place had been attended with such acts of carnage and barbarity, as could not be thought of without horror, and were a disgrace to humanity" (120). In Pybus's rhetoric, Turkey remained "the enemy" rather than a friend or ally, but while Whitbread had suggested Russia's imperial expansion mirrored Britain's past, Pybus insisted that Britain's future was reflected in the threat to Turkey: "the time might not be very remote, when the fleets of Russia would triumph in the Mediterranean, an object to the whole world, of her activity, adroitness, and power, and of our supineness, impotence, and disgrace" (120–21). Her power, our impotence: the terms of conflict begin to be sexually coded, as Russia's military force threatens to emasculate Britain's international reputation.

The Tory J. T. Stanley echoed the imperial paranoia of Pybus's warning, using still more extravagant hyperbole:

Let gentlemen but consider the character of the Sovereign, who refuses to accept our unenforced proffers of mediation, from the day she was seated on the throne of the Russias; did she not discover an insatiable thirst of power, and an unlimited desire of extending her territories, immense as they were, to still more distant boundaries? Was it not evident her ambition aimed at no less than the title of Empress of the East, and that she wished to be saluted as such on the ancient throne of the Eastern Emperors, while her ambition, unsatisfied with this object, still would lead her to be the directress of every cabinet and every council in the western division of the ancient world? (130)

Britain as well as Russia might be said to aim at the title of "Empress of the East" – and at the moment, Britain rather than Russia was attempting to direct the cabinets of other western nations: specifically, Britain was trying to dictate to Russia the terms of an acceptable peace treaty with Turkey. [7] Thus Stanley's hyperbolic account of Russia's imperial appetites works to ward off similarities between the two empires by shifting gender midstream:

But should a war ensue in consequence of these armaments; should the obstinacy of the Empress force the Minister to an opinion that a war was necessary, are we so much to dread it? Are there no reasons why Russia should not remain unmolested and mistress of *her* own will, in what concerns materially the interests of the great republics of Europe? Are there no reasons why we should not force *him* to listen to us, and to insist on *his* paying some attention to our negociation? (128; my italics)

Britain's use of force would in this case only be a response to the "force" of Russia's obstinacy, framed as an offensive power, capable of constraining the minister's opinion and choice. But in a debate where gallantry has been invoked, the image of Britain "molesting" a Russia no longer "mistress of her own will" could not be left unrevised: Russia must undergo a sudden sex change in order to justify Britain's own use of force to insist on "his" attention.

Sheridan finally turned the sexualization of Russia back on the ministry's supporters by involving the speakers themselves in the sexual excess they charted. Speaking after Sir William Young had described Russia's territories and conquests at length, Sheridan insisted that no one opposing Grey's motions had offered any substantial argument to support their position:

Not even any argument had been offered by the honourable Baronet who spoke last, and who had traversed over all Europe, traced the history of the navigation and commerce of Russia, from the earliest times; described her back frontiers, and all parts of her dominions, and expatiated with as much familiarity concerning the Dnieper and the Danube, as if he had been talking of the *Worcestershire* canal, and pictured the Empress as a female Colossus, standing with one foot on the banks of the Black Sea, and the other on the coast of the Baltic. (143)

Sheridan's phrasing cast doubt on the propriety of Young's familiarity with Russia's "back frontiers," but the prurient interest attributed to Young does not result in Russia's vulnerability to (sexual) penetration – rather, Sheridan encapsulated the gendered alarmism of his opponents in the mock-heroic figure of the *female* Colossus. The echo of *Julius Caesar* here salaciously reframed Young's investigations:

> Why man, he doth bestride the narrow world
> Like a Colossus, and we petty men
> Walk under his huge legs, and peep about
> To find ourselves dishonourable graves.   (1.2.135–38)

The thought of what Young might have been "peeping at," walking around under the empress's huge legs, dishonors him; so too the opposition argued that the war would lead to (dishonorable) deaths for British sailors and soldiers.

Sheridan's echo of *Julius Caesar* not only encapsulated Tory tendencies to exaggerate Russia's imperial threat by presenting her as a voracious and enormous female figure – it also (somewhat ambivalently) staged the Whig position that the balance of power most at risk in these deliberations was the balance of parliamentary power.[8] Throughout discussion of the armament, Tories repeatedly called for "confidence in ministers": i.e., support for Pitt's policies *without* a detailed account of the reasoning behind those policies. Pitt insisted that all specific information must remain confidential if negotiations with Russia were to proceed; Whigs saw this call for confidence as a thin excuse for ministerial conquest of parliamentary power and privilege. Behind the figure of the female Colossus (Russia) stood the more serious threat of Pitt's colossal ambitions. The irony seems all the more pointed, given that the last British figure to be caricatured as Colossus was Walpole, whose enormous power as prime minister sometimes seemed the goal of Pitt the younger. And concerns over this internal balance of power, rhetorically mirroring discussions of the balance of power in Europe, raised questions about Pitt's (and by extension, Britain's) own gender identity.

Sheridan's mockery of Tory rhetoric attacked the implicit transfer of power thus proposed by attacking the vainglory of Pitt's pretensions. Having invoked the image of the (female) Colossus, Sheridan went on to dismiss Pitt's claim to be acting as a peacemaker:

Let us call it any thing but a system of peace; let us say it is a system of ambition, of vain glory, to see the offspring of the immortal Chatham, intriguing in all the courts of Europe, and setting himself up as the great posture-master of the balance of power, as possessing an exclusive right to be the umpire of all, and to weigh out in patent scales of his own, the quantity of dominion that each power shall possess. (150)

Sheridan's wit worked by recombining images already put forth by other members of parliament. Grey had already implicitly cast Pitt as "offspring of the immortal Chatham," contrasting Pitt the younger's rash and warlike quest for power with the restraint practiced by his father under similar circumstances thirty years earlier (108). So too the Tory Stanley had earlier spoken for Pitt, insisting that the minister "asks for the exercise, in this *delicate posture of affairs*, of a discretionary power which the constitution allows to the executive Government" (128; my italics). Turning Pitt into the posture-master of Europe, Sheridan's sarcasm combined the rhetoric of both sides.

Encapsulating the relationship between domestic and international power relations, the image of the posture-master and that of the female Colossus were the most widely repeated and memorable of the entire debate: especially after James Gillray turned each into a caricature. The first, "A Female Colossus," emphasizes the monstrous size of the empress; the second, "The Balance of Power," implicitly brings Pitt's sexuality into play as he balances the sultan and the empress on a pole he swears to hold indifferently level between them (plate 17). This balance of power acts differently upon the empress and the sultan: Pitt's pole can be seen as penetrating the empress's back frontiers. But Isaac Cruikshank's "The Treaty of Peace; or, Satisfaction for all Parties" (May 3, 1791) offers perhaps the final word on the subject as it develops a carefully gendered compromise to the troubled balance of power (plate 18). Cruikshank's "Treaty of Peace" is accomplished in a Turkish harem, subordinating Catherine of Russia to the sultan of Turkey – yet all the men present in the harem are shown subordinated in turn to the sexual or physical power of women. The men all emphasize their sexual prowess, but the women's repeated questioning of that prowess takes its toll on all. If we read the print from left to right, as I think we are invited to do, the first figure presented is George III, paired with a black woman:

Plate 17 James Gillray, "The Balance of Power." April 21, 1791.

Plate 18 [?I. Cruikshank], "The Treaty of Peace; or Satisfaction for all Parties." May 3, 1791.

she remains silent in the print, but his response ("Yes yes yes yes very large very large!) gives her unwritten question away. To their right, Thurlow fondles another woman's breast while she tests the weight of the mace, his sign of office: "I dare say this thing of yours is very heavy?" she asks, and he responds complacently, "Dam-ned heavy my dear little Deary too heavy for you I fear." But her grasp of him and the mace together suggests that the latter may be too heavy for Thurlow. In the center of the print, Catherine II overwhelms the sultan, telling him to "Kick all those little Husseys out my dear boy I'll do your business for you." The sultan's response encapsulates the ambivalent sexual politics of the print as a whole: "Vat a fine large Girl as a Bear I fear she will be too much for me." Holland is interrogated more forthrightly by his companion: "Oh dear what large Breaches got anything in them." Like the king and Thurlow he too insists on his potency: "vel filld vel filld." But on the far right of the print, Pitt takes a drubbing from two women who tell him "We'll give it you for serving the pretty Ladies in England as you did & laying so much upon them." Pitt's response breaks in before the second woman can finish the complaint ("and for taxing their things") in order to play off the sexual sense of laying: "Indeed I never did lay too much upon them." The feminized Pitt, threatening to faint, is aligned with the sultan as the only other man unwilling or unable to assert his masculine sufficiency.

Gillray's and Cruikshank's prints suggest the extent to which Pitt and the empress could be linked through their similar military and political ambitions – and by their equally unnatural though very dissimilar sexual tendencies. If Catherine's sexual predations seemed monstrously transgressive, Pitt's rather aggressive chastity could be seen as equally unnatural, comically emasculating. Within a code of male gallantry, modesty, and humanity, neither Pitt nor the empress could appear a proper figure of political and military power. The fact that each held *immense* political and military power posed an ideological contradiction intensified by fears that the power of each might remain unchecked. In debates and caricatures, Russia was made female in order that she might be tamed, taught to underwrite Britain's more properly masculine power – but her insubordination could also be presented as an essentially female characteristic. The ambivalence of gender in the armament debates developed perhaps most clearly from the antagonism between Whig and Tory policies. To the proposed armament, the opposition party could be seen as posing a series of rhetorical questions linking Britain with Russia. The first question: what distinguishes one expanding maritime empire from another? The Tories responded by emphasizing the disorderly passions of the empress, but the Whigs – and the caricaturists responding to the debate – maintained their point by reframing the question: what distinguishes a militaristic, sexually voracious old woman from a militaristic, sexually abstemious young man? Answer (as Sheridan might have put it): not enough.

THE POWER OF LOVE

Hannah Cowley's "mixed drama," written during 1791 and performed both before and after a treaty of peace between Russia and Turkey was finally signed in January 1792, disrupted the gendered imagery of the published parliamentary debates as it played on public sympathies for Christian Russia against "her" Muslim enemy. Burke had claimed that aiding Turkey would reduce Christian nations "to the yoke of the infidels, and make them the miserable victims to these inhuman savages"; Cowley dramatized this scenario, but transformed both the misery of the Russian slaves and the inhumanity of their Turkish captors through the power of love. Countering the machismo of the parliamentary debates, Cowley's play replaced the voracious oversexed Russian empress with the chaste and beautiful Alexina, a Russian noblewoman under the "infidel yoke." Disputing the visual and verbal rhetoric which emphasized the monstrosity of women's supremacy, Cowley developed a benign and idealized empire of love, in which Russia and Italy combine to civilize Turkey through sentimental romance. Ostensibly developing in strictly local terms the sexualized power relations between male tyrants and female captives, however, Cowley's drama also engaged the global political issues of war, revolution, and slavery. The Oczakow parliamentary debates demonstrate the general analogy existing between sexual and imperial politics: in parliament and on the London stage alike, discussions of international politics could be inflected and informed by a rhetorical appeal to sexual norms. At the same time, members of parliament and female dramatists could each claim with impunity that the two interwoven topics had nothing to do with each other.

Cowley's *Day in Turkey* approached the conflict between nations through a mixed drama which offered a decidedly mixed view of politics. The sentimental plot of the comedy worked to reestablish clear gender roles, to set men and women back in their proper places: thus the play veers away from the oversexed empress and undersexed minister to focus on the relation between sex and politics in the harem of a Turkish pasha or "Bassa." Pointing toward a rather less bawdy treaty of peace and form of "satisfaction for all parties," Cowley rewrote *The Taming of the Shrew* as the *Taming of the Sultan*. Her revisions worked to raise the tone of political discussion, to erase the vulgarity of the debates. As Cowley's sentimental heroine rather awkwardly demanded, "Where shall honor be honor'd, if the mouth of woman casts on it contempt?" (39). While demonstrating respect for chastity and honor, however, Cowley's sentimental storyline also dramatized women's supremacy over men through the power of love and courtship (or, as Cruikshank would have it, sex). While Cowley insisted on distinguishing her politics from those of Wollstonecraft, Rousseau's anxieties about women gaining social power through the stage example of sentimental romance might seem prophetic here.

A Day in Turkey; or, The Russian Slaves tells the story of a sentimental heroine, Alexina, captured by Turkish raiders immediately after her wedding to the Russian noble Orloff. Though the raiders take her immediately to the Bassa's harem, the newly-wed (whose wedding remains unconsummated) is temporarily reprieved by her new master's absence in battle. The play begins a few weeks later, with the capture of a family of Russian peasants, the simultaneous capture of Orloff with his French *valet de chambre*, A la Greque, and the return of the Bassa Ibrahim to his harem. The plot alternates between the plight of Alexina, who would rather die than submit to Ibrahim, and the disruptions created by A la Greque, who refuses to recognize either the social or physical boundaries limiting his new existence. Lauretta, an Italian inmate of the harem, unites comedy and sentiment to save Alexina: first by teaching the Bassa to submit to the power of female chastity, then by presenting him with the peasant Paulina rather than Alexina as the object of his passion. Conquered by the force of love, the Bassa frees Alexina and Orloff and marries Paulina.

Countering the tone developed by the armament debates and caricatures, *A Day in Turkey* responded more loosely to the political issues at work. In performance, *The Russian Slaves* would have belittled Turkey and sided with Russia: to an English audience, the Turkish Bassa may have seemed admirably open to the civilizing force of western sentimentality, but in structural terms, he remains the butt of Lauretta's comic plotting. By contrast, the Russian nobility are consistently characterized by their honorable restraint. More generally, Cowley shows the conflict between nations resolved without English intervention: the play begins with Russian characters enslaved; it ends with a Turkish Bassa marrying a Russian peasant. Disruptive comic characters like the French A la Greque and the Italian Lauretta help produce the political inversions of the play, again suggesting the superfluity of English involvement. Morally rather than politically, France and Italy mediate between the extremes of the Orient (Turkey) and the ostensible virtues of the North (England and Russia). Still, the political implications persist: if a European balance of power exists, England need not, or perhaps could not, provide its point of leverage.

In keeping with the political complexities of the Oczakow dispute and Cowley's authorial stance, the relationship between sentiment and farce in *A Day in Turkey* seems unusually convoluted. Within the play, sentiment does the work performed by military action and international diplomacy in the "real world": it subordinates Turkey to Russia. Moments of farce undercut that sentimental subordination by exposing its despotic and erotic underpinnings. Yet in the play as a whole farce remains explicitly subordinate to sentiment: even the farcically plotting Lauretta "mean[s] to serve" the sentimental heroine Alexina (39). Conversely, however, discussions and enactments of sentiment throughout the play elaborate a farcical plotline: showing a Turkish despot erotically subdued by a Russian peasant he mistakes for a chaste aristocrat, the play produces itself as an extended orientalist joke. Operating both at the level of overall narrative structure and in particular episodes, farce remains unusually central to Cowley's mixed drama. Perhaps as a result, farce's political double edge shows itself with unusual clarity in this play: the farcical deployment of national stereotypes produces an orientalist narrative of civilized subordination even as farcical accounts of sentiment and of international affairs unravel the myth of western civilization.

The reading which follows moves among three different versions of the play: the Larpent manuscript submitted to the censor; the first edition of 1792; and the revised edition of 1813, printed in Cowley's collected works. Responding to the play's first performance, "Aesopus" had suggested that "if those parts were expunged which were apparently rejected by the audience, to those who are fond of stage pageantry, the Russian slaves might still prove acceptable."[9] Cowley's on-going revision of the play clarified the demure pageantry of sentimental femininity: the version of *A Day in Turkey* which was printed in 1792 offers a slightly modified acting script; her collected works, published in 1813, present a substantially altered *reading* version of the drama – one which works to articulate the play's orientalism and sentimental ideology more fully and more cautiously, even as it obscures the gender politics and topical references of the earlier edition.[10] Cowley's revisions shift the balance of power from farce toward sentiment and from South and East to the North, especially in the figure of Zilia, a Georgian woman who replaces the Italian Lauretta. Those revisions also underscore, however, the structural relationship between farce and sentiment, East and West, in this mixed drama.

In each version of the play, for instance, the largely sentimental plot of *A Day in Turkey* is based on an orientalist, classist joke more in keeping with farce than with sentiment. The Turkish Bassa, sentimentally captivated by a Russian peasant, frees both his Russian slaves and his entire seraglio in order to marry her. A more fully sentimental play would have made Paulina, like Richardson's Pamela, morally worthy of her social elevation, but Cowley's Paulina has to be bullied into playing a properly sentimental role. After emphasizing to Ibrahim the power of sentimental chastity, Lauretta/Zilia is repeatedly forced to school Paulina to stern and distant behavior with the Bassa. Having gone through three lovers, the pretty peasant is happy enough to bow to the desire of a man she believes is the Bassa's servant; only her indignation upon being told he might behead on his master's orders provides her with sufficient pique and disdain to keep the masquerade in motion. Paulina's lack of innate chastity does not seem to trouble the sentimental resolution of the plot: Ibrahim, thoroughly reformed by his experience of western love, is so relieved to find her unmarried that he makes no objection to her social status, and neglects to inquire into her previous life. While the play thus reaffirms class and national prejudices – i.e., lower-class women are naturally unchaste, but they can be palmed off on a Turk who knows no better – it also raises troubling questions about the performing and performative nature of sentimental love.

The mixed drama obscures these questions, however, by the parallels and oppositions it establishes. The performance of sentiment, for instance, is naturalized as class-specific within the play: Alexina "naturally" acts the part of a sentimental heroine; Paulina plays this role imperfectly at best, and only with much coaching; Lauretta, the outsider, refuses to *perform* sentiment, but directs the performances of Paulina and Ibrahim. The opposition established between Alexina and Paulina returns in the play's closing scene. *A Day in Turkey* ends by juxtaposing two couples: the proper, sentimental Orloff and Alexina and the farcical, inverted couple of Paulina and the Bassa. The sentimental heroine Alexina remains properly subordinated to her loving husband, while the once despotic Bassa is comically, improperly subordinated to his farcical wife-to-be. The relationships established at the beginning of the play further undermine the Bassa's position here, for Paulina, a vassal of Alexina's father, remains subordinate to Alexina and the men linked through her. If A la Greque at the beginning of the play finds himself "valet de chambre to a slave!" (3), Ibrahim at the end finds himself sentimentally enslaved to a member of the servant class. While Cowley's first farce asked the audience to decide *Who's the Dupe?*, her late mixed drama presents the Bassa duped through the machinations of his female slave, Lauretta.

Indeed, in an uncanny move, the Turkish seraglio becomes an unlikely "School for Sentiment" in which the instruction in and articulation of sentiment are both left to the unsentimental figure of Lauretta. Sentiment may rely, as Goldsmith suggested, on a performance of sincerity, but *A Day in Turkey* shows that sincerity inculcated by a cynical and self-interested figure. In 1792, the canny Lauretta operates as a figure for the female playwright, promising to "weave a web of amusement to crack the sides of half a dozen gloomy Harams with laughter – Mercy! what a sleepy life would our valiant Bassa & his Damsels live, but for my Talents at Invention" (1792: 21). The claims of chastity and sentiment are difficult to distinguish from Lauretta's imaginative inventions, her larger "web of amusement." In 1813, Zilia presents her sentimental instruction of the Bassa explicitly as a ploy to achieve freedom for herself and her female companions. In the midst of proclaiming to Ibrahim the power of beauty over male authority, she remarks in an aside to the female slaves, " – Hark ye! if I can tinge his mind with such feelings, real Love will take possession of it – he will determine on Marriage, and we shall escape from Slavery!" (1813: 258). Rebuked by Alexina for her lack of sentimental restraint, Zilia once again asserts her intention to win free of slavery through her comic plots. The ideals of sentimental courtship and female chastity are subordinated to an only partially covert struggle for greater freedom and self-determination.

Even more pointedly, the sentimental ideology presented by Lauretta and Zilia both replicates and inverts the master–slave relations of the seraglio. In 1792, the frivolous Italian Lauretta was presented as an expert in love on the basis of her nationality; this expert witness had assured the Bassa, "you must become the slave of your captive, if you ever mean to taste the sublime excesses of a mutual passion" (1792: 15). The compressed logic of mutual slavery and mutual passion was greatly expanded in the later version of the play. In the 1813 text, Lauretta

becomes the independent Georgian Zilia, whose advice is still more cosmopolitan – and orientalist: "Remember, Sir, she is no Asiatic slave, but
an European, born beyond the boundaries of Turkey and the region of
our manners!" (1813: 257). Zilia sets the love plot in motion by suggesting to Ibrahim the danger of falling in love with Alexina: "if she should
find you in love with her, and should ever condescend to listen to a sentence from you, she will deem herself intitled to treat you as she pleases,
and, instead of being *herself* a Slave, will assume unbounded authority
over *you*!" (257–58). When Ibrahim dismisses the possibility of such
indifference to his power, Zilia rebukes him, "You are thinking now of
your own power, when you should be sensible only of her's! You are powerful, and she is pretty, your empire is less absolute than her's – beware
of substituting Reproach for supplications! . . . Dominion and love are
very different things" (258).

   Dominion and love may indeed be separate things, but Zilia seems
able to describe romantic love only in terms of domination. She insists
that love overrides class distinctions, setting monarchs and peasants on
an equal plane, but as Ibrahim points out, "under such a System, the
Men must be the Slaves, and the empire of Love be transferred to the
Women!" (259). The doubled domination of Zilia's sentimental rhetoric
nonetheless catches Ibrahim's imagination: even as he exclaims against
the male slavery of this "empire of love" he pictures himself able to
conquer within that realm. He rejects sentiment on the basis of its inadequacy, not his own: " – Away with every thing so exotic! I'll waste no
time in mean conquest over female Caprice – victory over the Enemy is
alone worthy my Ambition!" But Zilia conquers his resistance through
the simple expedient of laughing at him, mocking his provincialism and
suggesting his heroic insufficiency: "Ha! ha! – there, now you are Turkish
again! – Sagacious Sir! if you would really be heroic as a Conqueror –
you must begin by being romantic in Love!" (259). Even as it challenges
masculine self-sufficiency, this last claim reinserts women's power over
men within a convention of separate spheres: male subordination to
women at home will simply make them more heroic, more successful,
more masculine in their conquests out of doors. A few scenes later,
Ibrahim shows that he has internalized Zilia's promise of superiority
through submission: "If I am distinguished amongst men, that which
best distinguishes man – refined love – ought in my breast to be more
tender, more powerful, than in the breast of others" (266). From this perspective, sentimental masculinity merely offers a new arena for the development of male prowess and distinction.

In both versions of the play, Cowley invoked orientalist and anti-Turkish tropes and sentiments to make her tale of women's romantic ascendancy more palatable to British audiences. In 1813, for instance, Zilia expanded on the faults of both eastern and western cultures, but she handled the follies of eastern manners much more harshly. "Ceremonious and uncommunicative," the men lack ideas of their own, and "[n]ever having known the advantages of elegant society, of Women they speak but as Slave-merchants." Similarly "excluded from rational society with men, and unrespected by them," eastern women's "Minds are uninformed, and their Manners ungraceful." Established as a cultural authority by her travels, Zilia concluded that "in the follies abroad there is a play of Mind that renders them interesting; your follies here – create but listlessness and Disgust!" (263–64). In taking the bait of romantic love, Ibrahim adopts the disdain toward eastern women expressed by Lauretta/Zilia – but the play's orientalism is undercut as its apparent distinction between bad sensuality and good sensibility comes unraveled. Told of Alexina's resistance to his summons, Ibrahim responds unexpectedly with respect for her honor, rejoicing (in 1792) that "at length I shall taste the joy of overcoming RESISTANCE." He goes on to describe the fatigue produced by the unremitting sexual submission the play attributes to eastern women; he turns the delay of sexual satisfaction into a new source of "satisfaction for all parties":

I am satiated, I am tired, with the dull acquiescence of our eastern slaves, and rejoice that I have at length found one, who will teach me to hope, and to *despair* . . . There is a transport which I have never yet experienced but which my soul longs to possess – yes, my heart languishes to remove the timid veil of coyness – to soften, by sweet degrees, the ice of chastity, and to see, for once, reserve sacrificed at the altar of desire; *these*, cruel Love, are luxuries thou hast never yet bestowed on me. (1792: 19)

The 1813 *A Day in Turkey* offers a heightened version of this opening claim: Ibrahim is now "disgusted with the abject submission of our Eastern Captives." Only a western European woman, he suggests, can teach him about love rather than lust. Yet the language of this passage reinstalls lust within love, sexuality within the hallowed precincts of sentimental courtship. As Ibrahim begins to contemplate with pleasure the prospect of becoming "the slave of his captive," he anticipates a lingering deferral of pleasure – and a series of luxuries cast in terms of sexualized, largely gothic imagery: veils he may remove, ice his passion will soften, reserve that will be sacrificed not on the altar of love, but on that of desire.

Indeed, Cowley's *Day in Turkey* shows the (western) romantic ideal of sentimental chastity constructed out of bits and pieces of oriental luxury and sexual domination. Even Alexina's stalwart refusal of sex can be seen in a sexual light. The heroine announces to Lauretta/Zilia that Ibrahim has sent for her, but vows, "I will first rush into the arms of death." In 1792, Lauretta laughs at her resolve, even as she reaffirms the sexualized orientalism of the play: "Rather rush into the arms of death, than into the arms of a handsome lover! the notion is exotic – it is an ice-plant of the North" (39–40). The notion *is* exotic (i.e., sexually perverse): Alexina sexualizes death (unconsciously, one presumes); Lauretta merely makes explicit the implied comparison between honorable and dishonorable lovers. In the process, however, western chastity becomes a phantasmatic, ghostly version of eastern sexuality.

The sado-masochistic elements of sentiment and sensibility have long been recognized in the work of Richardson, Rousseau, and other sentimental writers; yet for a female dramatist to draw the analogy quite so explicitly may have seemed somewhat scandalous. Both editions of the play allow Alexina a stinging rebuke of her companion. In 1792, for instance, Alexina asks scornfully, "Are you the friend who was to soothe my sorrows? Alas! where shall honor be honor'd, if the mouth of woman casts on it contempt?" Though Lauretta humbly begs pardon, Alexina continues to insist on the difference between them through a markedly insulting speech: "In you, the contented inhabitant of a seraglio, such profanation may be pardon'd; but alas! in the world, the grace of chastity is scarcely longer acknowledged! . . . Alas! so miserable is my situation, that I am obliged to accept services from those whom the feelings of my heart wou'd impel me to shun" (39–40). The 1813 edition retains Alexina's vow, but cuts Lauretta/Zilia's comparison of lovers. In its place, a rather wordy apology for cultural relativism develops into a paean to marital bliss:

ALEXINA. All allowance made for the force of Custom, in those who are ignorant of better, still you have elsewhere witnessed a happier System.

ZILIA. True I have, where the qualities of a Woman's MIND render her the object of Affection, where she is beloved as the participator in all the Interests of her husband's life, and is respected whilst she is beloved.

ALEXINA. Connubial love, Zilia, is the affection of a heart – all virtue. Its foundation is nobleness of mind; and, opening to a woman a more extended field for exercising all the charities of her nature, instead of degrading her in her society with a man, it gifts her with the loftiest Dignity, and throws a Grace around all her actions in life. (282–83)

In this exchange, the Georgian Zilia, a character raised as it were on the Russian borders, enters with Alexina into a joint performance of sentiment: a duet which the Italian Lauretta would surely have shunned. Here the noble Russian and her Georgian shadow agree that western marriage, rather than constraining women, offers a more extended field of endeavor, and a version of equality through participation in their husbands' interests. Yet Cowley was canny enough to make such a claim in a play designed to be read rather than performed: Alexina's last speech in particular seems not only overwritten but unstageable – too pompous to survive in a play as ideologically flippant as *A Day in Turkey* so often seems.

If the play's sentimental ideology is somewhat destabilized by its farcical framing, however, the real humor and subversive possibilities of *The Russian Slaves* exist in the middle ground created by the play's mixed characters. Against the sentimental pairing of Alexina and Orloff and the farcical coupling of Ibrahim and Paulina, we might set two other unromantic and unsentimental pairs of characters: Azim and Mustapha; and A la Greque and Lauretta. At once slaves of Ibrahim and masters of the seraglio, Azim and Mustapha take up a mixed-class position within the world of the play. Middlemen in the play's economy of slavery, they are quick to link the apparently divergent topics of sexism, racism, religious dissent, and trade. Their quips reveal fundamental similarities between the East and the West on points where differences are usually emphasized: slavery, religion, the treatment of women. Within Cowley's racist nationalism, meanwhile, the French A la Greque and the Italian Lauretta take up a mixed-race position – neither northern European nor oriental – and their speech and actions disrupt the relationships of class and subordination within the play. A la Greque's verbal enthusiasm for embracing slavery is matched only by his irrepressible egalitarianism of action, while Lauretta, choosing to serve Alexina rather than Ibrahim, inverts the gender politics of the seraglio and its rulers. Both of these comic pairs relate through competition rather than sentimental cooperation: Azim and Mustapha vie for power within the seraglio; A la Greque and Lauretta hold opposing views on women's rights. Together, however, both pairs bridge the ostensible gap between oriental barbarism and western civilization, showing the injustices underlying both social systems.

Within the pairing of Azim and Mustapha, Mustapha seems dominant, a comic in relation to whom both Russian women and Turkish
eunuchs become straight men. When Alexina begs Mustapha to inter-
cede with Ibrahim for her, for instance, he protests that he himself is also
a slave; she breaks into a highly sentimental song to move him to action:

> Thus, tho' a Slave, thy Soul's high State
> Shall prove it's origin divine
> Soar far above thy wretched fate,
> And o'er thy Chains sublimely shine!

Yet Mustapha, generally subdued by Alexina's noble virtue, responds in
1792 with marked flippancy: "Why, as to chastity and all that which you
make an orthodox article of, sweet one, we Turks are a sort of dissenters
– A woman's virtue with us, is to CHARM, & her religion should be
LOVE. – Ah, Ah! here comes Ibrahim & his whole haram – *His* creed is
love, and there is not a more orthodox man in the country" (1792: 10–11).
While Mustapha consistently tries to protect Alexina from the Bassa, his
humor refuses to value her standards of virtue over those of his master.
At the same time, the religious trappings of his joke, seen from an
English perspective, align Islamic orthodoxy with the sexual excesses
attributed to Methodism and dissenting sects, and thus suggest that dissenters and heathens alike confuse religion with sex. Admittedly,
however, the implications of the joke remain fairly subtle; meanwhile, its
blatant sexist emphasis on female charms aligns his stance with main-
stream British culture rather than with the side eddies of dissent.

Mustapha's quips also cap the humorous financial observations of the
Russian peasant Paulina. Captured with her family at the beginning of the
play, Paulina is struck by the paradoxical improvement in their material
circumstances: "So, we are made slaves to ride in our own carriage" (8).
Having been purchased by Mustapha as a Russian companion for Alexina,
however, Paulina is quick to protest her objectification: "Buy! buy! Why,
you talk of buying us, as though we were baskets of eggs, or bales of
cotton." Mustapha ignores her critique while granting its premise: "Yes, it
is the mode here – Every country has its fancies, and we are so fond of
liberty, that we always buy it up as a rarity" (35). This brazen contradiction
between the political ideal of liberty and the commercial action of a slave
trade reflects more soberly on England than on Turkey, for England alone
proclaimed its fondness for liberty loud and long. Unobtrusively yet repeatedly, the play highlights the rarity of freedom: a quality which it begins to
suggest can be experienced only by white, wealthy, northern men.

Still, the most thorough critique of English liberty comes in a three-way conversation among Alexina, Azim, and Mustapha, in which the Russian woman again provides merely the occasion for reflexive, oriental humor. When Alexina weeps at her captivity, the unsympathetic Azim ridicules her "wailing about freedom & liberty! Why the christians in one of the northern isles have established a slave trade, and have proved by act of parliament that freedom is no blessing at all." Mustapha objects to this wholesale dismissal of English liberty, but only to note the racist limitations of the act: "No, no – they have only proved that it does not suit dark complexions" (1792: 9). Remaining in character, he quickly links this racism to a familiar and supposedly flattering form of sexism: "To such a pretty creature as this, they'd think it a blessing to *give* every freedom, and *take* every freedom" (1792: 9). Sexual intimacies replace civil liberties for women: their bodies and beauties disqualify them for independent action, as dark complexions remain "unsuited" to freedom. Meanwhile, Alexina – or rather an English actress wailing about freedom and liberty on an English stage – is momentarily silenced. Costumed as oriental eunuchs, Azim and Mustapha would have embodied visible difference on the stage: Alexina, dressed as a westerner, would have seemed more purely English. Only humor, and the political critique it enables, underwrite the momentary moral subordination of this western woman to her eastern guards.

Neither eastern nor western, Lauretta and A la Greque allow Cowley to mediate more subtly between Russia and Turkey. While Cowley's *Belle's Stratagem* had presented France and Italy as purely antagonistic to England's native virtues, *A Day in Turkey* develops French and Italian characters as a middle ground between northern Europe and the Orient. The play's racism is unabashed but eminently comparative. On the first page, for instance, Paulina's father laments, "I shall see thee in a vile Turk's seraglio, no better as it were than the handmaid of a Jew" (1792: 1). Turk or Jew, French or Italian, Russian or English: the play operates through a series of racialized national analogies. In this context, Cowley's French and Italian characters register a certain social mobility derived from their racial indeterminacy. Neither oriental nor properly northern, they at once mediate between and disrupt these opposing worlds.

The figure of A la Greque, for instance, disrupts both the English ideal of liberty and the Turkish system of slavery by mingling an extravagant freedom of speech and action with an equally extravagant submission to authority. Freedom becomes as frivolous as dancing, and this (typically French) frivolity leads inevitably to the fact of enslavement. A la Greque claims that he "travell'd into Russia to polish the brutes a little, and to give them some ideas of the general equality of man," but his labor was lost: "Finding they would not learn liberty, I would have taught them dancing; but they seem'd as incapable of one blessing as the other – so now *I* am led a dance by this gentleman into your chains, in which, however, if I can but dance myself into your favour, I shall think it the best step I ever took" (1792: 18–19). A la Greque's shameless flattery of the Bassa undercuts all his vaunted rhetoric of equality, yet his actions on stage – in particular, pulling his Russian master Orloff back to exit ahead of him, and later invading the seraglio – speak still more powerfully of a leveling approach to social divisions.

In defending *A Day in Turkey* from the imputation of politics, Cowley singled out A la Greque as the source of the play's politics, yet insisted on her dramatic right to have a Frenchman speak of the revolution which must be at the forefront of his mind. A la Greque's exchange with the Bassa suggests some of the complexity of this political mediation. When Ibrahim tells A la Greque, "The freedom of thy speech does not displease me," the Frenchman responds again with abject submission, but that submission holds an edge: "Dear Sir, I am your most obedient humble slave, ready to bow my head to your sandals, & to lick the dust from your beautiful feet – (Ça ira!)" (Larpent, 17–18). The call to violent revolution ("Ça ira!") makes A la Greque's parody of submission ever so slightly threatening. Cowley's revisions of this line record her responses to the vicissitudes of the French revolution. To the published edition of 1792, she added the reflection that "chains were as natural t'other day to *Frenchmen* as mother's milk" (18); in 1813, by contrast, A la Greque asserts, "Chains! they wont weigh a rush with me! – *ils sont toujours à la mode à Paris!* I shall foot it to their clink, and feel myself at home again!" (266). In 1791, one could still believe that the revolution would put an end to absolute power in France; in 1813, after Napoleon's ravages, Cowley was less willing to subscribe to a model of French liberty.

Still, A la Greque seems so much the classic stage Frenchman, reconfirming the stereotypes of cowardice, bawdiness, and a terminal lack of seriousness, that his political views could hardly be seen as a challenge to conservative British politics. Even within the play, his attempt to convert the Russians to the doctrine of equality fails; his account of that failure ("they still continue to believe that a prince is more than a porter, & that a lord is a better gentleman than his slave – O, had they but been with me at Versailles, when I help'd to turn those things topsey-turvy there!" [18]) does not invite British sympathy. And in the 1792 script, Cowley used A la Greque to flatter her English audience. When Orloff tries to silence him with the command, "Peace!," A la Greque responds, "Peace! That's a bold demand! Your Empress can't find it at the head of one hundred thousand men, & the most sublime Grand Signior is obliged to put on his night-cap without it, tho' he has a million of these pretty Gentlemen to assist him – Besides, England has engrossed the commodity" (1792: 5–6). In 1813, this last line was cut: England's command of peace was rather less assured.

A la Greque on his own could hardly pose a political threat: protests about the play's politics seem more likely to have developed out of the intersection of the plotting Lauretta and the irrepressible A la Greque. These two together represent the intersection of two revolutions: the political revolution in France and the REVOLUTION IN MANNERS presented by Mary Wollstonecraft's *Vindication of the Rights of Woman*. A la Greque himself dramatizes the need for women's rights within a revolutionary context. Inserting himself into the harem and attempting to seduce the women there, he betrays his own failure to keep confidence with the indignant question, "Do you think that I, Madam, am a man to betray a lady's favours? I, who have been well receiv'd by duchesses and marchionesses?" When he is asked what duchesses and marchionesses are, he responds "in his usual tone" (in other words, carelessly): "They were a sort of female creatures, my dear, who once infested Paris . . . Now, my sweet charmer, there is not one in the country, I mean of native growth; and if the neighbouring nations do not now and then send them one for a sample, a duchess will be as rare an animal in France, as a crocodile" (67). Written before the Terror, his callousness to these women's fates nonetheless marks his irredeemable resistance to sentiment – and to women's claim to respect. At the same time, these lines feed English audiences' sense of superiority to the French, both before the revolution (when a duchess would sleep with a *valet de chambre*) and after (when the French threaten to extirpate duchesses altogether).

A la Greque is hardly a feminist, yet as a figure of the French revolution, he nonetheless holds out to women an important model of liberation. As Azim bursts into the harem in search of A la Greque, for instance, he warns the women to hide themselves from a man loose in the harem. Lauretta has already hidden A la Greque by sitting on him; she refuses to leave and engages Azim in a dialogue which bases the rights of women upon the rights of man asserted by the revolutionaries.

Once again, Cowley's revisions record the shifting politics of the play's reception and the dramatist's thinking over time. The Larpent manuscript of the play offers the most radical version of the exchange:

LAURA. And what are we to fly for? Is a man a tyger that we should be so
    scared? Who is he?
AZIM. The new French slave. Frenchmen, there is no being guarded against.
    They make free everywhere.
LAURA. At least they have made themselves free, ~~and all the nations of the
    Earth shall bless them for it.~~ Who knows, but at last, the spirit they have
    raised, may reach, even to a Turkish harem, and the rights of women be
    declared, as well as those of men.
AZIM. Don't talk to me of the rights of women; you would do right to go and
    conceal yourselves as I order'd ye . . . Rise up, and give me your Seat.
LAURA. I wonder at your impertinence. Surely we have not so entirely
    forfeited the rights of women, but we may keep our Seats, tho' we have
    lost our liberty. (59/72)

The words struck out of the manuscript were presumably cut by the censor: they do seem a little too explicitly (and objectionably) political, nor do they appear in the published version of the play. Indeed, the 1792 edition is milder on both French and feminist politics: the crossed out line reads simply, "they have made themselves free AT HOME," and the second reference to women's rights has also been cut so that the closing line reads, "Surely we may keep our Seats, tho' we have lost our liberty." The 1813 revisions were far more sweeping. To Zilia's question "Who is he?" Azim responds, "The new French slave. Frenchmen there is no being guarded against – at other's cost they make *themselves* free everywhere." All reference to women's rights and to the potential benefits of the French revolution have vanished. Yet in each edition of the play, the plotting female of the seraglio literally seats herself upon the debased figure of the French revolution: emblematically, this action speaks louder than many words could do.

Cowley's progressive retreat from the explicitly political claims on which the play originally turned does not erase the more pervasive gender politics of her mixed comedy – or the breadth of impact the playwright attributed to the comedy of women's private influence. *A Day in Turkey* responds to the unnatural images of male and female sexuality used to debate the wisdom of going to war with Russia by reestablishing proper gender roles for both men and women – but only under the rubric of performance. Alexina presents on stage a pure and highly moral Russian noblewoman, whose mere presence counters the sexually degrading popular images of Catherine II. But Lauretta and later Zilia, the true power behind the throne, remains like the Russian empress a woman whose passions do not blind her to her own interests. Lauretta/Zilia's crafty manipulation of the codes of sentiment work somewhat half-heartedly to blind the male audience (on stage and off) to her interests in the rights of women: Cowley's 1792 advertisement and 1813 revisions attempt to achieve a more extended conceptual blackout.

The parliamentary debates of 1791, when seen through Hannah Cowley's *A Day in Turkey; or, The Russian Slaves* (1791), suggest that the balance of power in turn-of-the-century Britain was maintained by various forms of negation, of knowledge disavowed. The political debates deny the relevance of sex and gender to the political issues under discussion – but members of both sides use sexually coded images and rhetoric to inflect their own arguments, to imply what they do not want to say directly, or to cast doubt on the probity of their opponents. Hannah Cowley's advertisement to *A Day in Turkey* similarly denied any involvement in politics for both the play and the playwright, yet the comedy intervened in a wide range of political debates – in part through its disavowal of public interests. While these overlapping modes of negation produced an odd double vision of sentimental and political romance, politicians and playwrights alike could profit from the juxtaposition of similar though ostensibly different categories. Disavowing politics while displaying political knowledge, Cowley's advertisement to *A Day in Turkey* might best be read in the French sense of a "warning" (*avertissement*) about the duplicity of Romantic politics and gender. Certainly the mixed drama thus advertised relies on the duplicity of farce to subordinate Turkey to Russia, the East to the West, while simultaneously making a mockery of the cultural differences summoned to justify that subordination. *A Day in Turkey* shows East and West equally seduced by erotic fantasies of conquest and absolute dominion, equally engaged in slave trading, equally culpable except perhaps in their treatment of women. Yet while Cowley shows Lauretta/Zilia able to manipulate the cult of sentiment on women's behalf, she also shows sentiment producing Alexina's passivity. Cowley's mixed drama suggests that in the disparate settings of an oriental seraglio, an English political debate, and a London theatre, a single warning holds true: a woman's best hope for freedom relies on the mimic plotting of the practiced farceuse.

CHAPTER SEVEN

The farce of subjection: Elizabeth Inchbald

For Elizabeth Inchbald, the image of the prison or dungeon seems to encapsulate the connections between English patriarchy, sentiment, and oriental despotism. In the sentimental comedy *Such Things Are* (1787), the plot of sentimental reformation focuses on freeing the prisoners of an East Indian sultan from the dungeons in which they have languished for decades. Yet the play also sketches subtler forms of despotism at work in the British ideal of (masculine) benevolence. So too the plot of the later comedy *Wives as They Were, Maids as They Are* (1797) turns on the threat of imprisonment for debt – a threat which in turn marks the collision of gender conflict and imperial concerns. A modified Nabob, Sir William Dorillon, returns to England disguised as a Mr. Mandred in order to spy on his daughter, believing quite rightly that she will not conceal from a stranger the faults she would try to hide from a father. When Miss Dorillon is pursued by a bailiff who wants to arrest her for gambling debts, she seeks refuge with her unrecognized father, but he refuses to protect her:

What! do you droop? Do you tremble? You, who at the ball tonight would have danced lightly, though your poor creditor had been perishing with want! You, who never asked yourself if your extravagance might not send an industrious father of a family to prison, can you feel on the prospect of going thither yourself.[1]

Throughout the play, Sir William reiterates his (paternal) industry and hard work in India: hearing that his daughter may be arrested for debt produces in his mind the image of just such an industrious father imprisoned for her excesses. The fantasy seems to suggest that one or the other will end in confinement: both cannot exist in plenty. Soon afterwards, Miss Dorillon produces a complementary fantasy of her father imprisoned: after the man she knows as Mandred has given money for her release from prison and announced his return to India, Maria Dorillon first imagines her father in poverty – then imprisoned and suffering. She urges Mandred, "release me instantly, and take me with you to the place of his confinement" (71). Father and daughter see their freedom and captivity oddly entangled: familial relations seem to produce a prison which in turn develops, if only belatedly, the "natural feelings" of fatherly or daughterly love it would seem to contradict.

In Inchbald's work, the image of the prison links colonial paranoia with the paranoia implicit in patriarchy. As we have seen, Homi Bhabha associates colonial paranoia with colonial narcissism: the colonizers' desire to see the colonized people as almost the same as themselves (but not quite). So too the men in Inchbald's plays develop an odd confusion of identity – in which their authority over a wife or daughter seems essential to the security of their own personae. Yet like colonial authority, the ambivalence of paternal authority repeatedly moves from narcissism to paranoia. In reading three of Inchbald's most popular plays, this chapter argues that Inchbald gradually superimposes the constraints of colonialism upon those of gender. More specifically, it suggests that the farce *A Mogul Tale* (1784) pokes fun at colonial paranoia: British fears of eastern power structures reappear as comedy; the potential for menace turns back to the farce of mimicry. Three years later, the sentimental comedy *Such Things Are* attempts to move beyond critique to a resolution of the problems inherent in colonialism. Yet while the play presents an apparently naïve reliance on the powers of sentimental benevolence, it nonetheless exposes willing slavery and female subjection as preconditions for resolving the contradictions of empire. This play's sentimental ideal internalizes the dichotomies parodied by farce. Finally, the late comedy *Wives as They Were, Maids as They Are* brings the gendered lessons of colonialism home to London: oriental subjection reappears in western guise as an antique form of marriage and a lowly debtor's prison. Inchbald's drama never quite abandons its orientalist perspective, but it does apply the ironic model of willing slavery to western contexts with a striking degree of exaggeration.

I

Inchbald's breakthrough as a playwright came with the production of her farcical afterpiece, *A Mogul Tale*, first staged at Covent Garden on July 6, 1784. The piece appealed to several sets of topical interests: most notably, the pseudo-sciences of quack medicine and balloon travel, and most importantly, concerns about British relations with the "East."

Three balloon travelers – a quack "doctor," a cobbler, and his wife – land by accident in the seraglio of the great mogul, and are led by their terror into a series of absurd and entertaining masquerades. Throughout these adventures, *A Mogul Tale* balances its frank display of British tyranny and paranoia with a narcissistic portrait of a mogul indistinguishable from contemporary European philosophers. In more specific political terms, *A Mogul Tale* implicitly sides with would-be reformers of the East India Company, even as its title parodies their fall from power: the educated mogul embodies Whig portraits of Indian culture, while the vulgar travelers parody the Company's lower-class factors and employees.

The play's topical appeal earned it a public hearing: George Colman, manager of Covent Garden, told Inchbald, "I wish to have the farce completed as soon as possible. The idea is droll, as well as temporary."[2] Inchbald's "idea" simply literalized a series of caricatures linking Indian affairs to the volatility of balloon travel. On December 4, 1783, for instance, W. Wells published an anonymous caricature entitled "The Political Balloon; or, the Fall of East India Stock" (plate 19). Recalling the excesses of the South Sea Bubble, the balloon caricature reframed Fox's reform bill as a vehicle for personal profit, one which toppled directors and functionaries from their own speculative heights of profit. Fox's India Bill was defeated on December 13th, the Fox–North coalition government was dismissed by the king on December 18th, and the "India Balloon" was well and truly punctured. A revised India Bill was passed only in July 1784 – the month in which *A Mogul Tale* had its debut.

The reception of the farce underscored its political allusions. One early reviewer, for instance, remarked that "[t]here are many laughable Circumstances to render this Farce agreeable; and among other Strokes, one at the Mogul's Officer, who the Cobler charges with having stole the Great Seal, which had a very good Effect."[3] The Great Seal had been stolen from the Chancellor's House on the night of March 23, 1784; parliament was supposed to have been dissolved on March 24th, but the theft of the seal, which was needed for the issuing of writs, delayed proceedings for a day. Since the theft seemed designed to slow down the dissolution of the Fox–North government, the action was generally attributed to Fox and his friends. The cobbler's accusation worked in part through its outlandishness – who could have stolen the seal? – and partly by equating Fox's friends with the mogul's chief eunuch. Enjoying Inchbald's jest and exploiting its popularity, the reviewer extended the metaphor to the trappings of the play: "The manager has bestowed (as indeed when does he not?) some excellent Scenery and very expensive

Plate 19 Anonymous, "The Political Balloon; or, the fall of East India Stock."
December 4, 1783.

Dresses, and it promises to afford much Pleasure to the Public, and we
hope it will likewise increase the Income of Mr. Colman's Treasury."[4] If
individual moments within the play took aim at Fox and his friends,
however, Inchbald's mogul more generally dramatized the reformers'
support for Indian self-government. In 1783, for instance, the Whig
Annual Register, a mouthpiece for the views of Burke and Fox, had
described one indigenous ruler in glowing terms:

Hyder Ally . . . establish[ed] so mild and equitable a system of government in
his dominions, that the new subjects of so many countries were not only
attached to his person in a most extraordinary degree, but the neighbouring
nations shewed on every occasion their wishes to come under his protection . . .
He might profitably have been considered as one of the first politicians of his
day, whether in Europe or in Asia.[5]

Inchbald's mogul is an equally wise and mild ruler. A philosopher who
is up to date with the recent French discovery of ballooning, he plays the
oriental despot simply to see how these Europeans will respond: "I mean
to save their lives, yet I want to see the effect of their fears; for I love to
contemplate that greatest work of Heaven, the mind of man!"[6] In his
cultural curiosity, the mogul mirrors French and British *philosophes*; in his
plotting, he seems rather to mimic the English playwright, Elizabeth
Inchbald.

Inchbald uses the mogul and his court to criticize English views of
national virtue: paranoia and vice structure the farce of national identity. The mogul's aide suggests to three terrified Englishmen a strategy
of hyperbolic self-representation – he introduces the doctor as an
ambassador from the British king, and the cobbler Johnny Atkins as the
Pope – and the characters' inept performances produce broad farce.
The doctor, for instance, offers only a parodic replication of imperial
grandeur:

The King, my master, is, by the Grace of God, King of Great Britain, France,
Ireland, Scotland, Northumberland, Lincolnshire, Sheffield, Birmingham –
giver of all green, Blue, Red, and pale Blue Ribbons, Sovereign of the most sur-
prising Order of the Bath, Sovereign of the most noble Order of St. Patrick –
Grand Master of every Mason Lodge in Christendom, Prince of the River
Thames, Trent, Severn, Tyne, New-River, Fleet-Ditch, and the Tweed –
Sovereign Lord, and master of many loyal subjects, husband of one good wife,
and father of eighteen fine children. (16)

The mogul's aide furnished the doctor with this roll of credentials, so the
ludicrous turn from the sultan's territories to the English king's ribbons,
rivers, and ditches may be an Indian (and Inchbaldian) satire on good

"Farmer George." At the same time, however, dominion over France slides easily into the list, and the conclusion of these credentials replaces the 8,000 islands and 1,000 wives of the sultan with George III's one wife and eighteen children: imperial rule and sexual extravagance are both contained within the king's prolific English family. The doctor's ambassadorial travesty may also have banished worries over a different kind of masquerade. Indicting Hastings in 1788, Burke described the East India Company as "a State in disguise of a Merchant, a great public office in disguise of a Countinghouse" (*Writings and Speeches*, 6.283–84). Here, power disguises itself in humbler form, extending its range by stealth. Inverting these relations, Inchbald's farce dramatized the East India Company's farcical pretence to represent Great Britain in India as it more literally portrayed humble persons disguising themselves as figures of state in order to preserve their lives.

Inchbald's mogul, for his part, satisfies the colonial narcissism of English audiences. Pronouncing judgment on the three invaders, the mogul first presents himself as the bogeyman of the European imagination: "Keep silence, while I pronounce judgment. – Tremble at your approaching doom! You are not now before the tribunal of a European, a man of your own colour. I am an Indian, a Mahometan; my laws are cruel and my nature savage!" While the audience has been privileged to see beyond this performance, the characters take this paranoiac vision at face value, producing the farcical spectacle of Englishmen deluded by their own fears and an Indian's ironic self-presentation. The mogul then sketches his own ostensible reform in language redolent of European missionaries: "[K]now that I have been taught mercy and compassion for the sufferings of human nature, however differing in laws, temper and colour from myself. Yes, from you christians, whose laws should teach charity to all the world, have I learnt these virtues!" Here, characters and audience alike are tempted to believe. Yet the mogul's closing lines rapidly invert this picture of reform, and the ideal of Christian English virtue it supports: "Your countrymen's cruelty to the poor Gentoos has shown me tyranny in so foul a light, that I have determined henceforth to be only mild, just, and merciful . . . You are too much in my power to be treated with severity – all three may freely depart!" (24–25). The mogul learns not from Christian benevolence, but from the negative mirror of Christian tyranny; the audience is invited to learn in turn from the ethical model of the mogul-philosopher. In *A Mogul Tale*, colonial narcissism requires the abjection of British vice and folly in order for the audience to maintain its identification with Enlightenment (oriental) benevolence.

Inversion defines the politics of *A Mogul Tale*: Christianity and British imperialism are unveiled as tyranny, while the oriental despot appears as a gentle ruler. Such inversions do not, however, apply to gender. The *Tale* opens with the women of the seraglio arguing over their standing in the mogul's favor – an image of sexual oppression unaltered by the mogul's modern philosophy. Indeed, Inchbald seems to present sexual inequity in eastern culture as more essential than constructed. The intoxicated Johnny is happy to court any of the "soul-less" women of the seraglio, yet he unerringly (and unknowingly) selects Fanny as his favorite of them all, as if she were indeed the only one to possess (an English) spirit. Joyce Zonana's account of feminist orientalism seems especially apt here: an underlying assumption of gender superiority licenses Inchbald's farcical critique of British nationalism and imperialism. Yet Inchbald's treatment of gender also sharpens her critique of English exploitation. Johnny, for instance, tries to use the "Muslim" belief that women have no souls as a strategy of seduction: "But if you have no soul, you have a pretty body, a very pretty body, – that I do assure you; – and I am a sweet soul, and what is a body good for without a soul?" When the Muslim Irene counters by asking, "Have your countrymen souls?," Johnny can only asssert "They have a great deal of spirit" (19). Englishmen have (or perhaps imbibe) a great deal of spirit – but this does not necessarily entitle them to the claim of a soul.

At other moments, the mimicry of *A Mogul Tale* draws attention to the gap between ideal and reality back in England: here, too, women bear the brunt of the discrepancy. The lament for home at the center of the farce, for instance, develops an ideal of bourgeois domesticity undercut in the very process of its presentation:

JOHN. Oh, Fan, Fan! if we were but once at Wapping again, mending of
    shoes, in our little two pair back room – with the bed just turned up on
    one side –
FANNY. My Johnny and I sitting so comfortable together at breakfast, and
    pawning your waistcoat to get it; with one child crying on my knee, and
    one on yours; my poor old mother, shaking with the ague, in a corner of
    the room, and the cat and dog fighting in the other. Oh, Johnny! the
    many happy mornings that we have got up together quaking with the
    cold! – No balloon to vex us –
JOHN. Ay, and the many times, after threshing you well, Fan, when we kissed
    and made it up again – (18)

As this English couple nostalgically insists "There's no place like home," their nostalgia merely highlights the sufferings of working-class domesticity. Their longed-for domestic space is cramped and invaded by labor;

poverty, tears, illness, and physical abuse represent the ideal of family intimacy. The working-class cobbler family mimics and thus parodies the bourgeois construction of domestic peace and love. While both husband and wife comically idealize their material constraints, Fanny's account sketches their farcical sufferings much more vividly. Johnny's loose syntax, meanwhile, turns his beating of Fanny into a communal project: "we" both "thresh . . . you" before kissing and making up. If the domestic relations of John and Fanny Atkins remain far from any bourgeois ideal, Fanny herself appears complicit in her husband's abuse of her. Both in the sultan's court and in working-class England, women seem content with their state of oppression: their contentment at once underwrites and highlights the inequities it ostensibly ignores.

II

A Mogul Tale played off eighteenth-century associations of farce with vulgar or working-class characters. In *Such Things Are*, however, Inchbald broadened her social scope, mingling the conventions of farce with those of romance, and (like Samuel Foote and David Garrick before her) deploying a farcical mimicry of famous men. Such mimicry was no respecter of social boundaries: indeed, it seemed to vulgarize whomever it attacked. Mimicry, itself a low form, exposed men of all classes to debasement through ridicule. Following the model set by Garrick and Foote, Inchbald's *Such Things Are* moved beyond the class assumptions of farce to use mimicry against characters at all levels of society. Yet even as Inchbald's use of mimicry intensified and extended the social (and critical) range of *Such Things Are*, her mixed drama attempted to move beyond farce to offer a model of positive colonial relations. The attempt to replace mimicry with benevolent despotism led to the mimic replications of farce (here, a repeated splitting or doubling of identity) and to the self-conscious performance of a benevolence dependent on the linked yet divided pairs of romance and farce, actor and spectator, master and slave.

Inchbald's preface to *Such Things Are* presents it as a *drame-à-clef* with a divided plot, based on the moral polarity of two famous men: Lord Chesterfield, whose posthumously published *Letters to his Son* were simultaneously a scandal and a best-seller; and John Howard, a prison reformer famous for his philanthropy both in England and abroad. The farcical character Twineall displays the absurdities of Chesterfield's cynical self-interest, while Haswell represents the opposing virtues of Howard's active benevolence as he traveled through Europe and Asia:

As Haswell is the hero of the serious part of this play, so is Twineall of the comic half. His character and conduct is formed on the plan of Lord Chesterfield's finished gentleman . . . [T]he public appeared to be as well acquainted with [Chesterfield's] despicable reputation, as with the highly honourable one of Howard.[7]

The farcical plot of *Such Things Are* focuses on relations among a British expatriate community, where the practice of shipping unmarried women to the colonies to find husbands results in the on-going marital skirmishes of Sir Luke and Lady Tremor, skirmishes complicated by the attentions of Lord Flint, an upper-class tool of local tyranny. The cycle of the marriage market repeats itself (with better results, presumably) in the more sentimental courtship of Elvirus and Aurelia, though their romance is complicated by the imprisonment of Elvirus's father for rebellion against the sultan. Twineall, newly arrived from England, attempts to manipulate this corrupt and imperfect society for his personal gain, and is nearly executed for his pains. In contrast to this farcical background, the sentimental plot of the comedy highlights the plight of the sultan, an oriental despot *malgré lui*, and his lost and much-lamented European wife. Haswell the savior serves as a lynchpin between the two plots, providing a model of virtue for the British as he labors to reform native abuses of power.

Even to begin with, however, the play's farcical response to Chesterfield is far more complicated and ambivalent than the preface would suggest. Within *Such Things Are*, Twineall performs in exaggerated fashion the various social sins against which Chesterfield attempted to warn and school his son. By contrast, Lord Flint displays a mixture of selfish policy, subservience to foreign despotism and manipulation of women: the worst traits Chesterfield's letters were thought to develop. The figure of Chesterfield within the play is thus split into a version of performance that undoes itself, and a more cynical performance that undoes others. Twineall's mimicry of Chesterfield produces farce, but the connection between this broad comedy and Lord Flint's more dangerous performance remains visible only to those already familiar with Chesterfield's system.

Chesterfield warns his son against dressing badly, muttering, and flattering by system or report; Twineall, by acting in contradiction to each of these warnings, suggests the validity rather than the folly of Chesterfield's advice. Chesterfield emphasizes the importance of first impressions, insisting that "A man of sense . . . dresses as well, and in the same manner, as the people of sense and fashion of the place where he is."[8] Yet Twineall first appears on the stage in a "fashionable undress" so *outré* that Sir Luke feels it necessary to inform Lady Tremor that "that is a gentleman, notwithstanding his appearance" (14–15). Worried over reports that his son muttered and spoke indistinctly, Chesterfield wrote attacking "the modern art *de persifler*" which "consists in picking out some grave, serious man, who neither understands nor expects raillery, and talking to him very quick, and in inarticulate sounds" (*Letters*, 1.90). Twineall exaggerates this "art" into a principle of evasive discourse:

> when a gentleman is asked a question which is either troublesome or improper to answer, he does not say he won't answer it, even though he speaks to an inferior; but he says, "Really it appears to me o-e-e-e-e – [*Mutters and shrugs.*] – that is – mo-mo-mo-mo-mo – [*Mutters.*] – if you see the thing – for my part – te-te-te-te – and that's all I can tell about it at present." (17)

Finally, while Chesterfield endeavors to teach his son the art of flattery, he carefully limits the practice of this art. Flattery, for Chesterfield, requires intensive knowledge of the world and of the people one would flatter: flattery becomes the art of social recognition. Twineall attempts to learn the world by description and to flatter by report. He asks Meanwright for intelligence of the Tremors and Flint: "Come, give me all their characters – all their little propensities – all their whims – in short, all I am to praise, and all I am to avoid praising, in order to endear myself to them" (23). Chesterfield would think Twineall's near-execution a just reward for this laziness, this unwillingness to learn his part. Twineall's flattery is deficient not only in preparation but also in execution: while Chesterfield warns against systematic or criminal flattery, Twineall practices both. In direct contradiction of Chesterfield's maxim ("flatter nobody's vices or crimes: on the contrary, abhor and discourage them" [*Letters*, 1.29]), Twineall boasts to Meanwright, "I will myself, undertake to praise the vices of a man of sentiment, till he shall think them so many virtues" (25). And Twineall's application of flattery is as indiscriminate as that of the system-monger Chesterfield attacks: "he daubs and besmears the piece he means to adorn. His flattery offends even his patron; and is almost too gross for his mistress" (*Letters*, 1.334–35). For Chesterfield as well as Inchbald, Twineall would provide a model of how *not* to behave.

Lord Flint, by contrast, displays the darker side of the nobleman's social cynicism. First mentioned for his manners and "*politesse*" (far more successful than Twineall's bungling), he nonetheless exhibits another of Chesterfield's pet peeves: in company, Flint, like the nobleman's son, is "frequently most PROVOKINGLY inattentive, absent, and distrait" (Chesterfield, *Letters*, 1.212). Flint's repeated distraction while in company confirms his contempt for those around him. As Sir Luke notes,

though he forgets his appointments with his tradesmen, did you ever hear of his forgetting to go to court when a place was to be disposed of? Did he ever make a blunder, and send a bribe to a man out of power? Did he ever forget to kneel before the prince of this island, or to look in his highness's presence like the statue of patient resignation, in humble expectation? (11)

Flint's contempt for English company is presented partly as a result of his upbringing. As Chesterfield sent his son to become familiar with the various courts of Europe, so Flint, "[s]ent from his own country in his very infancy, and brought up in the different courts of petty arbitrary princes here in Asia, . . . is the slave of every rich man, and the tyrant of every poor one" (11). Flint aspires to the powers of despotism for himself; he acts as the sultan's agent of surveillance in order to deal in decisions of life and death. Hearing that Twineall has insulted Lady Tremor, he responds that Twineall "is a disaffected person – boldly told me he doubted the Sultan's right to the throne. – I have informed against him; and his punishment is left to my discretion. I may have him imprisoned, shot, sent to the gallies, or his head cut off – but which does your lady-ship choose? – Which ever you choose is at your service [*Bowing*]" (53). Yet while Flint appears to give the decision over to Lady Tremor, she promptly hands it back to him, and Flint himself chooses execution as Twineall's fate. Indeed, Flint's apparent deferral to her opinion merely enacts Chesterfield's advice on how to win women's adoration: "being justly distrustful that men in general look upon them in a trifling light, [women] almost adore that man who talks more seriously to them, and who seems to consult and trust them; I say, who seems; for weak men really do, but wise ones only seem to do it" (*Letters*, 1.107). Unfortunately, Flint is neither wise nor weak; in his ability to influence as well as enact despotic power, he presents the dangers implicit in the social cynicism of Chesterfield's *Letters*.

Inchbald presents Chesterfield, split into the opposite figures of Flint and Twineall, as a negative model of masculine social performance. Yet naming Twineall alone as the figure for Chesterfield distracts attention from the subtler dangers of Flint: a spectator would need substantial familiarity with the *Letters* to recognize that the figure of Flint actually offers the critique of the *Letters* supposedly embodied in Twineall. The doubling of Chesterfield within the play may be designed to appeal to separate audiences: one which is able to interpret only broad farce, the other better read, if not more politically astute and socially discerning. Yet in any case, these figures of farce, paranoid and self-parodic, appear largely as a counterpoint to the performance of radical benevolence idealized in Haswell. Self-divided even in its duplicity, Inchbald's farcical plot increasingly verges on the serious.

With Haswell, Inchbald attempts to step outside the limits of farce. The play proposes Howard/Haswell's active benevolence as a real-life alternative to despotic injustice. Yet by representing Howard's benevolence on stage, *Such Things Are* begins to unravel the opposition it ostensibly creates between Chesterfield's hypocritical performance and Howard's sincere benevolence. The demands of theatre and the ubiquity of performance begin to infect and affect the ideal of manly sensibility with mimic duplicity. To maintain the distinction between performance and manly sensibility, Haswell must remain free of theatre, and so cannot call attention to his own performance of benevolence. As a result, however, benevolence as a performance, an "act" of virtue, is split into two parts within the world of the play: charity exists only when registered by a spectator or recipient. The sultan himself defines Haswell's virtue by report:

They tell me, that in our camps you visited each sick man's bed, administered yourself the healing draught, encouraged our savages with the hope of life, or pointed out their better hope in death. – The widow speaks your charities, the orphan lisps your bounties, and the rough Indian melts in tears to bless you. (44–45)

The hero's sensibility speaks not *in propria persona*, but through the figures of widows, orphans, savages, and observers: more than one person is required for its representation.

More ominously, the play's ideal of benevolence seems most clearly performed in an exchange between Haswell and the "tawny Indian" Zedan – an exchange which articulates quite clearly the roles of master and slave. As Haswell visits the prison, Zedan picks his pocket and steals his purse. Yet when Haswell, unaware of the theft, offers Zedan his pity and a pittance with which to relieve his immediate needs, Zedan's conversion is instantaneous. Returning the wallet, he articulates the power of benevolence: "'Tis something that I never felt before – it makes me like not only you, but all the world besides. – The love of my family was confined to them alone – but this sensation makes me love even my enemies" (34). Inchbald's biographer James Boaden described this scene as the climax of the drama:

Nature in a moment bursts through the villany [*sic*] which slavery had taught her; he throws himself upon his knees before Haswell, and with convulsive emotion restores the pocket-book. The effect was electric. Fearon [the actor], a rough but valuable man, struck it by his action into every heart; and Mrs. Inchbald must have trembled under the severe delight of applause that never was exceeded in a theatre.[9]

In the "electric" process of representation, benevolence splits into the linked figures of benefactor and recipient, explicitly aligned with the imperial pairing of master and slave. Haswell eventually secures Zedan's release, and the Indian comes to thank him and bid him farewell. Explaining that he departs only because he has "a family in sorrow till [his] return," Zedan insists that otherwise, "you [Haswell] should be my master, and I would be your slave" (76–77). The performance of benevolence paradoxically produces the figure of the willing slave: an oxymoron to which we (and Inchbald) will return. It may be worth noting, however, that this explicit statement of colonial relations made reviewers uncomfortable: a critic for the *Public Advertiser*, generally praising the play, nonetheless complained that "the thanks of the prisoner Zedan, at times prompted us to say 'somewhat too much of this.'"[10]

The master–slave performance of benevolence provides a dubious model for colonial reform. When, in colonial encounters, "a disembodied notion of cultural exchange merges 'love' [benevolence] with 'fear and loathing' [slavery]" this creates "a historical context where nationalism is synonymous with terror" (Suleri, *Rhetoric of English India*, 4). *Such Things Are* simultaneously domesticates and disavows that terror. If benevolence is performed through the relation of master and slave, *English* benevolence establishes itself as master over oriental despotism: Haswell's benevolence makes him nominal master not only of the tawny Indian Zedan, but also of the sultan himself. Haswell's Christian virtue calls forth from the sultan the confession of having once been a Christian himself, converted by his European wife. This confession rapidly becomes the fulcrum on which the sultan's life and the plot of the play together turn; he describes his Arabella as

a lovely European, sent hither in her youth, by her mercenary parents, to sell herself to the prince of all these territories. But 'twas my happy lot, in humble life, to win her love, snatch her from his expecting arms, and bear her far away; where, in peaceful solitude we lived, till, in the heat of the rebellion against the late Sultan, I was forced from my happy home to take a part. – I chose the imputed rebels' side, and fought for the young aspirer. – An arrow, in the midst of the engagement, pierced his heart; and his officers, alarmed at the terror this stroke of fate might cause among their troops, urged me (as I bore a strong resemblance to him,) to counterfeit a greater still, and show myself to the soldiers as their king recovered. I yielded to their suit, because it gave me ample power to avenge the loss of my Arabella, who had been taken from her home by the merciless foe, and barbarously murdered. (45–46)

This story, the secret heart of the sentimental comedy, establishes the sultan's despotism as a result of absence rather than presence: this counterfeit sultan's vengeance records the empty and thwarted domestic longings of romance (his desire for Arabella) rather than a will to power in its own right. Through this revelation, however, the omnipotent sultan stands revealed as a cipher, split between East and West: the inscrutability of oriental vengeance becomes remarkably difficult to distinguish from the internalized role of the devoted (westernized) husband. Romance unveiled replicates some of the internal divisions associated with farce.

Haswell offers a verbal performance of benevolence as comfort and cure to those internal divisions. He proposes to treat the sultan's dis-ease by further Anglicizing him, completing his domestication through the experience of benevolence.

SULTAN. What medecine will you apply?
HASWELL. Lead you to behold the wretched in their misery, and then show
    you yourself in their deliverer. – I have your promise for a boon – 'tis
    this: – give me the liberty of six whom I shall name, now in confinement,
    and be yourself a witness of their enlargement. – See joy lighted in the
    countenance where sorrow still has left its rough remains – behold the
    tear of rapture chase away that of anguish – hear the faultering voice,
    long used to lamentation, in broken accents utter thanks and blessings! –
    Behold this scene, and if you find the prescription ineffectual, dishonour
    your physician. (46–48)

Haswell's description reinstalls the sultan as master over slaves, but shows that mastery performed through deliverance and liberation. Within the logic of the play, the sultan's power to imprison is really impotence, for it keeps him from his heart's desire, the recovery of his European wife. For eastern rulers to gain real power, the play suggests they must become, like English gentlemen, exemplars of the hidden mastery of benevolence.

Ironically, Haswell as doctor and master of benevolence proposes to stage a *scene* of sentimentality: one which he anticipates in this verbal performance of tears and rapture. Inviting this patient to see himself in the role of deliverer, he asks the sultan simultaneously to occupy that role and stand outside it . Haswell's prescription of benevolence thus replaces one split subjectivity (native/Christian) with a slightly different mode of self-division. The splitting of despotic power into the actor/spectator of benevolence turns the antitheatrical ideal of virtue back into the kind of performance Chesterfield himself could espouse on the grounds of self-interest: "But am I blamable if I do a good action, upon account of the happiness which that honest consciousness will give me? Surely not" (*Letters*, 1.106). Haswell, urging the theatrical pleasures of benevolence on the sultan, sounds surprisingly like Chesterfield himself.

In Haswell's influence over the sultan we see "a complex strategy of reform, regulation and discipline, which 'appropriates' the Other as it visualizes power" (Bhabha, *Location of Culture*, 86). Yet Haswell's benevolent despotism also mimics the power it pretends to appropriate, developing into a model of moral surveillance and potential oppression. During the minor episode in which Elvirus masquerades as a Mr. Glanmore to hide his illicit courtship of Aurelia, Haswell sternly questions both partners in deception (i.e., "Why do you blush, Aurelia?" [56]). He proceeds to discipline Elvirus by playing on the son's fears for his father – whose liberty remains at Haswell's "benevolent" disposal. The sultan and Haswell become increasingly difficult to distinguish, as do Haswell's and Flint's relations to power. As the saintly Englishman teaches the sultan to see his mastery at once transformed and maintained through the performance of benevolence, he also allows the audience or careful reader to see the absolute power associated with oriental despotism installed at the heart of the West's claim to civilized and social virtue. That lesson could be applied back to the show trial of the Hastings impeachment: the 1789 caricature entitled "Such things may be" presented Burke as just such a civilized (pseudo-clerical) despot (plate 20).[11]

The mimicry of *Such Things Are* cuts in two directions: if the sultan, like the mogul, seems a fitting example of Bhabha's mimic man, Haswell's benevolence also replicates the internal divisions and power relations of "oriental" despotism. The scene of benevolence performed by these two men concludes the sultan's romance of longing for his absent wife – but the resolution of romance depends upon the willing subjection of that missing woman. Indeed, the virtuous Arabella might be considered an inverted "mimic woman," demonstrating the extent to which the ideal English heroine is just barely distinguishable from the stereotype of slavish oriental femininity – and then only on racial grounds. At first a

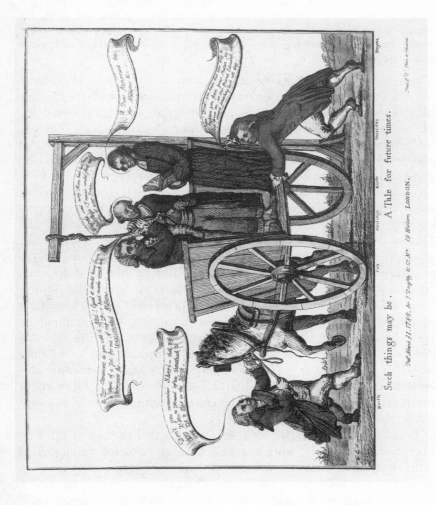

Plate 20 [P. J. Baldrey], "Such things may be. A Tale for future times." March 1, 1788.

generic female prisoner eager for freedom, Arabella rapidly resigns herself to continued imprisonment, telling Haswell,

When you first mentioned my release from this dark dreary place, my wild ideas included, with the light, all that had ever made the light a blessing. – 'Twas not the sun I saw in my mad transport, but a lost husband filled my imagination – 'twas his idea, that gave the colours of the world their beauty, and made me fondly hope to be cheered by its brightness . . . But in a happy world, where smiling nature pours her boundless gifts! oh! there his loss would be insupportable. (63)

This resignation – with its melancholy translation of the lost husband into the light of the world – also marks the moment at which the "female prisoner" of the play pronounces her own (European) name: Arabella. Haswell marks this transformation by "starting" and inquiring, "Are you a Christian? an European?" (63). In a much earlier scene, Arabella had rebuked Haswell for doubting her honesty, then apologized in racially coded terms: "Forgive me – I am mild with all these people – but from a countenance like yours – I could not bear reproach" (31). Despite her own racial pride, however, Arabella's race and religion remain imperceptible to other characters in the play until the closing action. She becomes visible as a Christian and a European in the moment she resigns herself to slavery. Brought before the sultan, whom she fails to recognize as her husband, Arabella explains to him that freedom without his companionship is a meaningless term: "were I free in this vast world, forlorn and friendless, 'tis but a prison still" (70). The sultan's identity once revealed, Arabella changes the context while retaining the concept of captivity: "[*Recovering*] Is this the light you promised? – [*To Haswell*] – Dear precious light! – Is this my freedom? to which I bind myself a slave for ever – [*Embracing the Sultan*] – Was I *your* captive? – Sweet captivity! more precious than an age of liberty!" (71). Life without her husband is a prison; life with him is sweet captivity: life without captivity appears unthinkable.

In *A Mogul Tale* Inchbald seemed to suggest that women of the East accept subjection and imprisonment because of some fundamental difference from western women; in *Such Things Are*, she shows a European woman embracing "eastern" captivity through marriage – and receiving general praise for her actions. A difficult moment to read, this sentimental resolution substitutes for the feminist orientalist equation of western men with eastern despots, the slightly different equation of western women with eastern subjection. Yet Inchbald balks at presenting on stage the figure of an Indian or Sumatran woman: the princess of this island can only be imagined as a European. The "oriental woman" remains obscure, inscrutable – literally invisible within the world of the play. As European women become defined by servitude and captivity (or vulgarity), East Indian women vanish entirely from the scene. Meanwhile, the mixed drama itself – mixing East and West as well as sentiment and farce – takes on the lineaments of femininity in the eyes of its beholders. The author of "Cursory Remarks on the New Play of 'Such Things Are,'" again in the *Public Advertiser*, made the connection explicit: "To speak briefly of this play, it may be compared to a woman, whom the painter, nor statuary can allow *true lines of beauty*, or *exact symmetry of shape*, yet she possesses a certain *je ne secai quoi* which is irresistible."[12]

III

Such Things Are and *Wives as They Were, Maids as They Are* stand separated by a decade of revolution and disillusionment, through which the intense and ultimately self-defeating scrutiny of the Hastings trial runs like a tangled thread. By the time Inchbald wrote *Wives as They Were, Maids as They Are*, the ideal of benevolence which gave *Such Things Are* its *raison d'être* had been undermined both by the Terror and by the excesses of the trial, with its use and abuse of the rhetoric of sensibility. During these years, Inchbald wrote two plays, two novels, and nine dramatic translations or adaptations, largely from the French. Despite the gap in time and sensibility between the two plays, I want to argue that *Wives/Maids* complements the earlier drama in political terms. *Such Things Are* uses colonial settings and characters to present opposing models of male conduct; *Wives as They Were, Maids as They Are* invokes the metaphor of antiquity (linked to the oppressions of the *ancien régime*) in order to develop a rather different conduct book for women. While *Such Things Are* offers an ambivalent critique of Chesterfield's *Letters*, *Wives as They Were, Maids as They Are* develops a revisionary reading of Hannah Cowley's *Belle's Stratagem* and Inchbald's own *Simple Story*.[13] At the same time, in an attempt to (re)produce a workable ideal of British womanhood, Inchbald brings home to London and potentially to her audiences the farce (and prison) of colonialism. Approaching the domestic female conduct book of *Wives/Maids* through the male colonial conduct book of *Such Things Are* offers some fruitful "ways to reinsert 'imperial' into 'national' without reducing the two terms to a single category."[14] Inchbald's juxtaposition of gothic and sentimental modes of performance continues to produce split characters and doubled speech, but as the playwright gradually abandons the ideal of universal benevolence, she also complicates the figure of the willing slave which underwrote that ideal.

In adapting Cowley's hit comedy to her own devices, for instance, Inchbald translates the issue of national identity into historical terms. While Cowley's hero Doricourt enters the world of *The Belle's Stratagem* preferring continental beauties to plain English virtue, the masquerade plot of the comedy demonstrates to him and to the audience that an Englishwoman, though naturally modest and retiring, is worth far more than an Italian marquizina or a French coquette. Rather than engaging directly with Cowley's nationalistic plot, *Wives/Maids* positions its narrative within the doubled figure of its own title – wives as they *were*, and maids as they *are* – yet this temporal division reintroduces a colonial context. As we have seen, half of the doubled plot of *Wives/Maids* addresses the eventual reconciliation of a father returning to England with an Indian fortune and his wayward daughter, Miss Dorillon. The latter persists in gambling, rejecting eligible suitors but encouraging ineligible rakes, and quarreling with her disguised and unrecognized father. The other half of the plot focuses on Lord Priory's attempts to rule his wife according to the manners of antique simplicity – and the rakish Mr. Bronzely's attempts to seduce Lady Priory according to "modern" social norms. "Antique" manners are presented in Inchbald's play by a revised version of the *Belle's* subplot – but Inchbald's revision mingles the norms of the *ancien régime* with those of the eastern harem.

Where Cowley sketches the *joint* education of a newly-wed husband and wife – the husband must learn to temper his jealousy and the wife to forsake the dangers of society – Inchbald introduces her comic couple in terms of a one-way Miltonic education in domestic femininity:

In ancient days, when manners were simple and pure, did not wives wait at the table of their husbands? and did not angels witness the subordination? I have taught Lady Priory to practise the same humble docile obedience – to pay respect to her husband in every shape and every form – no careless inattention to me – no smiling politeness to others in preference to me – no putting me up in a corner – in all assemblies, she considers her husband as the first person. (12)

This allusion to the dinner party of *Paradise Lost*, where Eve waited on Adam and the angel Raphael, sets the burden of female subordination firmly in a frame of British culture as well as antique simplicity.[15] Yet Lord Priory's unabashed demand for female subordination strikes even his male companions within the play as remarkable – and he himself tries to moderate their expectations: "But don't expect a fine lady with high feathers, and the et caetera of an eastern concubine; you will see a modest plain Englishwoman, with a cap on her head, a handkerchief on her neck, and a gown of our own manufacture" (13). Where one might expect to find a reference to contemporary French fashion, Inchbald turns instead to the orientalism of the eastern concubine. In contrast to Cowley, Inchbald excludes the possibility of continental competition – and were it not for a throw-away comparison such as this, one might think British femininity existed in total domestic isolation. While Letitia Hardy of *The Belle's Stratagem* must demonstrate her ability to encompass the varied charms of continental womanhood, Inchbald's domestic comedy focuses on the transformation of Maria Dorillon from a "maid" into a wife like those of ancient days – a woman who, except for the simplicity of her dress, might be mistaken for an eastern concubine.

As we have seen, *Wives/Maids* reproduces the sultan's dungeons as a debtor's prison, an alteration which highlights the importance of economic constraint within the play. Inchbald's preface apologetically draws the reader's attention to the disgraceful vulgarity of this prison: "Had the punishment of the two fashionable women been inflicted by a less disgraceful means than a prison for debt, and had the singular conduct of Lord and Lady Priory been supported by occurrences as pleasantly singular, this might have ranked among some very deserving comedies" (4). Inchbald introduces these two faults of the play as instances of her own lack of imagination, a fact which suggests the impoverished realism of her sketch (such things are).[16] Thus she indirectly highlights the difficulty of imagining a less disgraceful way to punish two fashionable women – or providing occurrences sufficiently unusual to "support" the singular conduct of Lord and Lady Priory.

In *Wives/Maids*, the paranoia and narcissism which comprise sentimental colonial relations also constitute the relationship between father and daughter or husband and wife under the dispensations of antique simplicity. Sir William, for example, returns to England under a false name, the better to maintain surveillance over his daughter. His disguise is explicitly a defense against mimicry: "had I come at present as her father, she might have deceived me with counterfeit manners, till time disclosed the imposition. – Now, at least, I am not imposed upon" (9). The resistance to mimicry produces oppression: Mr. Norberry, a friend to both father and daughter, accuses Sir William of "rigour." Lord Priory's rigor toward his wife likewise demonstrates a kind of paranoia. As Mr. Bronzely points out to the nobleman, "you live in continual fear

– for (without meaning any offense to Lady Priory's honour) you know you dare not trust her for one hour alone with any man under sixty . . . You constantly follow all her steps, watch all she says and does" (51–52). While *Such Things Are* repeatedly eased colonialist fears by turning menace to mimicry, paranoia to narcissism, *Wives/Maids* shows fatherly and husbandly narcissism fuelling paranoia. Having been persuaded by Bronzely to let the bachelor woo his wife, Lord Priory exclaims to himself: "I am passionate – I am precipitate – I have no command over my temper. – However, if a man cannot govern himself, yet he will never make any very despicable figure as long as he knows how to govern his wife" (54). The impossibility of male self-governance is masked through a confusion of identity that produces, in Blackstone's famous formulation, man and wife as one person: the man.

As Inchbald metaphorically replicates the figure of the prison within the settings of *Wives/Maids*, she shows how such confusion can lead to a double-edged operation of power. Trying to win Lady Priory's sexual submission, for instance, Mr. Bronzely remarks upon the gothic attributes of his own home: "Lady Priory, you are in a lonely house of mine, where I am sole master, and all the servants slaves to my will . . . [D]o not you fear me?" (64). The answer is a resounding "no." Of the three women in the play, Lady Priory best understands how to deal with such a prison and its threats. Having calmly taken out her knitting, she articulates a female defense based on the fears and limits of male dominance:

LADY PRIORY. No – for your fears will protect me – I have no occasion for mine.

MR. BRONZELY. What have I to fear?

LADY PRIORY. You fear to lounge no more at routs, at balls, at operas, and in Bond Street; no more to dance in circles, chat in side-boxes, or roar at taverns: for you have observed enough upon the events of life to know – that an atrocious offence, like violence to a woman, never escapes condign punishment.

MR. BRONZELY. Oh! for once let your mind be as feminine as your person – hear the vows – (65)

Lady Priory's mind lacks femininity because it remains unyielding: she sees with sometimes brutal clarity the benefits and liabilities of her own position – as well as the fears, both physical and social, that define and delimit male dominance. Unswayed by romance, she sees the farcical underside of seduction as clearly as the tyranny that more generally defines a woman's role in society.

Such Things Are presents benevolence as a strained resolution for the contradictions of colonialism; *Wives/Maids* attempts to resolve the inequities of domestic relations by turning to various unsatisfactory models of law and government. In particular, the language of the law court offers Miss Dorillon a temporary victory in her struggle for self-governance. When her father, disguised as Mr. Mandred, attempts to further Sir George's romantic aspirations, Maria replies in playful legalese:

To fit you for the tender task of advocate in the suit of love, have you ever been admitted an honourable member of that court? Have you, with all that solemn wisdom of which you are master, studied Ovid, as our great lawyers study Blackstone? If you have – show cause – why plaintiff has a right to defendant's heart.

Maria insists that the case of romantic love be as carefully argued as a law brief: more specifically, as a dispute over possession. Sir William naturally misses the point, as he takes for granted that "A man of fortune, of family, and of character, ought at least to be treated with respect and with honour." He considers the case strictly from the man's perspective, as his daughter is quick to note, though without disputing the point:

You mean to say, "That if A is beloved by B, why should not A be constrained to return B's love?" Counsellor for defendant – "Because, moreover, and besides B, who has a claim on defendant's heart, there are also C, D, E, F, and G; all of whom put in their separate claims – and what, in this case, can poor A do? She is willing to part and divide her love, share and share alike; but B will have all, or none: so poor A must remain A, by herself, A."

"A" has no defense from constraint by "B" – except for the similar attempts by C, D, E, F, and G to constrain her. Sir George, who remains a cipher within the play, no more than a man of fortune, family, and character, breaks in at this point to assert a claim to sole possession ("Do you think I would accept a share of your heart?") but Miss Dorillon parries this claim with a reassertion of her own economic/emotional constraints: "Do you think I could afford to give it to you all?"[17] She closes the argument by reintegrating sentiment with the terms of exchange:

"Besides," says defendant's counsellor, "I will prove that plaintiff B has no heart to give defendant in return – he has, indeed, a pulsation on the left side; but as it never beat with any thing but suspicion and jealousy; in the laws of love, it is not termed, admitted, or considered – a heart." (26–27)

This complaint, as it articulates the paranoia and surveillance which define Sir William's actions, addresses itself as much to the father (speaking for the suitor) as to the less definite Sir George. The parallel points up the extent to which the father seems a jealous suitor within his own masquerading plot: jealous of Bronzely, he tries to shape Miss Dorillon to his own desires (specifically, nostalgic memories of her look-alike mother) as Lord Priory has done with his wife. Antique manners support patriarchy, the rule of the father: Sir George seems little more than a necessary intermediary for the on-going relationship between father and daughter.

Maria's wits win her only a temporary reprieve – perhaps because the language of law and government serves less to defend her rights than to define her subordination. After the reconciliation of father and daughter, Sir William offers Sir George his daughter in marriage. When Sir George looks to Miss Dorillon for a response, she (playfully?) rejects the match, and is promptly overruled by her father speaking for her:

SIR GEORGE. And may I hope, Maria –
MISS DORILLON. No – I will instantly put an end to all your hopes.
SIR GEORGE. How?
SIR WILLIAM. By raising you to the summit of your wishes. Alarmed at my severity, she has owned her readiness to become the subject of a milder government.
SIR GEORGE. She shall never repine at the election she has made. (77–78)

Sir William's language seems to suggest a passage from the severities of an *ancien régime* to a more moderate marital state; Sir George's response ironically credits Maria with the power of "election" – a radical notion indeed. In response, Lord Priory instantly urges a return to a more despotic domestic state, guarded against (i.e., constantly fearing) a rebellion. And Lady Priory's assertion that she has never wished for the abolition of domestic laws is emphasized by Lady Raffle's echo: "Any control, rather than have no chief magistrate at all" (78). What are we to make of this willing, even eager submission to male authority?

Like Arabella in *Such Things Are*, Lady Priory has already articulated the absence of real alternatives. In an earlier conversation with Bronzely and her husband, Lady Priory points out, however "timidly," that

LADY PRIORY. To the best of my observation and understanding, your sex, in respect to us, are all tyrants. I was born to be the slave of some of you – I make the choice to obey my husband.
LORD PRIORY. Yes, Mr. Bronzely; and I believe it is more for her happiness to be my slave, than your friend – to live in fear of me, than in love with you. Lady Priory, leave the room. (51)

Lord Priory of course misses the point his wife so carefully makes here: while a woman has no choice but to be a slave, she can nonetheless choose to undo her tyrannical husband. His power depends on her choice – a fact which Lord Priory recognizes only belatedly, and promptly forgets. Yet, as Lady Priory later explains to Mr. Bronzely, abandoning a husband remains a bad bargain for a woman:

MR. BRONZELY. If, then, you have ever harboured one wish to revenge and forsake a churlish ungrateful partner, never return to him more – but remain with me.

LADY PRIORY. And what shall I have gained by the exchange, when you become churlish, when you become ungrateful? My children's shame! the world's contempt! and yours! [*Smiling*] Come, come; you are but jesting, Mr. Bronzely! You would not affront my little share of common sense, by making the serious offer of so bad a bargain. Come, own the jest, and take me home immediately. (64)

Lady Priory repeats to Bronzely the same point she made earlier: women are necessarily slaves, as men are tyrants. In asking Bronzely to acknowledge the farce of his "modern chivalry," she also explains *why* she chooses to obey her husband: leaving him would bring shame on her children and earn contempt for herself – without materially changing her position of subordination.

Lady Priory does not go so far as to explain why women are necessarily slaves, but much of the comedy suggests that this state of servitude derives from an economic imbalance, constituting (as it were) a debtor's prison.[18] This economic imbalance plays itself out in rhetorical terms: while a man's word is as good as money, a woman's word is equivalent only to submission. Charging into the prison to release Lady Mary Raffle (by mistake), Sir George exclaims, "Madam, you are free – the doors of the prison are open – my word is passed for the – "(72). He stops short as he realizes his word has just been passed as currency to pay the wrong woman's debts. A woman's word, by contrast, is only indirectly related to financial resources. Thus, Maria could have recourse to Sir George's fortune to pay her debts – but only by exploiting "the weakness of a lover" – something she claims she is too proud to do. Sir William tries, unsuccessfully, to buy his daughter's word in exchange for her freedom from prison:

SIR WILLIAM. You must promise, solemnly promise, never to return to your former follies and extravagancies. [*She looks down*] Do you hesitate? Do you refuse? – Won't you promise?

MISS DORILLON. I would, willingly – but for one reason.

SIR WILLIAM. And what is that?

MISS DORILLON. The fear I should not keep my word.

SIR WILLIAM. You, will, if your fear be real.

MISS DORILLON. It is real – it is even so great, that I have no hope.

SIR WILLIAM. You refuse my offer, then, and dismiss me? [*Rises*]

MISS DORILLON. [*Rising also*] With much reluctance. – But I cannot, – indeed I cannot make a promise, unless I were to feel my heart wholly subdued, and my mind entirely convinced that I should never break it. (69)

Maria's word, like that of Lady Priory, is "[m]ost sacred" (37). Yet unlike Lady Priory, she retains sole control over her words, and her self, until she believes her father's welfare is at stake. Then, although cautioned by Mandred/Sir William to consider the difficulty of keeping a promise, she swears, "Exact what vow you will on this occasion, I will make and keep it" (71). The scene ends with Mr. Norberry's revelation of Sir William's true identity and Maria's collapse into a sentimental faint. We never learn what vow may have been exacted. Yet when father and daughter reappear, Sir William is firmly in control, speaking over his daughter and putting words in her mouth. Miss Dorillon now speaks the role that has been scripted for her. Asked by Sir George for a response to Lady Priory's and Lady Mary Raffle's willing submission to authority, Miss Dorillon responds with "Simply one sentence – A maid of the present day, shall become a wife like those – of former times" (78). The play ends by abolishing one of its two central figures (the maid of the present day) and thus apparently resolves the division which defines its title (Wives/Maids) into a single unified figure of "ancient" domesticity.

Yet resolving the division between wives as they were and maids as they are seems to produce a form of language or verbal performance which is itself split and doubled. Lady Priory, our exemplar for the wife of former times, speaks with a forked tongue throughout the play. Bronzely, in making an assignation with her, makes her swear to come alone and tell no one of their meeting. When he checks her earnestness in this matter ("Your word is sacred, I rely?") she replies, " Most sacred" (37). When Bronzely later complains of her husband's presence at the *rendezvous*, she explains, "I thought you understood I could have no secrets from my husband." And when Bronzely charges her with breaking a promise that "no one should know it but [her]self" she asserts, "He is myself" (50–51). Lady Priory twists language, her "most sacred" word, to her own uses in exposing Bronzely's seduction plot. Hannah Cowley's popular comedy delineated the shifting forms of a *Belle's Stratagem* to win a husband and his heart; Inchbald's comedy might have been named by contrast *The Wife's Stratagem*. The unmarried Miss Dorillon scorns policy and self-disguise (except perhaps before her father) – yet these are precisely the traits she must learn in order to perform with Lady Priory the "primitive manners" of ancient simplicity. The wife's stratagem is duplicity.

Lady Priory's speeches in the last scene demonstrate a similar self-division. Lord Priory asserts the value and integrity of his wife's word ("the tongue which, for eleven years, has never in the slightest instance deceived me") and then commands its obedient performance: "My dear wife, boldly pronounce, before this company, that you return to me with the same affection and respect, and the self-same contempt for this man – [*To* BRONZELY] – you ever had" (76). Lady Priory resists this command, declaring she does not hate Bronzely and remaining silent when urged to declare her love for her husband, though she is quick to acknowledge her fear of him. Implying that she has indeed fallen in love with Bronzely, she asserts, "But to preserve ancient austerity, while, by my husband's consent, I am assailed by modern gallantry, would be the task of a stoic, and not of his female slave" (77). Yet as soon as her husband registers his horrified belief in her statement, she returns to the role of "Wives as they were": it gives her "excessive joy" to hear her husband say he cannot doubt her word, "because you will not then doubt me when I add – that gratitude, for his restoring me so soon to you, is the only sentiment he has inspired" (77). While Lord Priory takes this as a validation of his "management," one might also note that in returning to the role of the ancient wife, Lady Priory redefines that role as stoicism rather than slavery. Like a stoic, she has resisted Bronzely's gallantry – a female slave presumably would have lacked the intellectual and moral resources she brings to bear on her situation. Her assertion that "not all the rigour" of her husband's domestic laws "has ever induced me to wish them abolished" should come as no surprise: the abolition of these laws leads back to the threat of separation and divorce – shame for her children and contempt for herself – while Lady Priory has already demonstrated her ability to use this legal rigor to her own stoical ends. When Miss Dorillon closes the play with the general claim that "A maid of the present day, shall become a wife like those – of former times," that assertion marks a new beginning, rather than an end to female self-division. The play invites women whose minds, like those of Miss Dorillon and Lady Priory, are something less than "feminine" to take a stoic's perspective on the fact of female slavery. This role of the slave as stoic might be said to anticipate Irigaray's model of gender as mimicry: "One must assume the feminine role deliberately. Which means already to convert a form of subordination into an affirmation, and thus to begin to thwart it."

My emphasis on stoicism and mimicry may seem a misreading of the last scene – in which, after all, the women pronounce themselves subdued to male dominion. Yet their pronounced submission itself marks the "despotism" of this romance of domesticity: the vanishing point which defines this version of romance is the notion of female identity or transparency. Miss Dorillon's vivid personality, for instance, seems to vanish in this last scene, leaving a gap which disrupts the promise of resolution-through-marriage. The title of the play likewise retains the tensions exhibited throughout *Wives as They Were and Maids as They Are*, suggesting an on-going tension between these two figures even after marriage.

The duplicity portrayed by the close of *Wives/Maids* and by the wife's stratagem throughout echoes the kind of internal division demanded of a playwright. For Elizabeth Inchbald, the mimicry produced by femininity, by theatre, and by political farce all seem to overlap: the servitude and captivity she repeatedly presents as women's lot mirrors the limitations she describes playwrights suffering under the despotic rule of state and audience. In an 1807 essay to *The Artist*, Inchbald contrasted the freedom of the novelist with the constraints of the playwright:

The Novelist is a free agent. He lives in a land of liberty, whilst the Dramatic Writer exists but under a despotic government. – Passing over the subjection in which an author of plays is held by the Lord Chamberlain's office, and the degree of dependence which he has on his actors – he is the very slave of the audience. He must have their tastes and prejudices in view, not to correct, but to humour them. Some auditors of a theatre, like some aforesaid novel-readers, love to see that which they have seen before; and originality, under the opprobrious name of innovation, might be fatal to a drama, where the will of such critics is the law, and execution instantly follows judgment.[19]

Like executions in the sultan's prisons, the audience's condemnation brooks no delay or leisurely reflection. Yet while Inchbald asserts that the author of a play "is the very slave of the audience," the series of prohibitions she goes on to list are for the most part prohibitions she herself has transgressed. In particular, she claims that "A dramatist must not speak of national concerns, except in one dull round of panegyrick" – yet as we have seen, she undertook in her first drama to mock and critique Anglo-Indian relations. The playwright's art, like the role of the "willing" female slave, uses mimicry to expose the extent and prevalence

of slavery. In making visible, through the repetition of dramatic structure, setting, and role, the cover-up of a possible operation of the feminine (or culturally Other) in language, Inchbald both draws on and
"takes off" the tropes of despotism, replicating the mesconnaissances of
"benevolent" colonial expansion on the stages of London, as they in
turn are asked to mirror (and mimic) the domestic spaces of the empire.
The influence of her work in the mixed realms of literature, theatre, and
politics has yet to be fully acknowledged.

Epilogue: what is she?

I would have these criticks only consider, when they object against [my play] as a tragedy, that I design'd it something of a comedy; when they cavil at it as a comedy, that I had partly a view to pastoral; when they attack it as a pastoral, that my endeavours were in some degree to write a farce; and when they would destroy its character as a farce, that my design was a tragi-comi-pastoral . . . Yet that I might avoid the cavils and misinterpretations of severe criticks, I have not call'd it a tragedy, comedy, pastoral, or farce, but left the name entirely undetermin'd in the doubtful appellation of the What d'ye call it.

John Gay, preface to *The What D'Ye Call It* (London: Lintot, 1716)

Gay's preface presents his explicit evasion and mingling of forms as a defense against literary critics; some eighty years later, Charlotte Smith's *What Is She?* (1799) suggested that a similar generic evasiveness might protect women against the social constraints mobilized through generic definitions of femininity. Charlotte Smith's mixed drama presents social existence as a conflict between different genres, each with its own sedimented forms of literary meaning and social experience.[1] Setting the absurdities of one ready-made text against those of another, Smith's comedy problematizes the relationship between generic convention and social life. Aligning the prose genres of the gothic novel and travel book with the social follies of the bourgeoisie and aristocracy respectively, *What Is She?* remains at once most heavily invested in and distinctly hostile toward a third genre: the novel of sentiment, with its concomitant marriage plot.

Smith at once sets the story of her heroine off from the vulgar "ready done" plots of the bourgeois gothic *and* embeds it within the strict conventionality of the ready made. When gothic novelist Mrs. Gurnet asserts, "I should like to hear your history. Nay, if you will, I'll write – four volumes, interspersed with pieces of poetry – call it translated from

230

the German – 'twill be delightful. I have a moonlight scene, a dungeon, and a jealous husband – all ready done," Mrs. Derville rejects this off-the-rack fictional frame – paradoxically, by embracing it: "[*Gaily*] Oh! my history, madam, is the history of every body; and for that reason, nobody would read it. [*Ironically*] 'Tis so common for men to be base, and women weak, that the vices of one sex, and the follies of the other, are subjects for jests and *bon mots* rather than history" (242). Throughout the play, Mrs. Derville insists there is nothing new in the history of romance. There is, for instance, "nothing unusual" in "a pair of idiots conspiring against the peace of their whole lives" by planning to marry (225). And when her would-be suitor claims to be seeking her advice about marriage to another, she covers her sense of hurt with a brisk summary: "I dare say now your uncle has discovered you have a fancy for some farmer's daughter – very young, very blooming, very silly, and very credulous, whom you will adore the first month, neglect the second, and abandon the third. – 'Tis all in the usual course of things – nothing extraordinary in it; and I wonder you should come to consult me about such trifles" (248). The tedious familiarity of the marriage plot destroys its claim to attention.

Yet the insidious power of the sentimental marriage plot reveals itself most clearly through the figure of Mrs. Derville herself: she falls victim to the cultural norms of sensibility as soon as she attempts to distinguish herself from the generic narrative she so readily recounts. The moment the sentimental heroine substantiates a claim to her own exemplary history, a history different from that of "everybody," she loses control of sentimental narratives in the play. The melancholy widow can maintain her biting observations on the miseries of marriage only as long as her own narrative remains buried in the obscurity of common experience. As soon as she is revealed as a full sentimental heroine – orphaned, widowed, cheated of part of her fortune by her dissolute husband, oppressed by an evil guardian – her desire for self-determination is dramatically subordinated to the patriarch's well-intentioned plotting: Mrs. Derville finds herself assigned as a husband her rather sorry and suspicious would-be suitor. Smith's drama does not go so far as to imply that this will be an unhappy match – but then the play has very little to say about the match at all. Having ostensibly answered the question "What is she?" by recourse to sentiment, the play leaps to the most rapid possible conclusion, one clearly out of the heroine's control, and quite possibly beyond the dramatist's as well.

In the introduction to this book, I tried to suggest that literary genre and political appeals to national identity take shape through a similar process of negotiation and collaboration. Charlotte Smith's *What Is She?* suggests that gender, or at least femininity, likewise takes shape according to the logic of genre. But Smith's mixed drama merely shows more clearly what the work of other female playwrights has already suggested. Hannah Cowley's *Belle* Letitia Hardy insists "I can be any thing," but that open range of possibilities exists only within the framework of her lover's desires ("I can be anything *you want*"), and her own actions teach her lover to desire only English femininity. Elizabeth Inchbald's Arabella appears, according to the expectations of her audience, one of two different dramatic stereotypes: the epitome of the oppressed oriental female, or the long-suffering but stalwart western wife. Mary Robinson's array of poetic personae – from Sappho to Tabitha Bramble, likewise suggest a range of generic possibilities for female performance: Robinson's refusal to limit herself to any one role highlights the conventionality of each. But the popularity of Emma Hamilton's "Attitudes" reminds us that mobility and change were themselves considered eminently feminine. As Hayley's *Triumphs of Temper*, upon which Hamilton partially modeled her own behavior, described its heroine: "She's everything by starts and nothing long." Mobility *per se* does not constitute an evasion of generic models of femininity.

Indeed, this book has tried to suggest that generic models of femininity, like fantasies of national unity, are impossible to evade altogether. According to Benedict Anderson, "[i]n the modern world everyone can, should, will 'have' a nationality, as he or she 'has' a gender." [2] I would argue that the parallel functions more closely than Anderson intended, and that genre, loosely considered, serves to articulate the link between these two modes of identification. In this way, particular genres – within this book, particular modes of theatre – at once enabled and encumbered Romantic women's participation in the nation, while at the same time the nation might be said to have shaped itself upon different generic notions of sexual relations.

The first section of this book worked to reconstruct the performative politics shaping the public woman and her role in England's national romance. A handful of plays constructed as dramatic romances used prominent female actresses to embody the attractions of the state; those female bodies could also be used to represent what must be abjected from the state: the illusions of theatre, the cunning of subordinated people, the material needs underlying national ideologies. Mary "Perdita" Robinson and Emma Hamilton both relied on revisionary autobiography in crafting their public personae and as a result modeled a very different version of national identity: one more closely associated with a prose romance mingling of history and fantasy than with chapbook tales, the romance revival or the more constraining elements of dramatic romance. As these women performers drew on romance motifs in their lives and work, they mobilized the popular nationalist appeal of romance: Hamilton's affair with Nelson was an integral though generally depreciated part of his fame; the nicknames of "Perdita" and "Florizel" aspired to a certain sexual and national innocence that pamphleteers worked hard to correct. Yet the (temporary) political influence Hamilton and Robinson gained also raised questions about the shape of national romance and the limits of gender. Could romance be good if it allowed "dissolute" women to participate in power? Should the romance of nation include an active role for women at all?

Perhaps because these questions had already been engaged at least superficially by the romance revivalists and their literary musings, they seemed to invite a *pro tem* resolution through recourse to genre and generic distinctions. The backlash against Mary Robinson and later against Emma Hamilton reenclosed both women within the sequential logic of dramatic romance, according to which actresses were first privileged as an embodiment of the nation, only to be exiled from the nation they once represented, or clearly subordinated within it. The reaction against Robinson and Hamilton recast both women not as heroines of romance but as players of farce; in the process, they were reconceived not as ladies, but as prostitutes and the most vulgar of women. Yet the challenge posed to romance nationalism by women and performance was never fully vanquished: women performers remained on the scene as necessary opponents *and* companions to the romance of national destiny.[3] Thus the national "romance" developed by revivalists and expanded by poets such as Southey, Wordsworth, and Coleridge was above all a compromise formation, working to exploit the popularity of chapbook and heroic romance, while attempting to discipline the (feminine) excess and (working-class) naïveté of these popular forms.

The second half of this book tried to unravel the paradoxical mixed drama of sentiment and farce – a form in which women dramatists were able to engage the national issues of their day. Ironically, female dramatists like Hannah Cowley and Elizabeth Inchbald participated in the public debates of their time *by emphasizing* the domesticity and proper femininity of their subject matter. When parliament and public opinion debated the wisdom of defending Turkey against the Russian empress,

Hannah Cowley (surely tongue in cheek) replaced the prevalent images of a sexually voracious, monstrously large empress with a chaste and beautiful woman whose virtue made everyone, even a Turkish pashaw, want to help her. Her "advertisement" to the play nonetheless disclaimed all political intent. Likewise, Elizabeth Inchbald's most explicitly orientalist dramas were written during times of national debate over England's Indian empire: *A Mogul Tale* in 1784, with Fox's fall from power upon the defeat of his East India Bill still vivid, and *Such Things Are* in 1787, toward the end of the Hastings impeachment. Yet at least superficially, both plays were as concerned with social fashions as with political policies: *A Mogul Tale* staged the fad of hot-air ballooning as well as the stereotypical orientalist harem; the title of *Such Things Are*, while eventually applied to political caricature, might rather have been drawn from a purely social satire of sartorial excesses. *Wives as They Were, Maids as They Are* (1797), Inchbald's most successful comedy, was also one of her least explicitly political full-length plays, though it examined the financial, domestic, and emotional prisons within which women were forced to operate. Replicating Lady Priory's duplicity, the plays of Cowley and Inchbald take political stands in the act of disavowing politics; the female dramatist participates in politics through an overdone performance of innocent restraint.

As the theatrical modes of romance and mixed drama enabled different kinds of female participation in the British nation, they also showed the nation potentially shaping itself around different fantasies of sexual difference and sexual relations. In *Nationalism and Sexuality*, George Mosse argues that respectability or "middle-class morality" joined forces with nationalism in the late eighteenth and early nineteenth centuries to control broader social changes, "the ever more obvious results of industrialization and political upheaval."[4] The "sexuality" of Mosse's title thus registers a restraint on passion: "Nationalism helped control sexuality, yet also provided the means through which changing sexual attitudes could be absorbed and tamed into respectability. In addition, it assumed a sexual dimension of its own, coming to advocate a stereotype of supposedly 'passionless' beauty for both men and women" (10). National symbols like Britannia and Germania served as guardians of the nation's continuity, immutability, and respectability – but they also modeled for the nation's citizens a mode of inhabiting their physical bodies: "Men and women who rediscovered their bodies saw them taken away again, spiritualized and aestheticized, treated as national symbols of strength and beauty" (Mosse, *Nationalism and Sexuality*, 183).

In many ways, sentimental drama embodied on stage the "respect-ability" emphasized in Mosse's account; romance offered a much more licentious fantasy of national union, while mixed drama exposed senti-mental morality's reliance on the sexually coded despotism it supposedly had conquered. Within the mode of romance nationalism, public women like Hamilton and Robinson seemed to embody the nation through their perceived promiscuity: a model of public union which raised fears about infection, impotence, and prostitution operating within the body public. Anderson has argued that nationalism is experi-enced as a "deep, horizontal comradeship," also called a "fraternity": stage romance wondered aloud where women might fit within this fra-ternity. Hamilton and Robinson were both portrayed as articulating through sex the connections among men of national importance: Robinson linked the prince, the opposition leader and a military hero; Hamilton united Britain's ambassador to Naples with her greatest naval hero. This licentious national romance, while presenting women strictly as sexualized objects, nonetheless allowed for horizontal, or largely equal relationships between men and women, as opposed to the vertical rela-tions of explicit subordination. Unsurprisingly, perhaps, this particular vision of the nation evoked a whole complex of sexualized fears and dis-gusts: Robinson was accused of infecting the prince with pox *and* of profiting financially from her politically charged love affairs. More omi-nously, perhaps, caricatures showed both Hamilton and Robinson dom-inating their lovers. *The Rambler* had envisioned Robinson's affair with the prince in terms of England's loss of colonial power, with Robinson insisting on her financial and political independence before she would satisfy the royal will. Likewise, the size of Gillray's "Dido" completely overshadowed the figure of Sir William in bed beside her – but the mock heroine also dwarfed the fleet just visible through the window.

The reception of Robinson's and Hamilton's romance careers pre-sented female domination in clearly physical terms; yet despite the comic anxieties displayed by these satires, the bodies of public women could not be fully divorced from the body politic of the nation. Indeed, even as caricatures and satires attempted to remove women from the realm of public affairs, they helped to articulate a political dilemma, one which Linda Colley has summarized in terms of suffrage:

If men without land but possessed of movable property were to start campaign-ing for admission to the political process, as they were by the 1760s, and if some radicals were to advance further and demand universal manhood suffrage, as they had by the 1780s, what was there to stop single or widowed, and possibly in the end, even married women seeking access to similar rights? How were upwardly mobile and politically ambitious British men to legitimise their claims to active citizenship, without taking women along with them?[5]

Theatre offered one arena in which political legitimacy might be dramatized as intrinsically masculine. At the same time, however, women were increasingly prominent in late eighteenth-century theatre: as actresses, dramatists, and critics. As a result, Romantic theatre can be read as a somewhat eccentric public sphere, an arena in which performances of gender relations and national identity were oddly intertwined – and embattled. The reception of Robinson and Hamilton as dubious heroines of stage romance may well have helped distinguish between the rights of men and those of women by emphasizing the horrific yet also laughable consequences of allowing women an equal, unsubordinated role in the nation.

Mixed drama, exploring sexuality as domination, seemed to put women back into their proper places – yet as I have shown, women dramatists used the form to engage in political debate. More specifically, Hannah Cowley and Elizabeth Inchbald used the form of mixed drama to comment on "eastern" politics: the war between Russia and Turkey; England's management of its East Indian empire. In sexual terms, these plays invoke the familiar tropes of orientalism: images of sexual despotism and sado-masochistic domination are projected on to the East, then eagerly, voyeuristically, consumed by western audiences. Yet Cowley and Inchbald's dramas show the same structure of domination at the heart of western sentiment and benevolence. Cowley's *A Day in Turkey* promotes the idealized chastity of its Russian heroine – only to show that restrained sexual ideal constructed out of the same voluptuousness the play projects on to its Turkish characters. In Inchbald's *Such Things Are*, the antitypes of the benevolent Englishman and the despotic sultan are shown to be logically interchangeable: Haswell's benevolent powers incorporate the sultan's control over his prisons. An early review of the play gallantly replicated this blurring of western chivalry and eastern despotism, commenting of the captive Arabella, played by Mrs. Pope, that "had the Drama admitted of the change, there were few who would not wish her captivity prolonged."[6] Ten years later, in *Wives as They Were, Maids as They Are*, Inchbald largely removed the oriental parallel from the play, attributing exaggerated structures of domination to "antique manners" rather than foreign climes – but her imagery rather than setting or plot retained the orientalizing connection between antique subordination and eastern submissiveness. These plays reflect or possibly prefigure the way English society simultaneously abjected and internalized an absolutist model of power: embracing and idealizing it as a form of domestic relations while at the same time rejecting it politically as oriental despotism. Cowley both celebrates and manipulates this domestic despotism; Inchbald shows women manipulating male despots but also imprisoned by sentiment's masculinist conventions. The work of both dramatists suggests that the orientalizing projection of despotism remains inseparable from its internalization through sentiment.

The timing of these plays – coinciding with a reform of English imperialism and with the fall of France's *ancien régime* – underscores their larger political moral. As political absolutism was ostensibly defeated, banished from the realms of "rational–critical debate" undergirding western democracy, it reappeared, dominating the western imagination in a voyeuristic fascination with eastern despotism and sexuality, *and* dominating western social organization through the ideal of sentimental domesticity. Cowley's and Inchbald's heroines claim to be happy in their sentimental prisons: the farcical plotting of these plays grants dramatic power and license to these underdogs. But farce's claim to manipulate sentimental systems – and the despotic authority on which farce relies for its comic effects – must be read within a history of its reception. An early reviewer described Inchbald's *A Mogul Tale* as "one of that kind of pieces that divert us in spite of our better judgment" – and such dismissiveness sums up the more general reception of farce.[7] Sensibility may collude with the varied fictions of the emperor's new clothes, while farce is always at work undressing the emperor *and* the empire, exposing the threadbare illusions of reigning ideologies. Yet the political and theatrical history of the long eighteenth century teaches us that such exposure does not necessitate change. Truth appears, but disarmed of its potential to set free, to set at odds, or even to upset the status quo. This does not mean that the exposures accomplished by farce can never lead to action; merely that they need not. In responding to the political revelations of farce, as well as to its generic experiments, "we are left to our own Imaginations and Feelings, if we should happen to have any." Mimicry exposes our hypocrisies and hidden vices, but without attempting a wholesale cure.

Still, certain plays and certain moments have their salutary effects. Let me close with a brief glance at Mary Robinson's *Nobody* (1794), a two-act mixed drama, the insignificance of which it would be difficult to overstate. Robinson's *Nobody* antedates Smith's *What Is She?* by four years, but might otherwise be considered a response to her colleague's query.

Disjointed, rough, unfinished, the play seems likely to have failed on its own account – but it was emphatically "damned," hissed by a claque of the society women it meant to satirize. The writing within the play is often sloppy: while Inchbald was praised by reviewers for avoiding puns and cheap jokes, Robinson was much less restrained. In the first act, for instance, a foolish maid exposes her mistress to slander by mishandling the simple task of cleaning a gentleman visitor's boots; when the mistress, attacked by her so-called friends as a result of this blunder, feels faint, the maid Nelly Primrose announces, "I'll go fetch a lighted Match, or a burnt Feather, for I be Subject to Historicals myself and they do always bring me to" (22). Robinson's conflation of hysterical and historical registers both the romance passion for antiquities and an ostensibly female vulnerability to outside forces. Yet the pun replaces the externalities one might expect to see working here – history, sentimental physiology – with language itself, capable of conflating these two very different realms of experience. And Nelly Primrose's malapropism records her own (admittedly fatuous) freedom from the travails of language: her freedom to make the associations she pleases.

We too are subject to historicals: one of the greatest barriers to appreciating Romantic theatre remains the difficulty of recapturing its historical context: performance norms, political contexts, and so forth. Romantic drama makes aesthetic sense as well as political sense only when seen in its larger cultural context. Yet only by resisting labels and categories do new options arise: sometimes, it is only through negation (e.g., Robinson's *Nobody*) that fresh possibilities appear. Freud's famous query, "What does woman want?" points back to the older, eighteenth-century question, "What is she?" – but the women artists considered here ironize and transform that question by performing it. This book has focused on romance and farce, two minor trends within late eighteenth-century and Romantic theatre, as theatrical modes offering a space in which women writers, performers, and spectators might recreate themselves and their nation from scraps and patches of earlier forms. The work of these women writers and performers starts to suggest what we might see if we opened our eyes more fully to the theatricality as well as the antitheatricality of Romanticism: a liminal space in which the boundaries between theatre and politics, public and private, masculine and feminine Romanticisms becomes so permeable as to be in some cases barely distinguishable. Within that liminal space, we might begin to see more clearly the larger contours of Romantic ideology and the versions of national identity it proposed. We know a part of this national identity through the work of the canonical male poets, but only a part. Armed with that partial knowledge, we misread both the underlying shapes of Romantic literature and politics, and the shadows they cast across late twentieth-century approaches to genre and gender and nation. Topical and ephemeral, feminized and degraded, the theatrical forms of romance and sentimental farce can nonetheless help us remember what we prefer to forget: the extent to which we too remain subject to historicals, the extent to which sentimental hypocrisy continues to structure our fantasies of national and international agency.

Notes

PROLOGUE: THE FEMALE DRAMATIST AND THE MAN OF THE PEOPLE

1 Quoted in Mary E. Knapp, *Prologues and Epilogues of the Eighteenth Century* (New Haven: Yale University Press, 1961), p. 308.
2 George Colman, *The Female Dramatist* (Larpent Collection), p. 34.
3 George Colman, *Random Records*, 2 vols. (London: H. Colburn and R. Bentley, 1830), vol. i, pp. 112–13.
4 See Jürgen Habermas, *The Structural Transformation of the Public Sphere*, trans. Thomas Burger (Cambridge, MA: MIT Press, 1989).
5 For relevant work here, see Mita Choudhury, "Gazing at His Seraglio: Late Eighteenth-Century Women Playwrights as Orientalists," *Theatre Journal* 47.4 (1995), pp. 481–502; Joyce Zonana, "The Sultan and the Slave: Feminist Orientalism and the Structure of *Jane Eyre*," *Signs*, 18.3 (spring 1993), pp. 592–617; Nigel Leask, *British Romantic Writers and the East: The Anxieties of Empire* (Cambridge: Cambridge University Press, 1992); Sara Suleri, *The Rhetoric of English India* (Chicago: University of Chicago Press, 1992); Joseph Lew, "The Deceptive Other: Mary Shelley's Critique of Orientalism in *Frankenstein*," *Studies in Romanticism*, 30 (summer 1991), pp. 255–83; Eric Meyer, 'I Know Thee Not, I Loathe Thy Race': Romantic Orientalism in the Eye of the Other," *ELH*, 53 (fall 1991), pp. 657–99.

1 THE POLITICS OF ROMANTIC THEATRE

1 I take the notion of genre signaling membership in a class from Maureen Quilligan, *The Language of Allegory: Defining the Genre* (Ithaca, NY: Cornell University Press, 1979), p. 20. Obviously, one could argue that nation is a particular social form and thus analogous not to genre *per se*, but rather to a specific genre: epic, perhaps. But so many different genres have been aligned with nations and nationalisms in recent years that I prefer to emphasize the broader sense of formalism associated with genre proper.
2 Ernest Gellner, *Nations and Nationalism* (Ithaca, NY: Cornell University Press, 1983), p. 7.
3 For some recent theories of nationalism and nationhood, see Benedict Anderson, *Imagined Communities: Reflections on the Origin and Spread of*

Nationalism (London: Verso, 1983); George Mosse, *Nationalism and Sexuality: Respectability and Abnormal Sexuality in Modern Europe* (New York: Howard Fertig, 1985); Partha Chatterjee, *Nationalist Thought and the Colonial World* (Oxford: Oxford University Press, 1986); Gauri Viswanathan, *Masks of Conquest: Literary Study and British Rule in India* (London: Faber, 1989); Homi Bhabha, *Nation and Narration* (New York: Routledge, 1990) and *The Location of Culture* (New York: Routledge, 1994); Andrew Parker, Mary Russo, Doris Sommer, and Patricia Yaeger, eds. *Nationalisms and Sexualities* (New York: Routledge, 1992). For studies of more specifically Romantic nationalism, see especially Marlon Ross, "Romancing the Nation-State" in *Macropolitics of Nineteenth-Century Literature: Nationalism, Exoticism, Imperialism*, eds. Jonathan Arac and Harriet Ritvo (Philadelphia: University of Pennsylvania Press, 1991); Leask, *British Romantic Writers*; David Simpson, *Romanticism, Nationalism, and the Revolt Against Theory* (Chicago: University of Chicago Press, 1993); Carlson, *Theatre of Romanticism*.

4   Eve Sedgwick, *The Coherence of Gothic Conventions* (New York: Methuen, 1986), p. 10. Originally published 1976.

5   Gellner has argued that in the early stages of industrial society – stages marked by "egalitarian expectation, non-egalitarian reality, misery, and cultural homogeneity already desired but not yet implemented" – latent political tensions seek out "good symbols, good diacritical marks to separate ruler and ruled, privileged and underprivileged" (*Nations and Nationalisms*, pp. 73–74). In late eighteenth-century theatre, gender constituted just such a diacritical mark, one which could be used in complicated ways.

6   See Leo Hughes, *The Drama's Patrons: A Study of the Eighteenth-Century London Audience* (Austin: University of Texas Press, 1971), pp. 3–31.

7   *Bingley's Journal*, September 29, 1770. Quoted *ibid.*, p. 5.

8   *The Bystander*, 1790 (reprinted December 12, 1789). Quoted in Charles Gray, *Theatrical Criticism in London to 1795* (New York: B. Blom, 1931; rpt. 1964), p. 268.

9   The last number of *The Diary, or Woodfall's Register*, August 31, 1793. Quoted *ibid.*, p. 267.

10 See Marc Baer, *Theatre and Disorder in Late Georgian London* (Oxford: Clarendon Press, 1992) for more discussion of the nation coming together through theatre; see Paula Backscheider, *Spectacular Politics: Theatrical Power and Mass Culture in Early Modern England* (Baltimore: Johns Hopkins University Press, 1993), for more on connections between power and spectacle.

11 Jean-Christophe Agnew, *Worlds Apart: The Market and the Theater in Anglo-American Thought, 1550–1750* (Cambridge: Cambridge University Press, 1986), p. 160.

12 Until 1791 when it closed for reconstruction, Drury Lane seated roughly 2,300 spectators; after it reopened in 1794, its capacity was just over 3,600. Rebuilt in 1782, Covent Garden seated about 2,500 people; after it burnt down and was rebuilt in 1792, the theatre held 3,013.

13 Theophilus Cibber, *Two Dissertations on the Theatres* (London, 1756), p. 5.

14 Baer, *Theatre and Disorder*, pp. 142–43. See also Joseph Donohue, *Theatre in the Age of Kean* (Totowa, NJ: Rowman and Littlefield, 1975), p. 15.

15 Again, arrest records and newspaper accounts of the O.P. Riots suggest that disruption could occur in any section of the playhouse, and that the galleries were not solely occupied by members of the working classes.

16 *Dr. Campbell's Diary of a Visit to England in 1775*, ed. J. L. Clifford (1947), p. 45.

17 John Alexander Kelly, *German Visitors to English Theaters in the Eighteenth Century* (Princeton: Princeton University Press, 1936), p. 121. See Wendeborn, *A View of England towards the Close of the Eighteenth Century*, 2 vols. (London, 1791).

18 Dror Wahrman, *Imagining the Middle Class: The Political Representation of Class in Britain, c. 1780–1840* (Cambridge: Cambridge University Press, 1995), p. 36.

19 Mary Wollstonecraft, *An Historical and Moral View of the Origin and Progress of the French Revolution; and the effect it has produced in Europe* (1794) in Mary Wollstonecraft, *Political Writings*, ed. Janet Todd (Toronto: University of Toronto Press, 1993), p. 303.

20 [Scott], '*Life of Kemble*', pp. 200–1, quoted in Baer, *Theatre and Disorder*, p. 178.

21 Thomas Holcroft, *English Review*, May 1783, quoted in Gray, *Theatrical Criticism*, p. 298.

22 "Introductory Address to the Public" in *Devil's Pocket Book* (1786), quoted in Gray, *Theatrical Criticism*, p. 302.

23 Colman, *Random Records*, vol. I, pp. 251–52.

24 Edmund Burke, *The Writings and Speeches of Edmund Burke*, 9 vols., volume V, *India, Madras and Bengal, 1774–1785*, ed. P. J. Marshall (Oxford: Clarendon Press, 1991), p. 381.

25 Edmund Burke, *Reflections on the Revolution in France*, ed. Conor Cruise O'Brien (Harmondsworth: Penguin, 1968), p. 176, p. 171.

26 Quoted in Suleri, *Rhetoric of English India*, p. 68.

27 Thomas Paine, *The Complete Writings of Thomas Paine*, 2 vols., ed. Philip S. Foner (New York: Citadel Press, 1969), p. 373. See also pp. 366f.: "Hereditary succession is a burlesque upon monarchy."

28 Claudia Johnson, *Equivocal Beings* (Chicago: University of Chicago Press, 1992), p. 2.

29 Robert Markley, "Sentimentality as Performance: Shaftesbury, Sterne, and the Theatrics of Virtue" in *The New Eighteenth Century: Theory, Politics, English Literature*, ed. Felicity Nussbaum and Laura Brown (New York: Methuen, 1987), p. 211.

30 Jay Fliegelman, *Prodigals and Pilgrims: The American Revolution Against Patriarchal Authority, 1750–1800* (Cambridge: Cambridge University Press, 1982), p. 5.

31 Harry William Pedicord and Fredrick Louis Bergmann, eds. *The Plays of David Garrick*, 6 vols. (Carbondale: Southern Illinois University Press, 1980), vol. I, p. 72.

32 Quoted in Ernest Bernbaum, *The Drama of Sensibility: A Sketch of the History of English Sentimental Comedy and Domestic Tragedy, 1696–1780* (Gloucester, MA: Peter Smith, 1958), p. 248.

33 William Wordsworth and Samuel Taylor Coleridge, *Lyrical Ballads*, eds. R. L. Brett and A. R. Jones, 2nd edn (London: Routledge, 1991), p. 249.

34 See discussion of *Blue Beard* in chapter 2 below.

35 George Colman, *The Gentleman*, no. VI, in *Prose on Several Occasions* . . . (London, 1787), 1: 208–10; quoted in Arthur Sherbo, *English Sentimental Drama* (East Lansing, Michigan: State University Press, 1957), pp. 2–3.

36 Twentieth-century critics have emphasized the moral element at work in sentimental drama, along with a degree of artificiality, the presence of good characters, an appeal to the emotions rather than the intellect, and the evocation of pity. (See Arthur Sherbo's summary of common definitions in *English Sentimental Drama*, p. 21.) I would add that the "moral element" of sentimental drama often engaged social issues and familial tensions by presenting the problems of "the unfortunate": characters such as West Indians, Jews, gamesters, fallen women, and the poor more generally.

37 Oliver Goldsmith, "Comparison between Sentimental and Laughing Comedy" in *Westminster Magazine*, January 1773.

38 Quoted in Allardyce Nicoll, *A History of Late Eighteenth-Century Drama, 1750–1800* (Cambridge: Cambridge University Press, 1937), p. 112.

39 See for instance David Marshall, *The Surprising Effects of Sympathy: Marivaux, Diderot, Rousseau, and Mary Shelley* (Chicago: University of Chicago Press, 1988); Markley, "Sentimentality as Performance"; and Johnson, *Equivocal Beings*.

40 Raymond Williams, *The Long Revolution* (London: Chatto and Windus, 1961), p. 257.

41 See Richards, *Rise of the English Actress*, p. 45.

42 W. D. Archenholtz, German visitor, quoted in Philip Highfill, Jr., Kalman Burnim, and Edward Langhans, *A Biographical Dictionary of Actors, Actresses, Musicians, Dancers, Managers & Other Stage Personnel in London, 1660–1800*, 16 volumes (Carbondale: Southern Illinois University Press, 1973–93), vol. 1, p. 18.

43 Ralph G. Allen, "Irrational Entertainment in the Age of Reason" in *The Stage and the Page: London's "Whole Show" in the Eighteenth-Century Theatre*, ed. George Winchester Stone, Jr. (Berkeley: University of California Press, 1981), p. 101.

44 Lichtenberg, *Visits*, p. 69, quoted in Knapp, *Prologues and Epilogues of the Eighteenth Century*, pp. 78–79.

45 Quoted in M. D. George, *Catalogue of Political and Personal Satires Preserved in the Department of Prints and Drawings in the British Museum*, 11 vols. (London: Trustees of the British Museum, 1938), vol. VI, p. 106.

46 John Brewer, "Theater and Counter-Theater in Georgian Politics: The Mock Elections at Garrat," *Radical History Review*, 22 (winter 1979–80).

47 Robert R. Wark, *Drawings by Thomas Rowlandson in the Huntington Collection* (San Marino, CA: Huntington Library, 1975), no. 5, quoted *ibid.*, p. 30.

48 Elizabeth Inchbald, *Every One Has His Fault* (London, 1793), Act 3 Scene 1, line 281.

49 Quoted in James Boaden, *Memoirs of Mrs. Inchbald*, 2 vols. (London: Richard Bentley, 1833), vol. 1, p. 311.

50 Jean-Jacques Rousseau, *Lettre à d'Alembert sur les spectacles*, trans. Alan Bloom, *Politics and the Arts* (Ithaca, NY: Cornell University Press, 1960), p. 47. For the popularity of the *Letter*, see Edward Duffy, *Rousseau In England* (Berkeley: University of California Press, 1979), p. 11. The *drames* of Diderot were imported to England as sentimental drama, but Rousseau's antagonism toward women and actresses enacts the logic of English dramatic romance.

2 VARIETIES OF ROMANCE NATIONALISM

1 Linda Colley, *Britons: Forging the Nation, 1707–1837* (New Haven: Yale University Press, 1992).

2 Gillian Russell, *The Theatres of War: Performance, Politics and Society, 1793–1815* (Oxford: Clarendon Press, 1995), p. 52.

3 Ross, "Romancing the Nation-State," pp. 56–85. Other accounts of Romantic (as opposed to romance) nationalism stress the role of women novelists: see for instance Miranda Burgess, "Domesticating Gothic: Jane Austen, Ann Radcliffe, and National Romance" *in Lessons of Romanticism: A Critical Companion*, ed. Thomas Pfau and Robert Gleckner (Durham, NC: Duke University Press, 1998), pp. 392–412; Gary Kelly, "Women Writers and Romantic Nationalism in Britain" in *Literature of Region and Nation*, ed. Winnifred Bogaards (Saint John, NB: Social Sciences and Humanities Research Council of Canada with University of New Brunswick in Saint John, 1998), vol. 1, pp. 120–32; Ina Ferris, "Writing on the Border: The National Tale, Female Writing, and the Public Sphere" in *Romanticism, History and the Possibilities of Genre: Re-Forming Literature, 1789–1837*, ed. Tilottama Rajan and Julia Wright (Cambridge: Cambridge University Press, 1998), pp. 86–106. See also Simpson, *Romanticism, Nationalism, and the Revolt Against Theory*.

4 Useful Romanticist revisions of Habermas include Jon Klancher, *The Making of English Reading Audiences, 1790–1832* (Madison: University of Wisconsin Press, 1987); James Chandler, "Hallam, Tennyson, and the Poetry of Sensation: Aestheticist Allegories of a Counter-Public Sphere," *Studies in Romanticism*, 33 (winter 1994), pp. 527–37; Kevin Gilmartin, *Print Politics: The Press and Radical Opposition in Early Nineteenth-Century England* (Cambridge: Cambridge University Press, 1996). For more general revisions of Habermas, see *Habermas and the Public Sphere*, ed. Craig Calhoun (Cambridge, MA: MIT Press, 1992); Oscar Negt and Alexander Kluge, *Public Sphere and Experience: Toward an Analysis of the Bourgeois and Proletarian Public Sphere*, trans. Peter Labanyi, Jamie Oswen Daniel, and Assenka Oskiloff; with foreword by Miriam Hansen (Minneapolis: University of Minnesota Press, 1993); and *The Phantom Public Sphere*, ed. Bruce Robbins (Minneapolis: University of Minnesota Press, 1993).

5 John Shurley abridged and rewrote the romances of *Guy of Warwick* in 1681,

Don Bellianis of Greece in 1683, *Bevis of Southampton* in 1689, and *Amadis of Gaul* in 1702. *The Seven Champions of Christendom* was abridged in 1679, and printed steadily over the next 130 years, reaching a seventeenth edition in 1815. Johnson's story of St. George and Sabra, revised from *Bevis*, was extracted to form a shorter, separate romance. All of these romances were reproduced in chapbook form. See Arthur Johnston, *Enchanted Ground: The Study of Medieval Romance in the Eighteenth Century* (London: Athlone Press, 1964), pp. 29–30.

6 John Dryden, "Of Heroique Playes. An Essay," introduction to *Conquest of Granada, Part I* in *The Works of John Dryden*, 20 vols. (Berkeley: University of California Press, 1970), vol. XI, p. 12.

7 See E. K. Chambers, *The English Folk-Play* (Oxford: Clarendon Press, 1933), pp. 184–85.

8 According to William Nicolson, "King *Arthur*'s Story in *English*" was "often sold by the Ballad-singers, with the like Authentic Records of *Guy of Warwick* and *Bevis of Southampton*" (Nicolson, *The English Historical Library* [1714], p. 38). And Sir Walter Scott claimed that *Roswal and Lillian* was "the last metrical Romance of Chivalry which retained its popularity in Scotland, & indeed was sung in Edinbr. within these 20 years by a sort of reciter in the streets." Quoted in Johnston, *Enchanted Ground*, p. 28.

9 Negt and Kluge, *Public Sphere and Experience*, pp. 32–35.

10 See for instance John Clare, *Autobiographical Fragments*, ed. E. Robinson (Oxford: Oxford University Press, 1986), pp. 56–57, and Thomas Holcroft, *Hugh Trevor*, ed. S. Deanes (Oxford: Oxford University Press, 1973), p. 41.

11 *Life and Poetical Works of George Crabbe* (1847), p. 134.

12 Henry Fielding, *The Complete Works*, ed. W. E. Henley, 16 vols. (London: William Heinemann, 1903), vol. VIII, pp. 193–94. "Corinthian brass" may be a throw back to the Accession Day Tilts and/or to Sidney's *Arcadia*.

13 For more on the role of romance in the pamphlet wars of the 1790s, see David Duff, "The French Revolution and the Politics of Romance" in *Romance and Revolution: Shelley and the Politics of a Genre* (Cambridge: Cambridge University Press, 1994), pp. 8–53.

14 *Letters written by . . . Earl of Chesterfield to His Son . . .* (1774), vol. I, letter 3. Quoted in Ioan Williams, *Novel and Romance: A Documentary Record, 1700–1800* (New York: Barnes and Noble, 1970), pp. 100–1.

15 William Owen, *An Essay on the New Species of Writing founded by Mr. Fielding: with a Word or Two upon the Modern State of Criticism* (1751). Quoted in Williams, *Novel and Romance*, p. 151.

16 *Monthly Review*, 4 (March 1751).

17 Owen, *Essay on the New Species of Writing*, quoted in Williams, *Novel and Romance*, p. 151.

18 Richard Berenger, *The World*, Thursday, July 4, 1754, p. 79. See also Richard Cumberland, *The Observer* (1785), p. 27.

19 Thomas Munro, *Olla Podrida*, Saturday, June 23, 1787, p. 15.

20 Hugh Blair, "On Fictitious History," *Lectures on Rhetoric and Poetry* (1762). Quoted in Williams, *Novel and Romance*, p. 247.

21 Cleanth Brooks, ed., *Correspondence of Thomas Percy and Richard Farmer* (Baton Rouge, 1946), p. 7. Quoted in Johnston, *Enchanted Ground*, p. 73.

22 Richard Hurd, *Letters on Chivalry and Romance* (London, 1762), pp. 118–20.

23 *Correspondence of Thomas Percy and Evan Evans*, ed. A. Lewis (Baton Rouge, 1957), 84–5. Ironically, this argument for English nationalism was drawn from the *French* historian Paul-Henri Mallet's study of Norse antiquities, which Percy was then translating. See Johnston, *Enchanted Ground*, pp. 83–84.

24 Joseph Addison and Richard Steele, *The Spectator*, ed. Donald Bond, 5 vols. (Oxford: Clarendon Press, 1967), vol. III, p. 572.

25 Quoted in Knapp, *Prologues and Epilogues of the Eighteenth Century*, p. 201.

26 Nicoll, *History of Late Eighteenth Century Drama*, pp. 98–99.

27 Elizabeth Steele, *The Memoirs of Sophia Baddeley*, 3 vols. (Dublin, 1787), vol. I, pp. 226–28. See also Richards, *Rise of the English Actress*, pp. 66, 70.

28 Quoted in Highfill, Burnim, and Langhans, *Biographical Dictionary*, vol. I, p. 207.

29 George Colman, *Blue Beard* (London, 1798), p. iii.

30 George Colman, *Blue Beard* in *Plays by George Colman the Younger and Thomas Morton*, ed. Barry Sutcliffe (Cambridge: Cambridge University Press, 1983), pp. 190–91.

31 Adolphus, quoted in Sutcliffe, "Introduction" to *Plays by Colman the Younger and Morton*, p. 41.

32 Mary Robinson, *Thoughts on the Injustice of Mental Subordination* (London, 1799), p. 1.

33 For a discussion of the "lovely nation," see Carlson, *In the Theatre of Romanticism*, pp. 134–75. The phrase of course is Burke's.

34 Slavoj Žižek, *The Sublime Object of Ideology* (New York: Verso, 1989), p. 126.

3 PATRIOTIC ROMANCE: EMMA HAMILTON AND HORATIO NELSON

 1 The quotation is from Robert Southey, *The Life of Nelson*, 12th edn (London: John Murray, 1853), p. 350.

 2 For biographies, see Walter Sichel, *Memoir of Emma, Lady Hamilton, with Anecdotes of Her Friends and Contemporaries*, ed. W. H. Long (London: W. W. Gibbings, 1891); James Baily, *Emma, Lady Hamilton: A Biographical Essay with a Catalogue of Her Published Portraits* (London: W. G. Menzies, 1905); Walter Sichel, *Emma Lady Hamilton from New and Original Sources and Documents* (New York, 1906); Julia Frankau, *The Story of Emma, Lady Hamilton* (London: Macmillan, 1911); John Cordy Jeaffreson, *Lady Hamilton & Lord Nelson* (London: Grolier Society, n.d.); Marjorie Bowen, *Patriotic Lady: Emma, Lady Hamilton, the Neapolitan Revolution of 1799, and Horatio, Lord Nelson* (New York: D. Appleton-Century, 1936); Gerald Hamilton and Desmond Stewart, *Emma in Blue: A Romance of Friendship* (New York: Roy Publishers, 1958); Oliver Warner, *Emma Hamilton and Sir William* (London: Chatto and Windus, 1960); Jack Russell, *Nelson and the Hamiltons* (New York: Simon and Schuster, 1969); Norah Lofts, *Emma Hamilton* (New York: Coward, McCann and

Geoghegan, 1978); Colin Simpson, *Emma, The Life of Lady Hamilton* (London: Bodley Head, 1983); Flora Fraser, *Emma, Lady Hamilton* (New York: Knopf/Random House, 1986). For fictional accounts, all entitled "romance," see Lily Adams Beck, *The Divine Lady: A Romance of Nelson and Emma Hamilton* (New York: Dodd, Mead, and Co., 1924); Bradda Field, *Miledi: being the strange story of Emy Lyon, a blacksmith's daughter, who married his Britannic Majesty's Envoy Extraordinary and Minister Plenipotentiary at the court of Naples and became Emma, lady Hamilton, companion of royalty and the true friend of Vice-Admiral Lord Nelson, K.B., duke of Bronte. A romantic biography* (London: Constable, 1942); Susan Sontag, *The Volcano Lover: A Romance* (New York: Farrar, Straus and Giroux, 1992).

3 See Fraser, *Emma, Lady Hamilton*, p. 342.

4 Throughout this chapter, I will use "Hamilton" to refer to Emma, Lady Hamilton and "Sir William" to denote Sir William Hamilton.

5 The phrase is that of Horace Walpole: see *Correspondence*, ed. W. S. Lewis, 48 vols. (New Haven: Yale University Press, 1944), vol. XI, p. 337.

6 John Mitford, Esq., R.N., *The Adventures of Johnny Newcome in The Navy; A Poem in Four Cantos, with Notes*, 3rd edn (London: Sherwood, Neely, and Jones, 1823), p. 264n; Mitford's italics.

7 Peter Brooks, *The Melodramatic Imagination: Balzac, Henry James, Melodrama, and the Mode of Excess* (New Haven: Yale University Press, 1976), p. 18.

8 Addington MS 34,989 in the British Museum; quoted in Sichel, *Emma Lady Hamilton from New and Original Sources and Documents*, pp. 8–9. Note: quotations from letters throughout this chapter retain the original, often idiosyncratic, spelling.

9 In calling Hart a romance heroine, I mean to register both her similarity to Richardson's Pamela – both lower-class girls rise through a canny deployment of beauty, sensibility, and hyperbolically performed virtue – and her connections to romance heroines of the 1790s, whose lives were somewhat more adventurous.

10 William Hayley, *The Life of George Romney, Esq.* (London: T. Payne, 1809), p. 119.

11 In the eighteenth century, "attitude" referred either to the disposition of a figure in statuary, painting, drama, or dancing – or to "a posture of the body proper to, or implying, some action or mental state" (*OED*). "Attitudes" thus mediated between body and mind, between passion and expression.

12 She may have developed this technique out of her modeling experience: during his travels in Italy, Romney had become interested in the shadows and softened light produced by various kinds of headgear – and in his portraits Emma frequently appears draped in scarves, or other pieces of long, flowing material.

13 Comtesse de Boigne, *Memoirs*, trans. S. de Morier-Kotthaus (London, 1956), p. 34.

14 See Frederick Rehberg, *Emma Hamilton's Attitudes* (Cambridge, MA: Houghton Library, 1990).

15   Johann Wolfgang von Goethe, *Italian Journey*, trans. W. H. Auden and Elizabeth Mayer (New York: Schocken/Pantheon, 1968), pp. 199–200. Journal entry for March 16, 1787.

16   Mrs. St. George, *Journal*, pp. 75ff., quoted in E. Hallam Moorhouse, *Nelson's Lady Hamilton* (London: Methuen, 1906), p. 265.

17   Horace Walpole to Mary Berry, August 23, 1791. In Walpole, *Correspondence*, vol. XI, pp. 337ff. After seeing Emma give a performance of the mad scene in *Nina*, Walpole was much more enthusiastic.

18   Historians continue to dispute Emma's actual importance in Neapolitan politics of the period. For a more conservative view, see Brian Fothergill, *Sir William Hamilton; Envoy Extraordinary* (London: Faber and Faber, 1969).

19   Flora Fraser does, however, reproduce a Gillray caricature in which she identifies the key figures as Emma and Maria Carolina, Nelson's "female rival." See Fraser, *Emma, Lady Hamilton*.

20   *The Collection of Autograph Letters and Historical Documents formed by Alfred Morrison* (2nd series, 1882–93); the Hamilton and Nelson Papers, 2 vols. (printed for private circulation, 1893), vol. I, p. 156.

21   Egerton collection 2640 in the British Museum, quoted in Sichel, *Emma Lady Hamilton from New and Original Sources and Documents*, p. 199.

22   BM Egerton 1618, fo. 7, quoted in Sichel, *Emma Lady Hamilton from New and Original Sources and Documents*, p. 142.

23   Colley, *Britons: Forging the Nation*, p. 183.

24   Mrs. St. George's *Journal*, quoted in Moorhouse, *Nelson's Lady Hamilton*, pp. 263–67.

25   Elliott, *Memoirs*, vol. II, p. 242f., quoted in Sichel, *Emma Lady Hamilton from New and Original Sources and Documents*, p. 392.

26   See Sichel, *Emma Lady Hamilton from New and Original Sources and Documents*, p. 58.

27   William Hayley, *The Triumphs of Temper* (London: Cadell, 1780), canto 1.

28   Emma told the story to Romney, who promptly painted her in the costume of a lady's maid. See Sichel, *Emma Lady Hamilton from New and Original Sources and Documents*, p. 60, and John Romney, *Memoirs of the Life and Works of George Romney, etc.* (London: Baldwin and Cradock, 1830), p. 183.

29   Between January 10 and January 18, Emma's letters to Hamilton present her through the eyes of others both as a marble statue and as a marvelous combination of comedy and tragedy. Emma's "Attitudes," often described as the art of bringing antique statues to life, were consistently attributed to Sir William's ingenuity and interests. Yet these letters suggest that Emma herself at least planted the idea of bringing together her statuesque beauty with her emotional versatility. See Morrison, *Collection of Autograph Letters*, vol. I, pp. 160, 163.

30   Earl of Ilchester, ed., *Journal of Elizabeth, Lady Holland*, 2 vols. (London: Longmans, Green and Co., 1908), vol. I, p. 243.

31   According to Brian Fothergill, arming the Lazzaroni merely increased the bloodshed and anarchy of this tumultuous conquest (*Sir William Hamilton*, p. 356).

32 Paulson sees them both looking at her pubic area, but it seems to me that their gaze is aimed somewhat higher, perhaps as a reference to Emma's pregnancy?

33 The caricature is usually taken as referring to rumors that Emma had posed nude for drawing classes at the Royal Academy – but a more concrete model for the sketch may be found in a nude portrait by Romney, entitled "Lady Hamilton as the Goddess of Health." See the Huntington Library's photo collection of Romney portraits.

34 Sichel, however, suggests that Hamilton was at this time in serious financial trouble, and had borrowed some money from Nelson in efforts to remedy the situation.

35 In the seventeenth century, rakes would cut the noses of women accused of adultery. See G. J. Barker-Benfield, *The Culture of Sensibility: Sex and Society in Eighteenth-Century Britain* (Chicago: University of Chicago Press, 1992).

36 See Thomas Wright and R. H. Evan, *Historical and Descriptive Account of the Caricatures of James Gillray, Comprising a Political and Humorous History of the Latter Part of the Reign of George the Third* (New York: Benjamin Blom, 1968), p. 253. First published London, 1851.

37 Ronald Paulson, *Representations of Revolution* (New Haven: Yale University Press, 1983), p. 211.

4 (DIS)EMBODIED ROMANCE: "PERDITA" ROBINSON AND WILLIAM WORDSWORTH

1 See for instance Stuart Curran, "Mary Robinson's *Lyrical Tales* in Context" in *Revisioning Romanticism: British Women Writers, 1776–1837*, ed. Carol Shiner Wilson and Joel Haefner (Philadelphia: University of Pennsylvania Press, 1994) and Judith Pascoe, "The Spectacular Flaneuse" in *Romantic Theatricality*, pp. 130–62. "The participation of power" is a quotation from Mary Robinson's *Thoughts on the Injustice of Mental Subordination* (London, 1799), p. 1.

2 Judith Pascoe's "Performing Wordsworth" in *Romantic Theatricality* explores this question from a slightly different perspective.

3 Depending upon one's perspective, this bond was (1) extorted from an inexperienced lover as an advance payment for sexual favors; (2) an unsought and unexpected mark of princely generosity and love; (3) an appropriate consideration for the act of resigning a lucrative career at the prince's particular request. The first perspective is that recorded by various critical pamphleteers (see discussion below); the second is the position presented by Mary Robinson's memoir; the third is the voice of the "friend" who finished the memoir (generally assumed to be Robinson's daughter, Mary Elizabeth).

4 *The correspondence of King George the Third from 1760 to December 1783, printed from the original papers in the royal archives at Windsor castle*, ed. Sir John Fortesque, 6 vols. (London: Macmillan, 1927–28), vol. VI, p. 269.

5 M. J. Levy, "Introduction" to *Perdita: The Memoirs of Mary Robinson* (London: Peter Owen, 1994).

6 *Poetical Epistle from Florizel to Perdita: With Perdita's Answer. And a Preliminary Discourse upon the Education of Princes* (London: J. Stockdale, 1781), p. 17.

7 North may be included in this array because of his link to Fox in the coalition government; he was also the man instructed by George III to "pay off" Mary Robinson as a means of getting hold of the prince's politically indelicate letters to her.

8 *Letters from Perdita to a Certain Israelite and His Answers to Them* (London: J. Fielding, 1781), p. ii.

9 *Morning Post*, September 21, 1782.

10 The phrase "sexually impaled" is that of Jan Fergus and Janice Farrar Thaddeus in "Women, Publishers, and Money, 1790–1820" in *Studies in Eighteenth-Century Culture*, 27 vols. to date (Colleagues Press), vol. XVII, p. 194.

11 Originally published under the name Anne Frances Randall as *Letter to the Women of England, on the Injustice of Mental Subordination* (1798), the pamphlet was retitled and published under Robinson's own name in 1799.

12 See Dorothy's letter of September 10 and 12, 1800 in *The Letters of William and Dorothy Wordsworth*, ed. Ernest de Selincourt, 2nd edn, 8 vols. (Oxford: Clarendon Press, 1967–93), vol. I, p. 297.

13 William Wordsworth, *Lyrical Ballads*, ed. R. L. Brett and A. R. Jones (London: Methuen, 1963), pp. 242–43.

14 The first translation (1786) bore the title *Tales of the Twelfth and Thirteenth Centuries*; the second edition was retitled *Norman Tales* (1789). *Tales of the Minstrels* appears as an undated "fourth" edition: the British Library proposes a date of 1800 for this reprint. Steven Storace's musical farce *No Song, No Supper* was adapted from the tale of "The Poor Scholar"; and "The Three Hunchbacked Minstrels" furnished materials for another farce.

15 Quoted in Donald Reiman, "The Beauty of Buttermere as Fact and Romantic Symbol," *Criticism* 26.2 (spring 1984), p. 144.

16 See Kevis Goodman, "Making Time for History: Wordsworth, the New Historicism, and the Apocalyptic Fallacy" in *Studies in Romanticism*, 35 (winter 1996), pp. 563–77.

17 See Kristina Straub, *Sexual Suspects: Eighteenth-Century Players and Sexual Ideology* (Princeton: Princeton University Press, 1992). See also Antony Simpson, "Vulnerability and the Age of Female Consent" in *Sexual Underworlds of the Enlightenment*, ed. G. S. Rousseau and Roy Porter (Manchester: Manchester University Press, 1987), pp. 181–205. Simpson's discussion of rape trials between 1730 and 1830 leads into the related areas of child molestation and child prostitution; he suggests that sex with children was popular as a means of avoiding (or, according to popular myth, curing) sexually transmitted diseases.

18 Alan Richardson, *Literature, Education, and Romanticism: Reading as Social Practice, 1780–1832* (Cambridge: Cambridge University Press, 1994), p. 115.

19 Julie Carlson's *In the Theatre of Romanticism* argues that in Coleridge's later work, theatre links national politics with the imagination; I want to suggest that the same associations are made, more elliptically, by the 1805 *Prelude*.

20 See for instance lines 504–16.

21 Various critics have noted (or complained about) the incoherence of this

structure. Lawrence Kramer, for instance, remarks that "[t]he narrative illogic here, the lack of convincing transitions and the jumbling of ostensible topics are extreme even for Wordsworth" "Gender and Sexuality in *The Prelude*: The Question of Book Seven," *ELH*, 54 [1987], p. 620).

22 John Milton, *Paradise Lost* (New York: W. W. Norton, 1975), book 1, lines 63, 302–3, 341–44, and 268.

23 As Pascoe notes, the first version of "Winkfield Plain" was printed in the *Morning Post* on August 1, 1800 as "The Camp" and signed with one of Robinson's pseudonyms, but Robinson's daughter Mary Elizabeth claimed authorship of "Winkfield Plain" when printing it in *The Wild Wreath*. Still, a general confusion over authorship marked this collection of verse: Coleridge, for instance, may well have drawn Wordsworth's attention to the collection if only inadvertently – for Wordsworth's poem "The Mad Monk" appeared in *The Wild Wreath* above Coleridge's name.

24 Stuart Curran, "Romantic Poetry: The 'I' Altered" in *Romanticism and Feminism*, ed. Anne Mellor (Bloomington: Indiana University Press, 1988), pp. 191–92.

25 Coleridge, for instance, replied to Anna Barbauld's critique of meaninglessness in the "Rime of the Ancient Mariner" by paraphrasing the first story of the *Arabian Nights*.

5 MIMICRY, POLITICS, AND PLAYWRIGHTING

1 See Leo Hughes, *A Century of English Farce* (Oxford: Oxford University Press, 1956).

2 John Dryden, preface to *An Evening's Love, or the Mock-Astrologer* (1671) in *John Dryden: Four Comedies*, ed. L. A. Beaurline and Fredson Bowers (Chicago: University of Chicago Press, 1967).

3 Nahum Tate, preface to *A Duke and No Duke* (1693; 2nd edn) reprinted as "Nahum Tate's defense of farce," introduced and edited by Peter Holland, in *Farce, Themes in Drama*, vol. x (Cambridge: Cambridge University Press, 1988), pp. 106–10.

4 Fielding, *Complete Works*, vol. xi, p. 12.

5 Samuel Foote, preface to *Taste* (London, 1752).

6 *St. James Chronicle*, July 6–8, 1784.

7 Samuel Taylor Coleridge, *Shakespearean Criticism*, ed. Thomas Middleton Raysor (London: J. M. Dent, 1960), p. 89.

8 For more information see P. J. Crean, "The Stage Licensing Act of 1737," *Modern Philology*, 35 (1938), pp. 239–55.

9 Charles Churchill, *The Rosciad* in *Poetical Works of Charles Churchill*, ed. W. Tooke, 3 vols. (Boston: Little Brown and Co., 1854), vol. 1, pp. 1–110.

10 Ironically, perhaps, Foote's license at the Haymarket was itself designed as recompense for a purely physical limitation, a joke gone wrong. During a visit to a country estate, Foote was thrown by the Duke of York's horse; his leg, fractured in two places, was amputated. To compensate for the loss of

the leg, the duke acquired for Foote a royal patent to produce "plays and entertainments of the stage of all sorts" between May 15 and September 15.

11 *Henry Fielding: The Critical Heritage*, ed. Ronald Paulson and Thomas Lockwood (New York: Barnes and Noble, 1969), pp. 99–101.

12 Quoted in Mary Megie Belden, *The Dramatic Work of Samuel Foote* (New Haven: Yale University Press, 1929), p. 174.

13 *Letters*, vol. I, p. 88, quoted in Pedicord and Bergmann, eds., *Plays of Garrick*, vol. I, p. 391. Incidentally, Samuel Johnson's criticism of Foote as mimic both resists this claim to double vision and may help define it: Foote, according to Johnson, "gives you something different from himself, but not the character which he means to assume. He goes out of himself, without going into other people." (Quoted in *ibid.*, p. 6.)

14 *Public Advertiser*, March 1, 1763.

15 Henry Fielding, *The Jacobite's Journal and Related Writings*, ed. W. B. Coley (Middletown, CT: Wesleyan University Press, 1975), pp. 261–65.

16 Friedrich Wilhelm von Hassell, *Briefe aus England*, Hannover, 1792. Quoted in *Kelly, German Visitors to English Theaters*, p. 144.

17 Jacob Christian Gottlieb Schaeffer, *Briefe auf einter Reise durch Frankreich, England, Holland und Italien in den Jahren 1787 und 1788 geschrieben*, 2 vols. (Regensburg, 1794). Quoted in *ibid.*, p. 125.

18 Jacques Henri Meister, *Souvenirs de mes Voyages en Angleterre*, 2 vols. (Zürich, 1795). Quoted in *ibid.*, p. 134.

19 ?Peter Will, *Sittengemälde von London* (Gotha, 1801), p. 63. Quoted in *ibid.*, p. 161.

20 Quoted in *ibid.*, p. 149.

21 Abbé Jean Bernard le Blanc, *Lettres d'un françois*, 2 vols., trans. Dublin, 1747, vol. II, pp. 6–7. Quoted in Shearer West, *The Image of the Actor: Verbal and Visual Representation in the Age of Garrick and Kemble* (New York: St. Martin's Press, 1991), p. 131.

22 Schaeffer, *Briefe*, quoted in Kelly, *German Visitors to English Theaters*, p. 129.

23 Quoted in Hughes, *Century of English Farce*, p. 10.

24 Samuel Foote, *The Roman and English Comedy Consider'd and Compared* (London: T. Waller, 1747), p. 22. Quoted in West, *Image of the Actor*, p. 131.

25 "Honestus," "The Universal Farce display'd," *Town and Country Magazine* (January 1771), p. 8.

26 Pedicord and Bargmann, eds., *Plays of David Garrick*, vol. I, p. 72.

27 Henri Bergson, *Le Rire* (1900), trans. in Wylie Sypher, ed., *Comedy* (Garden City, NY: Doubleday, 1956), p. 77.

28 Daniel C. Gerould, "The Well-Made Play and its Heritage," pp. 43–44, quoted by Stuart Baker in *Georges Feydeau and the Aesthetics of Farce* (Ann Arbor, MI: University of Michigan Research Press, 1981), p. 20.

29 Mary Robinson, *Nobody*, pp. 11–12. A manuscript copy of the play resides in the Huntington Library's Larpent collection.

30 Charlotte Smith, *What Is She?* in *English and American Drama of the Nineteenth Century* (New Canaan, CT: Readex microform, 1985–), p. 236.

31 Hannah Cowley, prologue to *Who's the Dupe?* in *The Works of Mrs. Cowley; Dramas and Poems*, 3 vols. (London, Wilkie and Robinson, 1813), vol. I, n.p.
32 John Dryden, preface to *An Evening's Love*, p. 204.
33 "Theatrical Intelligence," *Morning Post and Daily Advertiser*, no. 3558, Wednesday, July 7, 1784. The play being reviewed is Inchbald's *A Mogul Tale*.
34 See Donkin, *Getting into the Act*, pp. 29–31.
35 Ellison, "Politics of Fancy," p. 229.
36 See for instance Moira Ferguson, *Subject to Others: British Women Writers and Colonial Slavery, 1670–1834* (New York: Routledge, 1992) and Markman Ellis, *The Politics of Sensibility: Race, Gender, and Commerce in the Sentimental Novel* (Cambridge: Cambridge University Press, 1996).
37 Williams, *Long Revolution*, pp. 260–1.
38 Christopher Newfield in *The Emerson Effect* sketches a tension between individualism and submission that offers a more structured analogy for the deflections of sentiment. In Newfield's reading, submission remains the hidden center of Emersonian individuality; in much the same way, I want to argue that deflection and conservation constitute the hidden center of sentimental calls for reform. See Newfield, *The Emerson Effect: Individualism and Submission in America* (Chicago: University of Chicago Press, 1996).
39 Zonana, "The Sultan and the Slave," p. 594.
40 Choudhury, "Gazing at His Seraglio," p. 486.
41 Samuel Foote, *The Nabob* in *The Works of Samuel Foote, Esq.*, 3 vols., ed. Jon Bee, Esq. (London: Sherwood, Gilbert and Piper, 1830), vol. III, pp. 213–14.
42 Burke, *Writings and Speeches*, vol. V, pp. 403–4.
43 *Ibid.*, vol. VI, pp. 292–93.
44 Luce Irigaray, "The Power of Discourse and the Subordination of the Feminine: Interview" in *This Sex Which Is Not One*, trans. Catherine Porter with Carolyn Burke (Ithaca, NY: Cornell University Press, 1985), p. 74.
45 *Ibid.*, p. 76.
46 Elizabeth Inchbald, *Lover's Vows* in *The British Theatre: or, A Collection of Plays*, 35 vols. (London: Longman, Hurst, Rees, and Orme, 1808), vol. XXIII, p. 5.
47 See William Cobbett's *The Porcupine and Anti-Gallican Monitor*, September 7, 1801 for a sharply critical review of *Lover's Vows*: "Amelia, notwithstanding the pains which Mrs. Inchbald, the adapter of the play, has taken to polish her, still remains coarse, forward, and disgusting, and, we trust, will never be imitated by the British fair."
48 Quoted in Gellner, *Nations and Nationalism*, p. x. I have not been able to place this citation in Santayana's work.

6 THE BALANCE OF POWER: HANNAH COWLEY'S *DAY IN TURKEY*

1 Hannah Cowley, *A Day in Turkey; or, The Russian Slaves* (London: G. G. J. and J. Robinson, 1792), n.p.
2 The editor of her collected work will point out Cowley's similar inability to "attend" to her own plays in production, asserting that she rarely attended

opening nights, and in general stayed away from the theatre. See *Works of Mrs. Cowley*, vol. 1, n.p.

3 *Morning Post, and Daily Advertiser*, no. 5808, Monday, December 5, 1791.

4 Barbara Freedman, "Frame-Up: Feminism, Psychoanalysis, Theatre" in *Performing Feminisms: Feminist Critical Theory and Theatre*, ed. Sue-Ellen Case (Baltimore: Johns Hopkins University Press, 1990), p. 58.

5 *The Parliamentary Register; or History of the proceedings and Debates of the House of Commons; containing an account of The most interesting Speeches and Motions; accurate Copies of the most remarkable Letters and Papers; of the most material Evidence, Petitions, &c. laid before and offered to the House, during the First Session of the Seventeenth Parliament of Great Britain* (London: J. Debrett, 1791), vol. XXIX, p. 50. Cited henceforth by page number; unless otherwise noted, all references are to volume XXIX.

6 Appealing to the British cult of commerce, Grey insisted that "trade with Russia was the most advantageous of any to Great Britain; it furnished materials for our manufactures, and proved an excellent nursery for seamen. Our exports to Russia amounted annually to about two millions sterling; and our imports to the amount of one million" (107–8). War would interrupt this trade, at great expense to English merchants.

7 Stanley's reference to Russia's western ambitions gestured to an earlier attempt to create an alliance with Baltic nations against Britain, as well as "her more late attempts to govern the two Courts of Sweden and of Denmark" and "her intrigues in the kingdom of Poland" (130).

8 The problem of course is that the image of the Colossus comes in a speech made by Cassius to Brutus, as he tries to persuade the latter to conspire against Caesar's life.

9 *Morning Post, and Daily Advertiser*, no. 5808, Monday, December 5, 1791.

10 See *Works of Mrs. Cowley*, vol. II.

7 THE FARCE OF SUBJECTION: ELIZABETH INCHBALD

1 Elizabeth Inchbald, *Wives as They Were, Maids as They Are* (London: Longman, Hurst, Rees, Orme, and Browne, 1797), p. 57.

2 Boaden, *Memoirs of Mrs. Inchbald*, vol. 1, p. 185.

3 *Public Advertiser*, no. 15636, Wednesday, July 7, 1784.

4 Ibid.

5 Quoted in George Bearce, *British Attitudes Towards India, 1784–1858* (New York and Oxford: Oxford University Press, 1961), p. 15.

6 Elizabeth Inchbald, *A Mogul Tale, or, The descent of the balloon: a farce* (London: Printed for F. Powell, 1796), p. 14.

7 Elizabeth Inchbald, *Such Things Are: a play, in five acts. As performed at the Theatre Royal, Covent Garden. Printed under the authority of the managers from the prompt book. With remarks by the author* (London: Longman, Hurst, Rees, and Orme, 1808), p. 5.

8 Lord Chesterfield, *Letters to his Son*, 2 vols. (Washington, DC: M. Walter Dunne, 1901), vol. I, p. 151.

9 Boaden, *Memoirs of Mrs. Inchbald*, vol. 1, p. 242.

10 *Public Advertiser*, no. 16452, Monday, February 12, 1787.

11 *Such things may be. A Tale for future times.* (London: J. Doughty & Co., March 1, 1788).

12 *Public Advertiser*, no. 16452, Monday, February 12, 1787.

13 As Terry Castle notes, "Hannah Cowley's *The Belle's Stratagem* (1781) seems in particular to have a bearing on *A Simple Story*. The hero's name, Doricourt, resembles Dorriforth's; the masquerade at Lady Brilliant's suggests the type of affair held by Mrs. G— in Inchbald's novel" (319n). Miss Dorillon in *Wives/Maids* seems to bear the heritage of these earlier names, and the play picks up on Cowley's plot and subplot both. The father/daughter or mentor/daughter theme of *A Simple Story* also seems relevant. Yet Inchbald's use of these earlier sources is much looser than her reading of Chesterfield's *Letters*.

14 Viswanathan, *Masks of Conquest*, p. 7.

15 The choice of Milton's Eve in place of a more contemporary reference to Rousseau's Sophie sidesteps the potential anti-Jacobin feeling mention of Rousseau could raise at this time.

16 Inchbald makes it clear, however, that what she points out as faults in no way hindered the reception of the play: "Yet even in its present imperfect state, assisted by the art of excellent acting, it was most favourably received on the stage; and may now, without the charm of scenic aid, afford an hour's amusement to the reader" (*Wives/Maids*, 4).

17 This seems to me an inverted echo of Cordelia in *Lear*: "Why have my sisters husbands, to love my father all?" In refusing to give all her heart to Sir George, Maria may be withholding at least a share of it for her father.

18 The situation is complicated by the fact that Miss Dorillon and Lady Mary Raffle are clearly in the wrong for having built up enormous *gambling* debts.

19 *The Artist: A Collection of Essays Relative to Painting, Poetry, Sculpture, Architecture, the Drama, Discoveries of Science, and Various Other Subjects*, ed. Prince Hoare, 2 vols. (London, 1802), vol. 1, no. 7.

EPILOGUE: WHAT IS SHE?

1 Charlotte Smith, *What Is She?* English and American Drama microfilm series (New Canaan, CT: Readox Microform), pp. 221–97.

2 Anderson, *Imagined Communities*, p. 5.

3 See for instance Carlson's discussion of Sarah Siddons in *In the Theater of Romanticism*.

4 Mosse, *Nationalism and Sexuality*, p. 9.

5 Colley, *Britons: Forging the Nation*, p. 239.

6 *Public Advertiser*, no. 16452, Monday, February 12, 1787.

7 *Morning Post and Daily Advertiser*, no. 3558, Wednesday, July 7, 1784.

Select bibliography

Addison, Joseph, and Steele, Richard, *The Spectator*, ed. Donald Bond, 5 vols., Oxford: Clarendon Press, 1967.

Agnew, Jean-Christophe, *Worlds Apart: The Market and the Theatre in Anglo-American Thought, 1550–1750*, Cambridge: Cambridge University Press, 1986.

Allen, Ralph G., "Irrational Entertainment in the Age of Reason" in *The Stage and the Page: London's "Whole Show" in the Eighteenth-Century Theatre*, ed. George Winchester Stone, Jr., Berkeley: University of California Press, 1981, pp. 90–112.

Anderson, Benedict, *Imagined Communities: Reflections on the Origin and Spread of Nationalism*, London: Verso, 1983.

Backscheider, Paula, *Spectacular Politics: Theatrical Power and Mass Culture in Early Modern England*, Baltimore: Johns Hopkins University Press, 1993.

Baer, Marc, *Theatre and Disorder in Late Georgian London*, Oxford: Clarendon Press, 1992.

Baily, James, *Emma, Lady Hamilton: A Biographical Essay with a Catalogue of Her Published Portraits*, London: W. G. Menzies, 1905.

Baker, Stuart, *Georges Feydeau and the Aesthetics of Farce*, Ann Arbor, MI: University of Michigan Research Press, 1981.

Barker-Benfield, G. J., *The Culture of Sensibility: Sex and Society in Eighteenth-Century Britain*, Chicago: University of Chicago Press, 1992.

Bearce, George, *British Attitudes Towards India, 1784–1858*, New York and Oxford: Oxford University Press, 1961.

Beck, Lily Adams, *The Divine Lady: A Romance of Nelson and Emma Hamilton*, New York: Dodd, Mead, and Co., 1924.

Belden, Mary Megie, *The Dramatic Work of Samuel Foote*, New Haven: Yale University Press, 1929.

Bergson, Henri, *Le Rire* (1900), trans. in Wylie Sypher, ed., *Comedy*, Garden City, NY: Doubleday, 1956.

Bernbaum, Ernest, *The Drama of Sensibility: A Sketch of the History of English Sentimental Comedy and Domestic Tragedy, 1696–1780*, Gloucester, MA: Peter Smith, 1958. Original copyright 1915, by Ginn and Co.

Bhabha, Homi, *The Location of Culture*, New York: Routledge, 1994.

Nation and Narration, New York: Routledge, 1990.

Boaden, James, *Memoirs of Mrs. Inchbald*, 2 vols., London: Richard Bentley, 1833.

Boigne, Louise-Eléanore-Charlotte-Adélaide d'Osmond, comtesse de, *Mémoirs de la comtesse de Boigne née d'Osmond; récits d'une tamte édition présentée et annotée par Jean-Claude Berchet* (Paris: Meraire de France, 1979).

Bowen, Marjorie, *Patriotic Lady: Emma, Lady Hamilton, the Neapolitan Revolution of 1799, and Horatio, Lord Nelson*, New York: D. Appleton-Century, 1936.

Brewer, John, "Theatre and Counter-Theatre in Georgian Politics: The Mock Elections at Garrat," *Radical History Review*, 22 (winter 1979–80), pp. 7–40.

Brooks, Peter, *The Melodramatic Imagination: Balzac, Henry James, Melodrama, and the Mode of Excess*, New Haven: Yale University Press, 1976.

Burgess, Miranda, "Domesticating Gothic: Jane Austen, Ann Radcliffe, and National Romance" in *Lessons of Romanticism: A Critical Companion*, ed. Thomas Pfau and Robert Gleckner, Durham, NC: Duke University Press, 1998, pp. 392–412.

Burke, Edmund, *Reflections on the Revolution in France*, ed. Conor Cruise O'Brien, Harmondsworth: Penguin, 1968.

   The Writings and Speeches of Edmund Burke, 9 vols., volume v, *India, Madras and Bengal, 1774–1785*, ed. P.J . Marshall, Oxford: Clarendon Press, 1991.

Burroughs, Catherine, *Closet Stages: Joanna Baillie and the Theater Theory of British Romantic Women Writers* (Philadelphia: University of Pennsylvania Press, 1997).

Butler, Marilyn, "Plotting the Revolution: The Political Narratives of Romantic Poetry and Criticism" in *Romantic Revolutions: Criticism and Theory*, ed. Kenneth Johnston, Gilbert Chaitin, Karen Hanson and Herbert Marks, Bloomington: Indiana University Press, 1990, pp. 133–57.

Calhoun, Craig, ed., *Habermas and the Public Sphere*, Cambridge, MA: MIT Press, 1992.

Carlson, Julie, *In the Theatre of Romanticism*, Cambridge: Cambridge University Press, 1994.

Chambers, E. K., *The English Folk-Play*, Oxford: Clarendon Press, 1933.

Chandler, James, "Hallam, Tennyson, and the Poetry of Sensation: Aestheticist Allegories of a Counter-Public Sphere," *Studies in Romanticism*, 33 (winter 1994), pp. 527–37.

Chatterjee, Partha, *Nationalist Thought and the Colonial World*, Oxford: Oxford University Press, 1986.

Chesterfield, Lord, *Letters to his Son*, 2 vols., Washington, DC: M. Walter Dunne, 1901.

Choudhury, Mita, "Gazing at His Seraglio: Late Eighteenth-Century Women Playwrights as Orientalists," *Theatre Journal*, 47.4 (December 1995), pp. 481–502.

Churchill, Charles, *The Rosciad* in *Poetical Works of Charles Churchill*, ed. W. Tooke, 3 vols., Boston: Little Brown and Co., 1854, vol. i, pp. 1–110.

Cibber, Theophilus, *Two Dissertations on the Theatres*, London, 1756.

Clare, John, *Autobiographical Fragments*, ed. E. Robinson, Oxford: Oxford University Press, 1986.

Coleridge, Samuel Taylor, *Collected Letters, 1772–1834*, ed. Earl Leslie Griggs, Oxford, Clarendon Press, 1956–.

Shakespearean Criticism, ed. Thomas Middleton Raysor, London: J. M. Dent, 1960.

Colley, Linda, *Britons: Forging the Nation, 1707–1837*, New Haven: Yale University Press, 1992.

Colman, George, *Blue Beard*, London, 1798. See also *Bluebeard* in *Plays by George Colman the Younger and Thomas Morton*, ed. Barry Sutcliffe, Cambridge: Cambridge University Press, 1983, pp. 181–210.

The Female Dramatist, Larpent Collection, Huntington Library.

Random Records, 2 vols., London: H. Colburn and R. Bentley, 1830.

Cowley, Hannah, *A Day in Turkey; or, The Russian Slaves*, London: G. G. J. and J. Robinson, 1792.

The Works of Mrs. Cowley. Dramas and Poems. In Three Volumes, London: Wilkie and Robinson, 1813.

Crabbe, George, *Life and Poetical Works of George Crabbe*, London, 1847.

Crean, P. J., "The Stage Licensing Act of 1737," *Modern Philology*, 35 (1938), pp. 239–55.

Curran, Stuart, "Mary Robinson's *Lyrical Tales* in Context" in *Revisioning Romanticism: British Women Writers, 1776–1837*, ed. Carol Shiner Wilson and Joel Haefner, Philadelphia: University of Pennsylvania Press, 1994, pp. 17–35.

Poetic Form and British Romanticism, New York: Oxford University Press, 1986.

"Romantic Poetry: The 'I' Altered" in *Romanticism and Feminism*, ed. Anne Mellor, Bloomington: Indiana University Press, 1988, pp. 279–93.

De Selincourt, Ernest, ed., *The Letters of William and Dorothy Wordsworth*, 2nd edn, 8 vols., Oxford: Clarendon Press, 1967–93.

Debrett, J., *The Parliamentary Register; or History of the proceedings and Debates of the House of Commons; containing an account of The most interesting Speeches and Motions; accurate Copies of the most remarkable Letters and Papers; of the most material Evidence, Petitions, &c. laid before and offered to the House, during the First Session of the Seventeenth Parliament of Great Britain*, London: J. Debrett, 1791.

Donkin, Ellen, *Getting into the Act: Women Playwrights in London, 1776–1829*, New York: Routledge, 1995.

Donohue, Joseph, *Theatre in the Age of Kean*, Totowa, NJ: Rowman and Littlefield, 1975.

Doody, Margaret, *Frances Burney: The Life in the Works*, Cambridge: Cambridge University Press, 1988.

Dryden, John, preface to *An Evening's Love, or the Mock-Astrologer* (1671) in *John Dryden: Four Comedies*, ed. L. A. Beaurline and Fredson Bowers, Chicago: University of Chicago Press, 1967.

The Works of John Dryden, 20 vols., Berkeley: University of California Press, 1970.

Duff, David, *Romance and Revolution: Shelley and the Politics of a Genre*, Cambridge: Cambridge University Press, 1994.

Duffy, Edward, *Rousseau In England*, Berkeley: University of California Press, 1979.

Ellis, Frank, *Sentimental Comedy: Theory and Practice*, Cambridge: Cambridge University Press, 1991.

Ellis, Markman, *The Politics of Sensibility: Race, Gender, and Commerce in the Sentimental Novel*, Cambridge: Cambridge University Press, 1996.

Ellison, Julie, "The Politics of Fancy in the Age of Sensibility" in *Revisioning Romanticism: British Women Writers, 1776–1837*, ed. Carol Shiner Wilson and Joel Haefner, Philadelphia: University of Pennsylvania Press, 1994, pp. 228–55.

Fergus, Jan, and Thaddeus, Janice Farrar, "Women, Publishers, and Money, 1790–1820" in *Studies in Eighteenth Century Culture*, 27 vols. (to date), Colleagues Press, 1988.

Ferguson, Moira, *Subject to Others: British Women Writers and Colonial Slavery, 1670–1834*, New York: Routledge, 1992.

Ferris, Ina, "Writing on the Border: The National Tale, Female Writing, and the Public Sphere" in *Romanticism, History and the Possibilities of Genre: Re-Forming Literature, 1789–1837*, ed. Tilottama Rajan and Julia Wright, Cambridge: Cambridge University Press, 1998, pp. 86–106.

Field, Bradda, *Miledi: being the strange story of Emy Lyon, a blacksmith's daughter, who married his Britannic Majesty's Envoy Extraordinary and Minister Plenipotentiary at the court of Naples and became Emma, lady Hamilton, companion of royalty and the true friend of Vice-Admiral Lord Nelson, K.B., duke of Bronte. A romantic biography*, London: Constable, 1942.

Fielding, Henry, *The Complete Works*, ed. William Ernest Henley, 16 vols., London: Heinemann, 1903.
  The Jacobite's Journal and Related Writings, ed. W. B. Coley, Middletown, CT: Wesleyan University Press, 1975.

Fliegelman, Jay, *Prodigals and Pilgrims: The American Revolution Against Patriarchal Authority, 1750–1800*, Cambridge: Cambridge University Press, 1982.

Foote, Samuel, *The Roman and English Comedy Consider'd and Compared*, London: T. Waller, 1747.
  The Works of Samuel Foote, Esq., 3 vols., ed. Jon Bee, Esq., London: Sherwood, Gilbert, and Piper, 1830.

Fothergill, Brian, *Sir William Hamilton; Envoy Extraordinary*, London: Faber and Faber, 1969.

Frankau, Julia, *The Story of Emma, Lady Hamilton*, London: Macmillan, 1911.

Fraser, Flora, *Emma, Lady Hamilton*, New York: Knopf/Random House, 1986.

Freedman, Barbara, "Frame-Up: Feminism, Psychoanalysis, Theatre" in *Performing Feminisms: Feminist Critical Theory and Theatre*, ed. Sue-Ellen Case, Baltimore: Johns Hopkins University Press, 1990, pp. 54–76.

Garrick, David, *The Plays of David Garrick*, ed. Harry William Pedicord and Fredrick Louis Bergmann, 6 vols., Carbondale: Southern Illinois University Press, 1980.

Gellner, Ernest, *Nations and Nationalism*, Ithaca, NY: Cornell University Press, 1983.

George III, *The Correspondence of King George the Third from 1760 to December 1783, printed from the original papers in the royal archives at Windsor castle*, ed. Sir John Fortesque, 6 vols., London: Macmillan, 1927–28.

George, M. D., *Catalogue of Political and Personal Satires Preserved in the Department of Prints and Drawings in the British Museum*, 11 vols., London: Trustees of the British Museum, 1938.

Gilmartin, Kevin, *Print Politics: The Press and Radical Opposition in Early Nineteenth-Century England*, Cambridge: Cambridge University Press, 1996.

Goethe, Johann Wolfgang von, *Italian Journey*, trans. W. H. Auden and Elizabeth Mayer, New York: Schocken/Pantheon, 1968.

Goodman, Kevis, "Making Time for History: Wordsworth, the New Historicism, and the Apocalyptic Fallacy" in *Studies in Romanticism*, 35 (winter 1996), pp. 563–77.

Gray, Charles, *Theatrical Criticism in London to 1795*, New York: B. Blom, 1931; rpt 1964.

Habermas, Jürgen, *The Structural Transformation of the Public Sphere*, trans. Thomas Burger, Cambridge, MA: MIT Press, 1989.

Hamilton, Gerald, and Stewart, Desmond, *Emma in Blue: A Romance of Friendship*, New York: Roy Publishers, 1958.

Hayley, William, *The Life of George Romney, Esq.*, London: T. Payne, 1809.

The Triumphs of Temper, London: Cadell, 1780.

Highfill, Philip Jr., Burnim, Kalman, and Langhans, Edward, *A Biographical Dictionary of Actors, Actresses, Musicians, Dancers, Managers & Other Stage Personnel in London, 1660–1800*, 16 vols., Carbondale: Southern Illinois University Press, 1973–93.

Hoare, Prince, ed., *The Artist: A Collection of Essays Relative to Painting, Poetry, Sculpture, Architecture, the Drama, Discoveries of Science, and Various Other Subjects*, 2 vols., London, 1802.

Hughes, Leo, *A Century of English Farce*, Oxford: Oxford University Press, 1956.

The Drama's Patrons: A Study of the Eighteenth-Century London Audience, Austin: University of Texas Press, 1971.

Hurd, Richard, *Letters on Chivalry and Romance*, London, 1762.

Ilchester, Earl of, ed., *Journal of Elizabeth, Lady Holland*, 2 vols., London: Longmans, Green and Co., 1909.

Inchbald, Elizabeth, *Lover's Vows* in *The British Theatre: or, A Collection of Plays*, 35 vols., London: Longman, Hurst, Rees, and Orme, 1808.

A Mogul Tale, or, The descent of the balloon: a farce, London: Printed for F. Powell, 1796.

Such Things Are: a play, in five acts. As performed at the Theatre Royal, Covent Garden. Printed under the authority of the managers from the prompt book. With remarks by the author, London: Longman, Hurst, Rees, and Orme, 1808.

Wives as They Were, Maids as They Are, London: Longman, Hurst, Rees, Orme, and Browne, 1797.

Irigaray, Luce, "The Power of Discourse and the Subordination of the Feminine: Interview" in *This Sex Which Is Not One*, trans. Catherine Porter with Carolyn Burke, Ithaca, NY: Cornell University Press, 1985.

Jacobus, Mary, "'The Science of Herself': Scenes of Female Enlightenment" in Tilottama Rajan and David Clark, ed., *Intersections: Nineteenth-Century*

Philosophy and Contemporary Theory, Albany: State University of New York Press, 1995, pp. 240–69.

Jameson, Fredric, *The Political Unconscious: Narrative as a Socially Symbolic Act*, Ithaca, NY: Cornell University Press, 1981.

Jeaffreson, John Cordy, *Lady Hamilton & Lord Nelson*, London: Grolier Society, n.d.

Johnson, Claudia, *Equivocal Beings*, Chicago: University of Chicago Press, 1992.

Johnston, Arthur, *Enchanted Ground: The Study of Medieval Romance in the Eighteenth Century*, London: Athlone Press, 1964.

Kelly, Gary, "Women Writers and Romantic Nationalism in Britain" in *Literature of Region and Nation*, ed. Winnifred Bogaards, Saint John, NB: Social Sciences and Humanities Research Council of Canada with University of New Brunswick in Saint John, 1998, vol. 1, pp. 120–32.

Kelly, John Alexander, *German Visitors to English Theatres in the Eighteenth Century*, Princeton: Princeton University Press, 1936.

Klancher, Jon, *The Making of English Reading Audiences, 1790–1832*, Madison: University of Wisconsin Press, 1987.

Knapp, Mary E., *Prologues and Epilogues of the Eighteenth Century*, New Haven: Yale University Press, 1961.

Kramer, Lawrence, "Gender and Sexuality in *The Prelude*: The Question of Book Seven," *ELH*, 54 (1987), pp. 619–37.

Leask, Nigel, *British Romantic Writers and the East: The Anxieties of Empire*, Cambridge: Cambridge University Press, 1992.

Letters from Perdita to a Certain Israelite and His Answers to Them, London: J. Fielding, 1781.

Levy, M. J., "Introduction" to *Perdita: The Memoirs of Mary Robinson*, London: Peter Owen, 1994.

Lew, Joseph, "The Deceptive Other: Mary Shelley's Critique of Orientalism in *Frankenstein*," *Studies in Romanticism*, 30 (summer 1991), pp. 255–83.

Lofts, Norah, *Emma Hamilton*, New York: Coward, McCann and Geoghegan, 1978.

Markley, Robert, "Sentimentality as Performance: Shaftesbury, Sterne, and the Theatrics of Virtue" in *The New Eighteenth Century: Theory, Politics, English Literature*, ed. Felicity Nussbaum and Laura Brown, New York: Methuen, 1987, pp. 210–30.

Marshall, David, *The Surprising Effects of Sympathy: Marivaux, Diderot, Rousseau, and Mary Shelley*, Chicago: University of Chicago Press, 1988.

Meyer, Eric, "'I Know Thee Not, I Loathe Thy Race': Romantic Orientalism in the Eye of the Other," in *ELH*, 53 (fall 1991), pp. 657–99.

Mitford, Esq. RN, John, *The Adventures of Johnny Newcome in The Navy; A Poem in Four Cantos, with Notes*, 3rd edn, London: Sherwood, Neely, and Jones, 1823.

Moorhouse, E. Hallam, *Nelson's Lady Hamilton*, London: Methuen and Co., 1906.

Morrison, Alfred, collector, *The Collection of Autograph Letters and Historical Documents formed by Alfred Morrison* (2nd series, 1882–93); the Hamilton and Nelson Papers, 2 vols., printed for private circulation, 1893.

Morrissey, L. J., "Introduction" to Henry Fielding, *Tom Thumb and The Tragedy of Tragedies*, Edinburgh: Oliver and Boyd, 1970.

Mosse, George, *Nationalism and Sexuality: Respectability and Abnormal Sexuality in Modern Europe*, New York: Howard Fertig, 1985.

Negt, Oscar, and Kluge, Alexander, *Public Sphere and Experience: Toward an Analysis of the Bourgeois and Proletarian Public Sphere*, trans. Peter Labanyi, Jamie Oswen Daniel, and Assenka Oskiloff with foreword by Miriam Hansen, Minneapolis: University of Minnesota Press, 1993.

Newfield, Christopher, *The Emerson Effect: Individualism and Submission in America*, Chicago: University of Chicago Press, 1996.

Nicoll, Allardyce, *A History of Late Eighteenth-Century Drama, 1750–1800*, Cambridge: Cambridge University Press, 1937.

Paine, Thomas, *The Complete Writings of Thomas Paine*, 2 vols., ed. Philip S. Foner, New York: Citadel Press, 1969.

Parker, Andrew, Russo, Mary, Sommer, Doris, and Yaeger, Patricia, eds., *Nationalisms and Sexualities*, New York: Routledge, 1992.

Parrish, Stephen, *The Art of the Lyrical Ballads*, Cambridge, MA: Harvard University Press, 1973.

Pascoe, Judith, *Romantic Theatricality: Gender, Poetry and Spectatorship*, Ithaca, NY: Cornell University Press, 1997.

Paulson, Ronald, *Representations of Revolution*, New Haven: Yale University Press, 1983.

Paulson, Ronald, and Lockwood, Thomas, eds., *Henry Fielding: The Critical Heritage*, New York: Barnes and Noble, 1969.

Pearson, Jacqueline, *The Prostituted Muse: Images of Women and Women Dramatists, 1642–1737*, New York: St. Martin's Press, 1988.

Poetical Epistle from Florizel to Perdita: With Perdita's Answer. And a Preliminary Discourse upon the education of Princes, London: J. Stockdale, 1781.

Quilligan, Maureen, *The Language of Allegory: Defining the Genre*, Ithaca, NY: Cornell University Press, 1979.

Randall, Anne Frances, *Letter to the Women of England on the Injustice of Mental Subordination*, London, 1798.

Rehberg, Frederick, *Emma Hamilton's Attitudes*, Cambridge, MA: Houghton Library, 1990.

Reiman, Donald, "The Beauty of Buttermere as Fact and Romantic Symbol," *Criticism*, 26.2 (spring 1984), pp.   .

Richards, Sandra, *The Rise of the English Actress*, New York: St. Martin's Press, 1993.

Richardson, Alan, *Literature, Education, and Romanticism: Reading as Social Practice, 1780–1832*, Cambridge: Cambridge University Press, 1994.

Robbins, Bruce, ed., *The Phantom Public Sphere*, Minneapolis: University of Minnesota Press, 1993.

Robinson, Mary, *Lyrical Tales*, London: Longman, 1800.

Nobody, Larpent Collection, Huntington Library.

Thoughts on the Condition of Women and on the Injustice of Mental Subordination, London, 1799.

Romney, John, *Memoirs of the Life and Works of George Romney, etc.*, London: Baldwin and Cradock, 1830.

Ross, Marlon, "Romancing the Nation-State" in *Macropolitics of Nineteenth-Century Literature: Nationalism, Exoticism, Imperialism*, ed. Jonathan Arac and Harriet Ritvo, Philadelphia: University of Pennsylvania Press, 1991, pp. 56–85.

Rousseau, Jean-Jacques, *Lettre à d'Alembert sur les spectacles*, trans. Alan Bloom, *Politics and the Arts*, Ithaca, NY: Cornell University Press, 1960.

Russell, Gillian, *The Theatres of War: Performance, Politics and Society, 1793–1815*, Oxford: Clarendon Press, 1995.

Russell, Jack, *Nelson and the Hamiltons*, New York: Simon and Schuster, 1969.

Sedgwick, Eve, *The Coherence of Gothic Conventions*, rpt., New York: Methuen, 1986.

Sherbo, Arthur, *English Sentimental Drama*, East Lansing: Michigan State University Press, 1957.

Sichel, Walter, *Emma Lady Hamilton from New and Original Sources and Documents*, New York: Dodd, Mead, 1906.

Memoir of Emma, Lady Hamilton, with Anecdotes of Her Friends and Contemporaries, ed. W. H. Long, London: W. W. Gibbings, 1891.

Simpson, Antony, "Vulnerability and the Age of Female Consent" in *Sexual Underworlds of the Enlightenment*, ed. G. S. Rousseau and Roy Porter, Manchester: Manchester University Press, 1987.

Simpson, Colin, *Emma, The Life of Lady Hamilton*, London: Bodley Head, 1983.

Simpson, David, *Romanticism, Nationalism, and the Revolt Against Theory*, Chicago: University of Chicago Press, 1993.

Smith, Charlotte, *What Is She?* in English and American Drama of the Nineteenth Century, microfilm series, New Canaan, CT: Readex Microform, 1985– .

Sontag, Susan, *The Volcano Lover: A Romance*, New York: Farrar, Straus, and Giroux, 1992.

Southey, Robert, *The Life of Nelson*, 12th edn, London: John Murray, 1853.

Stedman Jones, Gareth, *Languages of Class: Studies in English Working-Class History, 1832–1982*, Cambridge: Cambridge University Press, 1983.

Steele, Elizabeth, *The Memoirs of Sophia Baddeley*, 3 vols., Dublin, 1787.

Stone, George Winchester, Jr., ed., *The Stage and the Page: London's "Whole Show" in the Eighteenth-Century Theatre*, Berkeley: University of California Press, 1981.

Straub, Kristina, *Sexual Suspects: Eighteenth-Century Players and Sexual Ideology*, Princeton, NJ: Princeton University Press, 1992.

Suleri, Sara, *The Rhetoric of English India*, Chicago: University of Chicago Press, 1992.

Tate, Nahum, "Preface" to *A Duke and No Duke* (1693; 2nd edn), reprinted as "Nahum Tate's defense of farce," introduced and edited by Peter Holland, in *Farce, Themes in Drama*, ed. James Redmond, vol. x, Cambridge: Cambridge University Press, 1988, pp. 99–113.

Viswanathan, Gauri, *Masks of Conquest: Literary Study and British Rule in India*, London: Faber, 1989.

Wahrman, Dror, *Imagining the Middle Class: The Political Representation of Class in Britain, c. 1780–1840*, Cambridge: Cambridge University Press, 1995.

Walpole, Horace, *Correspondence*, ed. W. S. Lewis, 48 vols., New Haven: Yale University Press, 1944.

Wark, Robert R., *Drawings by Thomas Rowlandson in the Huntington Collection*, San Marino, CA: Huntington Library, 1975.

Warner, Oliver, *Emma Hamilton and Sir William*, London: Chatto and Windus, 1960.

Warton, Thomas, *The History of English Poetry, from the close of the eleventh and to the commencement of the eighteenth century*, ed. Richard Price and Richard Taylor (London: Thomas Tegg, 1840), 3 vols.

    Observations on the Faerie Queene, 2 vols., London, 1762.

Weber, Samuel, "The Sideshow, or: Remarks on a Canny Moment," *MLN*, 88.6 (1973).

Wellek, René, and Warren, Austin, *Theory of Literature*, New York: Harcourt, Brace, 1949.

West, Shearer, *The Image of the Actor: Verbal and Visual Representation in the Age of Garrick and Kemble*, New York: St. Martin's Press, 1991.

Williams, Ioan, *Novel and Romance: A Documentary Record, 1700–1800*, New York: Barnes and Noble, 1970.

Williams, Raymond, *The Long Revolution*, London: Chatto and Windus, 1961.

Wollstonecraft, Mary, *Political Writings*, ed. Janet Todd, Toronto: University of Toronto Press, 1993.

Wordsworth, William and Samuel Taylor Coleridge, *Lyrical Ballads*, ed. R. L. Brett and A. R. Jones, 2nd edn, London: Routledge, 1991.

    The Prelude 1799, 1805, 1850, ed. Jonathan Wordsworth, M. H. Abrams and Stephen Gill, New York: Norton, 1979.

Wright, Thomas, and Evan, R. H., *Historical and Descriptive Account of the Caricatures of James Gillray, Comprising a Political and Humorous History of the Latter Part of the Reign of George the Third*, rpt., New York: Benjamin Blom, 1968.

Žižek, Slavoj, *The Sublime Object of Ideology*, New York: Verso, 1989.

Zonana, Joyce, "The Sultan and the Slave: Feminist Orientalism and the Structure of *Jane Eyre*," *Signs: Journal of Women in Culture and Society*, 18.3 (spring 1993), pp. 592–617.

Index

265

CAMBRIDGE STUDIES IN ROMANTICISM

General editors
MARILYN BUTLER
University of Oxford
JAMES CHANDLER
University of Chicago